The Dao of the Press
A Humanocentric Theory

THE HAMPTON PRESS COMMUNICATION SERIES
Communication, Globalization and Cultural Identity
Jan Servaes, series editor

The Dao of the Press
A Humanocentric Theory

Shelton A. Gunaratne

Minnesota State University Moorhead

HAMPTON PRESS, INC.
CRESSKILL, NEW JERSEY

Printed in the United States of America

Library of Congress Cataloging-in-Publication Data

Gunaratne, Shelton A.
    The dao of the press : a humanocentric theory / Shelton Gunaratne
        p. cm. -- (The Hampton Press communication series)
    Includes bibliographic references and index.
    ISBN 1-57273-616-X (cl) -- ISBN 1-57273-617-8 (pb)
     1. Journalism--philosophy. 2. Journalism--Social aspects. I. Title.
    II. Series.

    PN4731.G86 2005
    070'.01--dc22

                        2005046041

Hampton Press, Inc.
23 Broadway
Cresskill, NJ 07626

To my family

Yoke-Sim
Junius Asela
and
Carmel Maya

Contents

Preface

This book combines the Eastern cosmological notion of *yin-yang*, which has some resemblance to the thesis-antithesis dialectic of Western philosophy, with the "new" systems thinking implicit in the theory of living systems to derive a dynamic humanocentric theory of communication outlets and free expression. The theory asserts that the dialectical interaction of the libertarian-authoritarian antinomy across space time produces various shades of social responsibility. The antinomy represents the autopoietic interaction of energy/matter/information at both the micro- and macro levels of a living system. Cognition, the process of life, which conjoins the micro with the macro, enables the antinomy at its particular level of operation to sense the sociocultural factors relevant to its environment in producing these shades. The theory presumes an operationally *closed*, but cognitively open, *far from equilibrium* structure of communication outlets and free expression at the main levels of the world system (e.g., the world/nation-state/individual levels or the core/semiperiphery/periphery levels).

The book critically examines the West-centric biases of the classic *Four Theories* of press (Siebert, Peterson, & Schramm, 1956) and subsequent improvements. It goes on to show that some contemporary scholars have confused the so-called *press theories* with varying genres of journalism. The *Four Theories* and its offshoots are based on West-centric history, theory, and practice. West-centrism and universalism are presumed to be one and the same. These normative theories are routinely used to evaluate the mass media of the entire world even though they are oblivious to non-Western history and philosophy. Habermas' public sphere suffers from the same ethnocentric fallibility.

This book represents a modest attempt to help reverse the current imbalance in mass communication literature and to motivate more communication scholars from non-Europe to use Eastern theories to analyze various aspects of communication outlets and free expression. The book examines how the mass media systems, or what I prefer to call *systems of communication outlets*, evolve through the lens of the emerging theory of living systems—combining the theories of autopoiesis, cognition, and dissipative structures—and world systems analysis.

I have looked at democracy, journalism, libertarianism, social responsibility, and authoritarianism from the perspective of Eastern philosophies—Buddhism, Hinduism, Confucianism, Daoism, and Legalism. I have also used the perspective of postcolonial subaltern studies to examine the relevance of concepts derived from ancient Eastern philosophy to the theory and practice of contemporary state-press relations.

The globalization of West-centric press theories is a reflection of the intellectual domination of the West from the time of Enlightenment. The highly lopsided global communication infrastructure that we see at the beginning of the 21st century makes it difficult to escape the continuing reality of domination. Autopoiesis of social systems is the natural defense that prevents cultural annihilation of non-Europe. The subaltern studies' project of provincializing Europe (Chakrabarty, 2000), calls for the selective retention of universals applicable to the modern state while discarding totalizing Eurocentrism. Such a response is consistent with the autopoietic operation of living systems.

Some may see my analysis of state-press relations from the perspective of Eastern philosophies as a shift from empirical-analytic (technical) approach to mysticism. However, as Capra (1996, [1975]1999, 2002) and others (e.g., Goswami, 1993; Zukav, 1979) have documented, the basic presumptions of the main strands of Eastern philosophy—the unity, dynamism, and part-whole interdependence of the universe—are remarkably in accord with the presumptions of both quantum physics and deep ecology. I take the view that transcendental philosophy offers useful insights that science can neither prove nor disprove. Science cannot handle the mystery of subatomic physics or the mysticism of Eastern philosophy. All phenomena cannot be reduced to empirical laws.

This book's origin goes back to a paper I prepared in 2001 for an ASEAN symposium on communication and media studies at Universiti Kebangssaan Malaysia and later presented to the Communication Theory and Methodology Division of the Association for Education in Journalism and Mass Communication at the annual convention in

Miami Beach in August 2002. I have benefited from the many sharp criticisms of various anonymous reviewers from the time I submitted the basic idea of this book as a conference paper.

Positivists (adherents of empirical-analytic science), historicists (adherents of historical-hermeneutic disciplines), and emancipatory critical theorists are all likely to see my theoretical approach in different ways. Neither Eastern philosophy nor complexity science—two of the main ingredients used to derive my theoretical framework—has yet penetrated the citadels of Western social science. However, if Laozi's mysticism is close to the reality of quantum physics, then the mystery of the *Dao* may also help our understanding of social science, including state-media/press relations.

Social scientists who continue to devalue Eastern philosophy, however, are implicitly following the West-centric modernization paradigm laid out by Montesquieu, Hegel, and Marx, all of whom justified European imperialism because the "most advanced people" had an obligation to help human emancipation. Ali Mirsepassi, the author of *Intellectual Discourse and the Politics of Modernization* (2000), has analyzed the work of these three intellectual luminaries to demonstrate their deep prejudice against non-Western cultures. Mirsepassi traces the "clash of civilizations" thesis conceptualized by Bernard Lewis and elaborated by Samuel Huntington to the same line of thinking. I call on my readers to "unthink" the prejudices of these Western intellectual luminaries and engage in humanocentric theory building.

Acknowledgments

Anonymous reviewers determined the shape of this book from the time I wrote the seed paper titled "Theory of Communication Outlets and Free Expression: A Humanocentric Exploration" in 2001. Cliff Christians, research professor at University of Illinois, was kind enough to discuss the seed paper with me at some length over coffee at an annual convention of the Association for Education in Journalism. and Mass Communication. He encouraged me to submit it as a conference paper.

Although my attempt to publish an expanded version in a communication anthology failed, the editor sent me lengthy reviews by my peers who offered numerous suggestions. One wrote, "This is an extremely ambitious manuscript that reads more like a précis for a book than a book chapter." Another reviewer wrote, "This manuscript represents an ambitious attempt to propose a global press philosophy . . . that would synthesize a number of perennial issues ranging across philosophical, political, and even religious topics related to public communication." Although I may not have met the high expectations of these two reviewers, their comments were instrumental in egging me on to write this book. I am deeply grateful to them whoever they are.

I must also acknowledge my debt to another anonymous reviewer who read the draft of the book manuscript. This reviewer wrote, "Let me say at the very outset that this manuscript is animated by a very important idea that is central to communication studies, namely, the need to move away from restrictive Eurocentric ideas of the press and to adopt a more inclusive attitude drawing on the wisdom of the East." I implemented many of the recommendations of this reviewer.

Those who wrote negative reviews of the project also served me well. Although my final product may not agree with their thinking, I appreciate their help for alerting me to pitfalls that I might not have otherwise noticed.

Crispin Maslog, visiting professor at Nanyang Technological University, provided me with feedback on Chapter 6, "The theory of communication outlets and free expression," from the graduate students enrolled in his Comparative Global Media course. Because their feedback reached me at the end of November 2004, two months after the manuscript went into production, I was unable to revise the text to incorporate some of their impressive suggestions. Eric Loo, University of Wollongong, interviewed me on several aspects of the book for an article that he published in the *Asia-Pacific Media Educator*.

I thank my faculty colleague Camilla Wilson for drawing my attention to *The Dao of Pooh*, which enabled me to grasp that the Pooh Way (or *wuwei*) was not the only way. Other ways—those of Rabbit, Tigger, and Eeyore—will continue to coexist in the world. Graphic artist Jody Bendel helped me with refining the graphic, and office manger Deb Hval helped me with copying, binding, and mailing the manuscript.

Jan Servaes, editor of the Hampton book series Communication, Globalization and Cultural Diversity, deserves special mention for his valiant attempt to find reviewers who were willing to read my manuscript. Barbara Bernstein, president of Hampton Press Inc., encouraged me from the outset.

Shelton Gunaratne
February 2005

One

What is Democracy?

Our understanding of democracy[1] should go beyond West-centric definitions based on the ideas of Enlightenment, the era of the new Cartesian, scientific approach in 18th-century Europe. This era also marked the age of imperialism and colonialism when, metaphorically speaking, Eastern thinking was dismissed as entropy and Western thinking was elevated as energy. Today, it appears that much of Eastern thinking— still identified as mysticism—is highly consistent with the new paradigms of physics, biology, and cognitive science (Capra, 1996, [1975]1999, 2002). The science of complexity has challenged Enlightenment's Newtonian model, which presumed that everything in nature is reducible to simple covering laws.

Although postcolonial subaltern studies (e.g., Chakrabarty, 2000) see the virtues of the ideas that emerged during Enlightenment (e.g., liberty, equality, pluralism, rationality, nation-state, liberal democracy, etc.) because non-Europe used these concepts in its struggle for freedom from imperialism, the subaltern project of provincializing Europe does not entail the wholesale acceptance of Enlightenment-backed definition of democracy, Fourth Estate, and so on. The globalization of these universals requires an adjustment for *glocalization*—a term Robertson

1

(1994) used to signify the heterogenizing aspect of the same phenomenon. Ritzer (2003) saw glocalization as "the interpenetration of the global and the local resulting in unique outcomes in different geographic areas" (p. 192).

In this chapter, I examine the concept of democracy from the standpoints of East and West (including the controversy on the East–West dichotomy). The concept of freedom of expression (and, therefore, freedom of the press) is intimately connected to the concept of democracy. In the language of systems theory, these two conceptual systems are operationally coupled. That is, they interpenetrate each other.

DEMOCRACY AND HISTORY

Democracy derives from the Greek words *demos* (the people) and *kratein* (to rule). The term stands for "rule by the people," although historically it had come to mean "rule by majority decision." In the latter sense, one could identify three types of democracy: direct democracy (as in ancient Greek city-states and New England town meetings), representative democracy (wherein people exercise their rights through elected representatives), and liberal/constitutional democracy (wherein elected representatives abide by constitutional restraints to ensure fundamental minority rights). Held (1995) conceded that many elements of democratic heritage are traceable to the older civilizations of the East. For example, the city-state or polis society existed in Mesopotamia long before it emerged in the West.

Indian political history documents that all three types of democracy, in varying forms, were known in North India from *Rigvedic* times (Perera, 1989; Sharma, 1968) although West-centric (Euro-American) history tends to concentrate primarily on ancient Greece and Rome. For example, Siddhartha Gautama (c. 563–483 BCE) had grown up in a tribal republic ruled by council or assembly (Macy, 1991). During the lifetime of the Buddha, who was a stanch republican in political views, the Sakyas and the Vajjians formed the most important republics in eastern India.

> It is especially remarkable that, during the near-millennium
> [between 500 BCE and CE 400], we find republics almost anywhere
> in India that our sources allow us to examine society in any detail.
> Unless those sources, not least our Greek sources, are extremely
> deceptive, the republics of India were very likely more extensive and
> populous than the *poleis* of the Greeks. One cannot help wondering
> how in many other parts of Eurasia republican and democratic
> states may have co-existed with the royal dynasties that are a staple

of both ancient and modern chronology and conceptualization. (Muhlberger, 1998)

Sarkar (1918b) pointed out that republics with sovereign authority, which originated early in India, survived with complete or modified independence down to the 4th century BCE as documented not only in Buddhist and Jain literature, but also in Greek and Latin literature on India and Alexander, as well as in Sanskrit epics and treatises on politics. Sharma (1968), who studied original sources written in Pali, Prakrit, and Sanskrit, in addition to non-Indian sources, traced the origin, development, organization, and administration of the republican and quasi-republican institutions in ancient India. Sharma paid particular attention to the Vajjian Confederacy, the Licchavis, the Videhas, the Nayas, the Mallas, the Sakyas, the Koliyas, and four lesser known republics—the Moriyas of Pipphalivana, the Bulis of Allahappa, the Bhaggas of Susumaragiri, and the Kalamas of Kesaputta.

> Republican ideas, attitudes, and practices survived until long after the days of the Buddha and Mahavira. The classical historians refer to a number of northwestern republics during the 4th century B.C., and numerous inscriptions and coins from northwest and western India clearly show that republics flourished, at least until the date when the Allahabad Pillar Inscription of Samudra Gupta was engraved. It is probable that the democratic spirit of the early Vedic aristocracies of the northwest did not completely vanish under the monarchies of the Brahmanic period. (Sharma, 1968, p. 238)

The inscriptions and edicts of Mauryan Emperor Asoka (c. 269–232 BCE) emphatically advocated the tolerance of pluralism and the protection of minorities (Sen, 2001). Asoka's seventh rock edict pleads for tolerance among all sects, and his second separate rock edict calls on the officials to create confidence in the government among the tribes on the eastern frontier (Thapar, 1961). Gokhale (1966) and Nikam and McKeon (1958) provided more details on Asoka's edicts. Inden (1990), who exposed the biases of Orientalism, pointed out that "political society in 'ancient' India has seldom been the direct center of focus in Indological discourse" (p. 164).

WESTERN VIEW OF DEMOCRACY

As Robert Dahl (1963) pointed out, there is no single theory of democracy—only theories. Held (1996) set out four classic models of democracy: the classical Athenian idea of democracy, the republican idea of self-governing community (and its two variants—protective and developmental), liberal democracy (and its two variants—protective and developmental), and the Marxist idea of direct democracy. Held also identified four 20th century models that have spawned intensive political discussion and conflict: *competitive elitist* democracy, *pluralism, legal* democracy, and *participatory* democracy. Held (1995, 2000) took the stance that the growing interconnections between states and societies resulting from globalization require a reconfiguration of the global political system as a cosmopolitan democracy, which entails the entrenchment of autonomy in regional and global networks, as well as in local and national polities.

Most agree that the two main traditions of Western democracy are the evolving liberal tradition and the civic republican tradition. Terchek and Conte (2001) said that the liberal tradition is reflected in the works of Locke, Paine, Madison, De Tocqueville, Mill, and John Rawls. The republican tradition is reflected in the works of Aristotle, Machiavelli, Rousseau, John Winthrop, and Horace Mann. Communitarianism, whose best-known exponent is Robert Bellah, is often categorized with the republican tradition. Terchek and Conte said that supplementing these two traditions are four contemporary Western theories of democracy: *protective* democracy (an extension of early liberal theories by Friedrich Hayek and Milton Friedman), *pluralist* democracy (whose exponents— Arthur Bentley and Robert Dahl—focus on interest groups), *performance* democracy (whose exponents—Joseph Schumpeter and Anthony Downs—promote a market model), and *participatory* democracy (whose exponents—John Dewey and Benjamin Barber—see the importance of high levels of citizen intervention in the tasks of governing).

All the Western theories of democracy generally deal with power, equality, freedom, justice, and interests. Not all these concepts are congruent with Eastern thinking. However, the West's attempt to propagate the liberal democratic tradition in the postcolonial world has met with resistance. Terchek and Conte (2001) correctly pointed out that many in the non-Western world take exception to the "universalizing impulse of Western democratic theory . . . because they want their democracy to reflect their own conceptions of the good community and fear that Western theories sometimes restrict this possibility or do not speak to their specific circumstances" (p. 279).

Freedom House (2003) identified five types of representative and/or liberal/constitutional democracies (Table 1.1), with presidential-parliamentary democracy and parliamentary democracy topping the list. This assessment pertains to 121 countries, thereby excluding from the fold of democracy some 70 countries—including the so-called dominant-party countries (Malaysia and Singapore), as well as Bhutan, Brunei Darussalam, Cambodia, China, Laos, Maldives, Myanmar, Nepal, North

Table 1.1. Types of Electoral Democracies 2003

Type	Number of countries
Presidential-parliamentary democracy	57[*]
Parliamentary democracy	51
Parliamentary democracy (federal)	6
Presidential-parliamentary democracy (federal)	4
Presidential democracy and traditional chiefs	3
Total number of electoral democracies	121
Not recognized as electoral democracies	71

[*]Includes Taiwan
Source: Freedom House (2003) <http://www.freedomhouse.org/research/free-world/2003/democracies.pdf>

Korea, Pakistan, and Vietnam in Asia Proper. All the Islamic countries in North Africa and the Middle East except Turkey, as well as in Central Asia, have been excluded, in addition to 28 countries in Sub-Saharan Africa (Table 1.2). However, many of the excluded countries may well claim that they meet the requirements of the respective articles in the Universal Declaration of Human Rights and the International Covenant on Civil and Political Rights. For example, the Freedom House's exclusion of Sudan as an electoral democracy has compelled Sudan to raise objections. The exclusion of Malaysia and Singapore also indicate a bias toward a West-centric definition of *democracy*.

It is noteworthy that despite Freedom House's negative view of democracy in Islamic countries, Moussalli (2001) asserted that "notions of democracy, pluralism, and human rights are not only in harmony with Islamic thought, but their seeds are embedded in many notions of government and politics found in Islamic religious thought" (p. 2). He drew attention to the Islamic concepts of *shura* (consultation), *bay'a* (the oath of allegiance), *ikhtiyar* (choice), *ijma'* (consensus), and *ikhtilaf* (tolerance of differences). Moussalli argued that, although the history of the highest Islamic political institution, the caliphate, is mostly a history of authoritarian governments, the economic, social, political, and intellectual history of Islam abounds with liberal doctrines and institutions.

U.N. VIEW OF DEMOCRACY

The United Nations has implicitly declared democracy a human right in broad terms. Article 21 of the Universal Declaration of Human Rights says:

Table 1.2. Countries Not Recognized by Freedom House as Electoral Democracies

Africa	Asia and the Pacific	Middle East and North Africa	Eastern Europe and N.I.S	Americas and the Caribbean
Angola	Bhutan	Afghanistan	Azerbaijan	**Antigua and Barbuda**
Burkina Faso	Brunei	Algeria	Belarus	Cuba
Burundi	Cambodia	Bahrain	**Bosnia and**	
Cameroon	China	Egypt	**Herzegovina**	
Central African Republic	Korea, North	Iran	Kazakhstan	
Chad	Laos	Iraq	Kyrgyzstan	
Comoros	Malaysia	Jordan	Tajikistan	
Congo	Maldives	**Kuwait**	Turkmenistan	
Congo, D.R.	Myanmar	Lebanon	Uzbekistan	
Cote d'Ivoire	Nepal	Libya		
Djibouti	**Pakistan**	**Morocco**		
Equatorial Guinea	Singapore	Oman		
Eritrea	**Tonga**	Qatar		
Ethiopia	Vietman	Saudi Arabia		
Gabon		Syria		
Gambia		Tunisia		
Guinea		U.A.E.		
Liberia		Yemen		
Mauritania				
Rwanda				
Somalia				
Sudan				
Swaziland				
Tanzania				
Togo				
Uganda				
Zambia				
Zimbabwe				
Total 28	Total 14	Total 18	Total 8	Total 2

Countries in bold-face had a partly-free press in 2002
Source: Freedom House <http://www.freedomhouse.org/research/freeworld/2003/democracies.pdf>

6

1. Everyone has the right to take part in the government of his country, directly or through freely chosen representatives.
2. Everyone has the right to equal access to public service in his country.
3. The will of the people shall be the basis of the authority of government; this will shall be expressed in periodic and genuine elections which shall be by universal and equal suffrage and shall be held by secret vote or by equivalent free voting procedures.

Although the declaration does not use the term *democracy*, it explicitly or implicitly approves the three main concepts associated with Westcentric liberal democracy: equality, liberty, and pluralism. It underscores *equality* in three articles: "All human beings are born free and *equal* in dignity and rights" (Article 1), "All are *equal* before the law" (Article 7), and "Everyone is entitled in full *equality* to a fair and public hearing" (Article 10). It underscores *liberty* in one article: "Everyone has the right to life, liberty and security of person" (Article 3), and it *implies* pluralism in three articles: "Everyone has the right to freedom of thought, conscience and religion" (Article 18), "Everyone has the right to freedom of opinion and expression" (Article 19), and "Everyone has the right to freedom of peaceful assembly and association" (Article 20).

Article 25 of the International Covenant on Civil and Political Rights amplifies Article 21 of the UDHR in specific and enforceable terms as follows:

> Every citizen shall have the right and the opportunity, without any of the distinctions mentioned in Article 2 [such as race, color, sex, language, religion, political or other opinion, national or social origin, property, birth, or other status] and without unreasonable restrictions
> (a) To take part in the conduct of public affairs, directly or through freely chosen representatives;
> (b) To vote and to be elected at genuine periodic elections which shall be by universal and equal suffrage and shall be held by secret ballot, guaranteeing the free expression of the will of the electors;
> (c) To have access, on general terms of equality, to public service in his country.

It is noteworthy that neither the declaration nor the covenant specifies a preferred form of democracy, thereby permitting the nation-states to choose among direct democracy, representative democracy, and liberal/constitutional democracy. Free voting, periodic elections, and access to public service are the specified requirements. Thus, from a systems (holistic) perspective, one can place types of "democracy," which adhere to these specified requirements, along a continuum of complexity—from simple direct democracy to more complex forms (Table 1.3). This is similar to Held's (1995) concept of "different types of democracy . . . forming a continuum from the local to the global" (p. 280). Each type has its own layers of complexity. Moreover, each type may also have hybrid layers; for example, authoritarianism at a family level and representative democracy at a state or national level. India, the largest democracy in the world, illustrates the systemic complexity of democracy. The intracaste arranged-marriage practice denotes shades of feudalism and authoritarianism at the family level. Within the structure of a federal republic of 28 states and seven union territories, it has been able to accommodate communist governments at the state level in Kerala (from 1957–1959, 1967–1971, and 1980–1984), West Bengal (from 1977 onward), and Tripura (from 1977–1989). The world system comprises at least 192 political structures of varying complexity.

Some of these political structures may supplant representative democracy with the legal procedures of recall and referendum. Another model (e.g., the United States, Sri Lanka) may require the election of both the executive head of government and the legislature. However, in typical constitutional monarchies or dominions (e.g., the United Kingdom, Norway, and Australia), the unelected monarch or his or her representative selects a prime minister and a cabinet from among the elected legislators. Moreover, the terms *democracy* and *republic* may have different connotations. Although both types of systems delegate the power to govern to their elected representatives, officials in a democracy are generally expected to subordinate their judgment so as to reflect the known or ascertained views of their constituents, whereas officials in a republic are generally expected to act on their own best judgment of the needs and interests of the country.

EASTERN VIEW OF DEMOCRACY

Quantum physics asserts that at a subatomic level, every particle has an antiparticle—just like the archetypical polar opposites *yin* and *yang,* which form the basis of Chinese thought (Capra, [1975]1999). The dynamic interplay of these two opposites generates all manifestations of the *Dao*—the ultimate, indefinable reality or oneness of things. These opposites interact to reproduce themselves in different shapes and forms (what physicists call *coherent superposition*[2]) along the continuum of n-dimensional space time. The principle of the dialectical completion of relative polarities (Cheng, 1987) tells us that libertarianism (or liberal democracy) cannot exist without authoritarianism because one is

Table 1.3. A Systemic View of Types of Democracy/Government

Complexity increases when there is a mixture of types of democracy/government at different layers

Libertarianism (State of nature)	Direct democracy	Representative democracy	Constitutional democracy	Communism	Authoritarianism
Layer n	Layer n	Layer n	Layer n	Layer n	Layer n
Layer 4 Nation	Layer 4 Nation	Layer 4 Nation	Layer 4 Nation	Layer 4 Nation	Layer 4 Nation
Layer 3 Region	Layer 3 State/Province	Layer 3 State/Province	Layer 3 State/Province	Layer 3 State/Province	Layer 3 State/Province
Layer 2 Tribe/Locality	Layer 2 Town/City/County	Layer 2 Town/City/County	Layer 2 Town/City/County	Layer 2 Town/City/County	Layer 2 Town/City/County
Layer 1 Family	Layer 1 Family	Layer 1	Layer 1	Layer 1 Family	Layer 1 Family

Types of democracy/government

Levels of complexity

the complement of the other. These interactions produce various shapes and forms of democracy and authoritarianism. These shapes and forms, as Hindus and Buddhists believe, are illusions (*maya*) because they are in a constant state of flux The Buddhist theory of causality asserts that "everything undergoes fluid, dynamic change, a perpetual flowing—with no experiencer in the stream of experience" (Goonatilake, 1998, p. 229). Thus, any attempt to reduce all nation-states of the world to a preferred form of Westcentric democracy goes against the ways of nature. The polarities represent an essential aspect of the oneness of things or what the Chinese call the *Dao* (Copleston, 1982) and the Hindus call the *Brahman*.

Life at all levels of living systems—organisms, social systems, and ecosystems—represents networks of interdependence (Capra, 2002). Asian philosophy is congruent with the holistic-worldview paradigm of seeing the world as an integrated whole rather than as a collection of isolated objects—a very different view from the traditional Cartesian mechanism. The Buddhist notion of dependent co-arising (*paticca samuppada*)[3] establishes the interdependence of person and community. Macy (1991) pointed out that, from the Buddhist perspective of mutual causality, "the individual self is both unique and inseparable from its natural and social matrix" (p. 183). Buddhism helps us "understand that not only are we related to each other personally and socially, but that we are related to a whole universe, materially and spiritually, stretching beyond the artificial boundaries of human beings" (Thayer-Bacon, 2003, p. 36). Buddhist philosophy is highly congruent with modern systems thinking: Both recognize "the flowering of integrated heterogeneity" (p. 187). Sri Lankan Buddhist scholars Jayatilleke (1974) and Kalupahana (1976) explained the centrality of *paticca samuppada* from the *Hinayana* perspective. Diversity and distinctiveness are consistent with both democracy and Buddhist philosophy.

Perera (1989) agreed with the connection between democratic values and Buddhism. Peek (1995) made this connection explicit by assembling the central components of a bill of rights consistent with Buddhism:

1. Freedom to select the government;
2. Right to petition the government for a redress of grievances, and to receive just compensation;
3. Freedom from cruel and unusual punishment such as torture, the death penalty, and inhuman internment;
4. Right to equal and fair treatment under the law;
5. Freedom of religion and conscience;
6. Freedom from discrimination on the basis of race, creed, economic class, or gender;

7. Right to education;
8. Right to work and receive just compensation including health care;
9. Freedom from want for those unable to work through social security programs;
10. Right to a clean environment. (p. 540)

Macy (1991) asserted that the systems view of mutual causality illustrated in the *Aggañña Sutta* has been recognized as the first expression in Indian political thought of a theory of social contract. The story presents self, society, and world as evolving by interaction and progressive differentiation. Buddha traces the origin of kingship to *Mahasammata*, the great elected one, whom the people chose to act on their behalf. The Buddhist order of the Sangha followed Buddha's advocacy of government by open assembly and consensus. Putuwar (1988) asserted that the Sangha, governed by advanced discipline, represents an ideal society in the democratic manner. The vinaya rules act as the constitutional law connecting the Sangha with the laity. Tolerance of dissent was another feature of Buddhist governance.

In Peek's (1995) view, the impact of Buddhism on Japanese culture explains the speed with which the Japanese embraced the principles of popular sovereignty and individual rights contained in the "Occupation Constitution." The current or recent political setbacks in at least four traditionally Buddhist countries in Asia (i.e., Cambodia, Laos, Myanmar, and Vietnam) are incompatible with the Buddhist bill of rights, particularly the freedom to select the government.

We can easily add to this list another fundamental human right: right of free expression consonant with the universal norm of righteousness. This implies a positive freedom, not the negative freedom associated with the Occidental concept of liberal democracy. The effects of negative freedom would have a recursive impact on all living beings through the causal law of dependent co-arising (*paticca samuppada*), which some describe as Buddhism's cardinal doctrine.

Fukuyama (1995), on the other hand, argues that "the contours of Asian democracy may be very different from those of contemporary American democracy" (p. 21). Even China can claim to be practicing an Asian type of democracy at different levels of its governmental structure. China is culturally a Confucian-Daoist-Buddhist country. Because Daoism reflects libertarianism and Buddhism is consistent with democratic principles, China can philosophically absorb democracy even though Confucianism may not endorse liberty, equality, and pluralism to the extent that liberal democracy does. However, one could also argue that the *yin-yang* polarity immanent in Chinese philosophy signifies the recognition of pluralism—the multitude of shades spanning the two polarities.

Moreover, Fukuyama sees egalitarian implications in Confucianism's meritocratic examination system and its emphasis on education. He sees the compatibility of Confucianism with democracy in the sense that Confucianism "builds a well-ordered society from the ground up rather than the top down, stressing the moral obligations of family life as the basic building block of society" (Fukuyama, 1995, p. 25). Whereas the Occidental concept of democracy emphasizes individualism embedded in Judeo-Christian culture, the Oriental concept of democracy emphasizes the individual's moral obligations to family life and the community, as well as other interpersonal networks. Article 29 of the Universal Declaration of Human Rights acknowledges this aspect as well: "Everyone has duties to the community in which alone the free and full development of his personality is possible." (Some branches of Western social science—e.g., phenomenological sociology and symbolic interactionism—place supreme emphasis on the individual [Huysmans, 2003]. The action theory built into the systems approaches of Weber, Parsons, and Habermas also reflects the concern with individualism.)

COSMOPOLITAN DEMOCRACY

Examining the growing interconnections between states and societies, Held (2000) foresaw transformations in the form and nature of political community. He argued that globalization has wrought a reconfiguration of political power and created new forms of governance and politics both within states and beyond their boundaries. He held that one can no longer defend the idea of government or the state as an idea suitable to a particular closed political community or nation-state. He pointed out that the new forms of governance, which are emerging regionally, internationally and globally, require us to think in terms of a "cosmopolitan conception of democratic governance" (p. 394).

Held (2000) went on to say that contemporary governments and states have helped create an array of intergovernmental organizations, international agencies and regimes, as well as quasi-supranational institutions like the European Union (EU). Moreover, nonstate actors or transnational bodies also have emerged as participants in global politics. These developments have produced a more complex picture of regional and global governance. The global economy, which has become more open, fluid, and volatile, has turned our attention to the need for greater accountability.

Thus, Held (2000) argued, "the locus of effective political power can no longer be assumed to be national governments"; "the idea of a political community of fate . . . can no longer be meaningfully located within the boundaries of a single nation-state alone"; the complex global and regional systems have cut into the autonomy and sovereignty of states; and these developments are marked by a significant series of new types of "boundary problems" (p. 399).

Held (2000) has introduced the cosmopolitan conception of democratic governance to match the emerging global reality, "a world where citizens enjoy multiple citizenships," and where democracy needs to be thought of as a "double-sided process"— deepening of democracy within a national community combined with "the extension of democratic forms and processes across territorial borders" (p. 402). Cosmopolitan democracy is predicated on the principle of autonomy that "requires entrenchment in regional and global networks as well as in national and local polities" (Held, 1996, p. 358).

Held (1995, 1996) spelled out the key short- and long-term features for a model of cosmopolitan democracy. In the short term, Held called for reform of leading U.N. governing institutions such as the Security Council, creation of a U.N. second chamber, enhanced political regionalization, creation of a new international human rights court, establishment of an international military force, enhancement of nonstate/nonmarket solutions in organizing the civil society, experimentation with different democratic organizational forms in the economy, and provision of resources to the socially disadvantaged to defend and articulate their interests.

In the long term, Held (1995, 1996) called for a new charter of rights and obligations, a global parliament, separation of political and economic interests, an interconnected global legal system, shift of some state coercive capability to regional and global institutions, creation of a diversity of self-regulating associations and groups in civil society, a multisectoral economy and pluralization of ownership patterns, and public framework investment priorities with extensive market regulation of goods and labor.

Held's macroscopic view of cosmopolitan democracy has some commonalities with Eastern philosophy and the theory of living systems, which provide the theoretical framework of this book, because of its emphasis on the interconnections of the world system and the interaction between the macro and the micro. However, Held's model of cosmopolitan democracy, despite the claim that it reflects unfolding global reality, still has a West-centric bias because it presupposes man's superiority over nature. It relies on top–down intervention to achieve what it claims to be global reality already. It pays inadequate attention to autopoiesis at the microlevels of the world system as a far-from-equilibrium dissipative structure. It is more or less a linear model. (Chapter 3 provides a critique of linearity.) The future of democracy will indeed be cosmopolitan—a concept that needs further refinement to accommodate

Eastern thinking, which looks at "the entire cosmos as a cooperative" (Sivaraksa, 2002, p. 58).

In summary, this book posits that democracy takes various shades along a continuum stretching from libertarianism (*yin*) to authoritarianism (*yang*). Broadly, it means rule of the people. The sociocultural characteristics of a nation-state (or any of its variants) determine the type of democracy it practices across space time. The Judeo-Christian tradition's emphasis on individualism clashes with the obligations to family in the Eastern tradition, which emphasizes the unity and mutual interrelation of all things and events. The Freedom House's exclusion of many countries from the fold of electoral democracy shows the bias of the Judeo-Christian tradition. Because libertarianism and authoritarianism are the complements of each other, one cannot exist without the other.

I examine the connection between democracy and journalism in chapter 7 after developing our theory of communication outlets and free expression.

EXCURSUS: EAST–WEST DICHOTOMY

The broad bifurcation between East and West adopted in this book may elicit some critical reactions because it appears to perpetuate the simplistic dichotomy that Rudyard Kipling's *Ballad of East and West* stereotyped in the lines, "Oh, East is East, West is West, and never the twain shall meet Till Earth and Sky stand presently at God's great Judgment Seat."

This book attempts to merge the ancient Eastern wisdoms and modern Western scientific thinking to produce a humanocentric (a horizontally integrative macrohistory-oriented) theory. However, this should not be misconstrued as yielding to the common impulse with deep historical roots to portray the East as an essentialized, immutable, and fixed entity and the West as a constantly changing ontology. I concede that the discursive boundaries of the various societies that constitute the East are constantly changing. This undermines the impulse to essentialize. Moreover, the Enlightenment project and the modern knowledge systems continue to influence the ancient Eastern traditions through complex and powerful ways.

Servaes (1999), who recognized the high risks involved in making cross-cultural comparisons, has nevertheless attempted to show the distinctions between East and West in terms of ideal-typical examples. In his view, the sociocultural pattern of the (Confucian-Buddhist) East places emphasis on cosmocentric thinking, group orientation, asymmetry/hierarchy, harmony, passive outlook, and being, whereas the (Anglo-Saxon) West places emphasis on anthropocentric thinking, individualism, symmetry/horizontality, power/conflict, active outlook, and doing. Servaes (1999) also saw 13 distinguishing characteristics in communication patterns between East and West. For example, Eastern communication is Platonic, indirect, intermediate, situational, receiver-oriented, dialectical/dialogic, deductive, and affective, whereas Western communication is Aristotelian, direct, face to face, instrumental, source-oriented, linear/monologic, inductive, and assertive.

Tillis (2003), among others, contended that the East–West dichotomy has outlived its usefulness because the dichotomy is based on assumptions that are at once factually untrue and profoundly Eurocentric. One assumption is that East and West are coherent cultural entities. And another is that East and West are roughly of the same magnitude and, between them, comprehend the world. Tillis suggested that a multiregional perspective would offer a more sound framework for scholarship.

Tillis (2003) said that no justification exists to posit a single East in the place of various Asian cultures perhaps as different from one another as they are from Europe. He said that truly distinct and coherent cultures should not be subsumed under a totalizing label whose primary motive has been to define an undifferentiated other from the perspective of Europe. He added that this dichotomy connotes xenophobia and perhaps even racism. Tillis said the second assumption also does not stand up to reality because the aggregate cultures of the putative East actually dwarf the West. Moreover, much of the world is not comprehended by the East–West dichotomy, and a vast swath of Eurasia turns out to be neither East nor West. Tillis believed that the insidious effect of this assumption is the illegitimate aggrandizement of European culture, which has allowed itself to believe it makes up *half* the world.

The *diaspora* evident in the immigrant communities in Western metropolises such as Los Angeles, London, and Toronto also attests to the expansion of the discursive boundaries of societies that constitute the East. Tambiah (2000) analyzed the cultural and political life of such diaspora communities. Tu Weiming (2000) provided an estimate of 36 million ethnic Chinese overseas who belong to this diaspora. The U.S. Census Bureau states that 10.2 million people of Asian origin live in the United States. Great Britain is home for 1.5 million people of South Asian origin. From another perspective, the collapse of the Soviet Union also expanded the discursive boundaries of the East through the re-inclusion of Central Asia.

Despite the foregoing contentions and facts, we continue to use the East-West dichotomy to signify the basic cultural differences arising from Sino-Indian civilization and the European civilization. The myth of the East (broadly equivalent to the mythical Orient) continues to persist. Several scholarly journals perpetuate the myth in their titles (e.g., *Comparative Medicine East & West, East West Journal, Historiography East and West, Literature East and West*, and *Philosophy East & West*). Mosco (2004) said, "Myths are not true or false, but living or dead" (p. 3). Disproving a myth with evidence does little to dispel it.

Inden (1990) objected to terms such as *East* and *Orient* because they "have displaced human agency to essences in the first place" (p. 264). He said that Europeans and North Americans have produced many overlapping images of "the Orient" or "the East" as the Other. Hegel and his contemporaries were the first to make "sharp and essential distinctions between the different parts of Asia" (p. 50)—to contrast them with Semitic Near East and Aryan Persia. However, nowadays the terms *Orient* and *East* are loosely used to refer to Asia, which has no Asian equivalent.

Geographically, the East comprises West Asia, Central Asia, South Asia, Southeast Asia, and East Asia. However, West Asia (better known as the Middle East) and Central Asia (associated with the Commonwealth of Independent States), both of which belong to the Islamic world, appear to have gained distinct identities that de-link them from the myth of the East. At the dawn of the 21st century, the myth of the East seems to apply to the other three areas that, according to Holcombe (2001), historically came under the cultural influence of China and India.

The objection to the East–West dichotomy (on the basis that modern knowledge systems are impacting ancient Eastern traditions through complex and powerful ways) deserves a separate discussion (see chap. 2). This book retains the terms *East* and *West*, having warned the reader about the myth. I have used the terms in a cultural and civilizational sense (devoid of the sense of inferiority that Kipling attached to the East) while conceding the validity of the objections to the dichotomy. Kim (2000) also used this broad dichotomy in her attempt to validate the concept of *intercultural personhood* by demonstrating the complementarity of Eastern and Western cultural traditions, which are often looked upon as "unbridgeably incompatible" (p. 431). Northrop (1946/1966) was another thinker who drew attention to East–West complementarity.

NOTES

1. I have based this discussion of democracy on a previous essay (Gunaratne, in press).

2. "A coherent superposition is a thing-in-itself which is as distinct from its components as its components are from each other" (Zukav, 1979, p. 285). Goswami (1993) defined *coherent superposition* as "a multi-faceted quantum state with phase relations among its different facets (or possibilities)" (p. 276).

3. *The International Dictionary of Buddhism* (www.orientalia. org/term21828.html) contains the following entry on *paticca samuppada*: Dependent co-arising; dependent origination. A map showing the way the aggregates (*khandha*) and sense media (*ayatana*) interact with ignorance (*avijja*) and craving (*tanha*) to bring about stress and suffering (*dukkha*). As the interactions are complex, there are several different versions of *paticca samuppada* given in the suttas. In the most common one, the map starts with ignorance. In another common one, the map starts with the interrelation between name (*nama*) and form (*rupa*), on the one hand, and sensory consciousness (*vinnana*), on the other. Skt *pratitya-samutpada*.

Two

Eastern Philosophy
Congruence with Quantum Physics

> Quantum mechanics and the relativity theory have confirmed that no component of the atom can be adequately understood or explained except through the "totality" of its relations to all other components. Buddhism purports that this claim must be evinced also in regard to the macrocosmic universe and to the human consciousness which this universe houses. (Verdu, 1981, p. 167)

> The study of complementarity, the uncertainty principle, quantum field theory, and the Copenhagen Interpretation of Quantum Mechanics produces insights into the nature of reality very similar to those produced by the study of Eastern philosophy. (Zukav, 1979, p. 330)

Whereas Weber, Hegel, and their followers saw the negatives of Eastern mysticism, physicist Fritjof Capra ([1975]1999), in addition to Verdu (1981) and Zukav (1979), saw a remarkable congruence between Eastern mysticism—Hinduism, Buddhism, Confucianism, and Daoism— and quantum physics.

> The most important characteristic of the Eastern world view—one could almost say the essence of it—is the awareness of the unity and

mutual interrelation of all things and events. . . . The Eastern traditions constantly refer to this ultimate, indivisible reality which manifests itself in all things, and of which all things are parts. It is called
Brahman in Hinduism, *Dharmakaya* in Buddhism, *Dao* in Daoism.
Because it transcends all concepts and categories, Buddhists also call
it *Tathata*, or Suchness. . . . The basic oneness of the universe . . . is
also one of the most important revelations of modern physics.
(Capra, [1975]1999, pp. 130–131)[1]

Writing on Buddhism, Ratanakul (2002) pointed out the many similarities between Buddhist concepts and scientific discoveries, particularly with regard to the evolution of the universe and life, the nature of
physical reality, and the dynamic relationship between space and time.
The Buddhist worldview sees the universe as a process—a complex of
causal relationships. Whereas science helps "unlock the mystery of
physical reality, the Buddhist investigation shows that the reality of
moral and spiritual phenomena is open to human discovery, one in
which the law of cause and effect operates as in the physical world" (p.
116). I further elucidate the complementarity between Buddhism and
science in chapter 4.

Elaborating on the Hindu concept of *Brahman*, Raman (2003)
explained that it comes close to the idea of *transcendence* related to
modern scientific discourse. If *nature* is the totality of the material universe, then *transcendence* implicitly refers to something that goes
beyond the physical world—the supernatural. Hinduism, however,
regards transcendence "as a layer of reality, as a substratum, indeed,
the ultimate essence, of the experienced world" (p. 823). Thus, the
Hindu worldview goes beyond the empirical and the intellectually
grasped features of the universe to a third level—the nonmanifest
dimension. *Brahman* is the transcendent principle in the Hindu framework. *Brahman* is "like electrons and matter-waves" or "multidimensional space" (p. 825). Inasmuch as modern physics has unveiled that
virtual particles are responsible for all the known fundamental interactions, Raman says that *transcendence*, in the Hindu sense, "is the intan-
gible principle that breathes life into inert matter" (p. 835). Goswami
(1993) asserted that science—quantum physics, biology, cognitive psychology, and parapsychology—is now capable of validating the existence
of a transcendental domain of reality. His paradigm of "monistic idealism" takes the view that consciousness, not matter, is the foundation of
everything that is.

As for Chinese philosophy, Daoism has much in common with complexity science because both deal with "how the systems of nature flourish and diminish and how patterns emerge from the various interactive
components of the natural world" (Jones & Culliney, 1999, p. 644). The

self in Daoism is a fractal self. *Dao* is the seamless dimensionality in nature, which is congruent with the string theory of the universe. Jones and Culliney (1999) wrote, "Perhaps nowhere is there a better model for the edge of chaos than at the interface of *yin* and *yang* [through the interaction of which] order arises among the myriad things as they are blended in the world" (p. 649). They asserted that emergence seems to be clearly anticipated by Daoism.

Weber, in contrast, looks at Eastern philosophy from the perspective of West-centrism. Weber (1951) asserted that, *inter alia*, unlike the Puritan, the Confucian lacks the emotional tension to drive him to remake the world according to God's ethical imperatives. He said that Confucianism provides neither inducement nor sanction to rebel against the established social order or even to upset its equilibrium. Although he conceded that Daoism has certain features favoring innovation, he contended that its otherworldly orientation and its traditionalist qualities have led to the same consequences as those that stemmed from Confucianism. Focusing on India, Weber ([1921]1958) perceived orthodox Buddhism as a salvation religion that has no "concept of neighborly love, at least in the sense of the great Christian virtuosi of brotherliness" (p. 208). He observed that Buddhism regards women as irrational beings incapable of supreme spiritual power. As for Hinduism, Weber said it provides "an incomparable religious support for the legitimation interest of the ruling strata as determined by the social conditions of India" (p. 18). Indian religion, he reasoned, is one factor among many that obstructed the development of capitalism in the Occidental sense. Inden (1990) said that Weber, the "totem of post-Second World War conservative liberalism" (p. 77), simplistically identified the caste order as the essence of Indian civilization.

These contrasting views provide adequate proof of the subjective nature of social analysis irrespective of the method used—historical-hermeneutical, empirical-analytic, or critical theory. Servaes (1999) argued that "objectivity is nothing more than inter-subjectivity, principles, and parameters that people agree to agree on" (p. 116). Quantum mechanics asserts that there is no such thing as objectivity (Zukav, 1979). Keeping this in mind, I use a selection of authoritative sources to sketch the Oriental philosophies of China and India[2] to ferret out elements related to communication and democracy. I intend these sketches to convey a fuller sense of each philosophy than the basic elements needed to analyze the relationship between state and communication-outlets. In this exposition, I point out the salient connections to Eastern philosophy that the authors of the classic *Four Theories* (Siebert, Peterson, & Schramm, 1956) omitted because of their West-centrism.

[The terms *press system* and *press theory* are restrictive because they tend to limit the scope and history of freedom of expression (speech) to the post-Gutenberg print press. This imparts a West-centric bias at the outset. If our intent were to capture the freedom of expression (or the right to communicate) available within broad social systems across space time, better substitute terms would be *system of communication outlets* and *theories of communication outlets.*[3] The term *communication outlets* would include all public modes of conveying news, information, and opinion at least from the first communication revolution—the emergence of writing—onward. This term includes, but is not limited to, *mass media*, which Luhmann (2000) defined as "all those institutions of society which make use of copying technologies to disseminate communication . . . [as well as] the dissemination of communication via broadcasting" (p. 2). The term *free expression* denotes the broad intent of Article 19 of the Universal Declaration of Human Rights: "Everyone has the right to freedom of opinion and expression; this right includes the freedom to hold opinions without interference and to seek, receive and impart information and ideas though any media and regardless of frontiers." This right is presumed to entail positive freedom—rather than negative freedom—that is compatible with both Eastern and Western cultural traditions. The evolving right to communicate would not only include Article 19's *information* rights—to inform, to be informed, and to inquire, but also *association* rights—assembly, speech, and participation—and *global* rights—privacy, choice, and culture (see Harms, 2003).]

CHINESE PHILOSOPHY AND THEORY

The classical period of Chinese philosophy dawned with the Eastern Zhou dynasty's late spring and autumn period (722–479 BCE) and flourished during the Warring States period (479-221 BCE). Commonly known as the period of the "hundred schools" of thought, it produced China's renowned philosophers: Confucius, Mo Di (Mozi), Mencius, Laozi, Zhuangzi, Shang Yang, Xunzi, Sunzi, and Han Fei. They formed three main schools of thought: the Legalists (*Fajia*), the Confucians (*Rujia*), and their opposites, the Daoists (*Daojia*) and two supplementary schools—the Mohists (*Mojia*), and the Naturalists (*Yin-yangjia*). The last two, as well as the Legalist school, subsequently disappeared into the mainstream philosophies. Scholars carved out a sixth school, the Logicians (*Mingjia*), from among the mainstreams at a later stage.

Fajia

The Legalists were the followers of Shang Yang (?–338 BCE), Shen Buhai (?–337 BCE), Shen Dao (350–275? BCE), Han Fei (280?–233 BCE), and Li Si (?-208 BCE). Their ideas went back to those of the 7th-century BCE statesman, Guan Zhong, who worked to make Qi the strongest state of his time by increasing the power of the ruler. *Guanzi*, the text bearing his name, served as the earliest reference to issues such as law and order (De Bary & Bloom, 1999). Devoted to the codification of law, the Legalists advocated an authoritarianism that came close to fascism. They were instrumental in replacing feudalism with the feudal-bureau-cratic state. Rubin (1976) showed resemblances between Legalism and Machiavellism. Both "freed the political actor from the need to observe the norms of morality and deemed all means acceptable in the struggle for power" (p. 62). However, unlike the Legalists, Machiavelli did not see despotic violence as an end in itself. The Legalists asserted that the people were a mere tool or raw material in the hands of the ruler. The Legalists' concept of law was devoid of all moral and religious sanctions. They stressed punishment and rewards as the two handles the ruler could use "to govern effectively and achieve power and authority" (p. 66). They argued that "a dull and ignorant population [was] a source of great strength" in contrast to the Confucians' push for education (p. 72). The Legalists represented the far right in political tendency, whereas the Daoists represented the far left.[4]

Siebert (in Siebert, Peterson, & Schramm, 1956) traced the authori-tarian theory to Plato who "idealized the aristocratic form of govern-ment" (p. 12), but neglected to mention Plato's East Asian contempo-raries—Shang Yang and Shen Buhai—who expounded authoritarian views on the relation of man to the state.

Rujia

Confucians were the followers of Confucius (551–479 BCE), aka Kong Qiu Zhong-Ni. Mencius (385?–312? BCE), aka Meng Ke, was one of his great followers. Xunzi (310?–219? BCE) was another. The Confucians propagated social justice within the framework of the feudal, or feudal bureaucratic, social order. Needham (1956) said their advocacy of free-ing education from the barriers of privilege and social class was revolu-tionary because "it embodied some of the essential elements of modern democratic thought" (p. 7). They believed that the purpose of govern-ment was to bring about "the welfare and happiness of the whole peo-ple" through the "subtle administration of customs generally accepted as good and having the sanction of natural law" (pp. 7–8). Birth, wealth, or position had no necessary connection with the capacity to govern. The goal of Confucianism was "intellectual democracy" (p. 8). Government was to be paternalistic. The Confucians' picture of nature envisaged that "man is born for uprightness" (p. 12). Mencius "developed the democratic conception that the goodwill of the people was essential in government" (p. 16). Legge (1895) quoted Mencius thus: "The people are the most important element in a nation; . . . the sovereign is the lightest" (p. 483), and "Benevolence is the distinguishing characteristic of man" (p. 485). Confucians believed that knowledge was the beginning of action and action the consummation of knowledge (Jung, 1999). Another element of Confucianism is the doctrine of the mean (*Zhongyong*), traditionally ascribed to Zisi, the grandson of Confucius: "Let the states of equilibrium and harmony exist in perfection, and a happy order will prevail throughout heaven and earth, and all things will be nourished and flourish" (Legge, 1893, p. 385). Rubin (1976) pointed out that Confucians had understood the "idea of man as a harmonious and fully developed person" long before Renaissance humanism (p. 25). Xunzi, a humanist, viewed human culture as the noblest thing in the world.[5] Byun and Lee (2001) pointed out that Confucianism presents five key interrelated sets of foundational moral principles or insights collectively called *Five Constants: ren* or *in* (human-heartedness), *yi* or *ui* (righteousness, proper character, and a principle of rationality), *li* or *ye* (rituals and ceremonies), *zhi* or *ji* (wisdom), and *xin* or *shin* (trust). Yum (2000) outlined the impact of Confucianism on communication patterns in East Asia. These patterns include the perception of communication as a process of infinite interpretation, the use of different linguistic codes depending on the persons involved and the situations, the emphasis on indirect communication, and receiver-centered interpretation of meaning.

Although Confucianism included numerous elements linked to the ethos of social responsibility (e.g., emphasis on knowledge and education, intellectual democracy, natural law, and moral obligations), Peterson (in Siebert, Peterson, & Schramm, 1956) thought of the social responsibility theory as essentially a Western construct born out of the "intellectual climate of the twentieth century" (p. 81). This conveys the incorrect impression that the notion of social responsibility originated as a reaction to the peculiar conditions of American communication outlets in the last century. Nuyen (2001) pointed out that Confucianism placed "a supreme value on personal freedom and autonomy" (p. 70), as well as equality, within a horizontal and vertical structure of social responsibility similar to the Western liberal tradition.[6] Had Peterson examined the social responsibility of communication outlets within a Confucian framework as well, he could have developed a more humanocentric theory. The Confucian concept of social responsibility was based on the coupling of the Five Constants with five social relationships—those between husband and wife, parent and child, ruler and subject, sibling and sibling, and friend and friend. Its aim was to produce social harmony. (Frank [1998] used the term *humanocentric* to refer to what historian Fletcher [1985] called the horizontally integrative macrohistory approach, which takes into account human developments across space-time rather than vertically focusing on one civilization or region, e.g., Western or European.)

Daojia

Daoists were the followers of Laozi (6th–5th century BCE) and Zhuangzi (369–286 BCE). Their insight into nature was comparable to pre-Aristotelian Greek thought. They rejected the feudal society and provided the basis for Chinese science. As Rubin (1976) explained, they "looked on society as evil and called on mankind to break loose from society's tenacious embrace, shake off the fetters of false duties and obligations, return to nature, and merge with the unsullied, simple, and genuine life of the universe" (p. 89). *Dao* meant *the way of man* (more precisely, the way of nature/universe that man should follow). Daoism, as Needham (1956) pointed out, was religious and poetical, as well as "strongly magical, scientific, democratic and politically revolutionary" (p. 35). Above all, the Daoists emphasized the unity of nature. They considered social knowledge valued by the Confucians and Legalists as rational, but false. What they wished to acquire was knowledge of nature—"empirical, perhaps even liable to transcend human logic, but impersonal, universal and true" (p. 98). They opposed the feudal nobility and merchants alike, and they yearned for "some kind of primitive agrarian collectivism" (p. 100), an undifferentiated natural condition of life or pure primitive solidarity. The *Daodejing* calls on people to abandon language and return "once more to the use of knotted ropes," a system used for record keeping before the invention of writing (De Bary & Bloom, 1999, p. 94).

Siebert (in Siebert, Peterson, & Schramm, 1956), however, saw the libertarian theory too as essentially a modern Western construct born out of "the theological doctrines of early Christianity" on "the nature of knowledge and of truth" (p. 41). The salience of Daoism to libertarian theory escaped Siebert's mind. In Daoism, "the individual and his free expression become the end and justification of everything" (Lin, 1947, p. 259). Critics may argue that, although Daoists had a strong sense of freedom in mind, they had no concerns with the freedom of expression they did not care about worldly affairs or the state at all. In fact, Lin (1947) pointed out that Daoist freedom was the freedom of a pre- or asocial being in comparison to the freedom of the socially conscious man in Western libertarianism. Daoism, Lin asserted, postulated generalized freedom without giving it content. However, one has to bear in mind that Daoism describes two approaches for practicing *pu* (unassuming attitude) and exercising *de* (power) so as to adhere to the Daoist principle of *wuwei* (effortlessness)—the ideal way to act, live, and think. One approach, directed to those engaged in public affairs, focuses on not impinging on the dictates of other people's *de* in the exercise of one's own. The other approach, directed to those who want to achieve their freedom in solitude, acknowledges the problems imposed by a complex society on one's desire to achieve freedom in consonance with one's *de*. Thus, those who see no connection between Daoism and freedom of expression have overlooked the Daoist advice for those engaged in public affairs.

The same critics may also argue that Laozi did not care about physics, although much of *Daodejing* is close to modern (quantum) physics. The penultimate chapter of *Daodejing* also says:

> Let [the people] savor their food and find beauty in their clothing,
> Peace in their dwellings, and joy in their customs. (chap. 80)

This shows that Daoism's main concern was happiness of the people. It follows the "small is beautiful" motto and even discourages the use of machines. The Daoist state is a retrenchment from civilization. Obviously, computers and Internet hosts were not a matter of concern in ancient China. From the viewpoint of subaltern studies (Chakrabarty, 2000), we have to be careful about how we interpret the ancient Laozi text—well known for its vagueness, ambiguity, and subtlety of thought—in relation to the citizens of the modern "nation-state." The path of *wuwei* guides the Daoist to follow the way of nature, which is invariably in a state of flux. The ambiguity of *Daodejing* was perhaps intended to allow for different interpretations in the context of the inevitability of change. Can a contemporary Daoist literally abandon the language and shun the mass media?[7]

Mojia

The Mohists were the followers of Mo Di (c. 479-381 BCE). They were chivalrous military pacifists who dabbled in the scientific method. Needham (1956) said that, although the earliest Mohists were interested in ethics, social life, and religion, the later Mohists were more concerned with scientific logic, science, and military technology. The Mohists showed an ambiguous attitude toward feudal society. In certain places, they condemned primitive society or the state of nature, almost in anticipation of Hobbes' description in the *Leviathan*, as a war of each against all: "In the beginning of human life . . . each man had his own idea, two men had two different ideas, and ten men had ten different ideas . . . ; so arose mutual disapproval among men. . . . The disorder in the human life could be compared to that among birds and beasts" (Mo Di, cited in Needham, p. 166). However, elsewhere they adopted an attitude similar to that of Daoists. Overall, they were not fundamentally against feudalism as such. They were similar to the Confucians except for "their greater interest in all that would benefit the people" (p. 168). Rubin (1976) said this concept of Mohist utilitarianism is comparable to that of the English philosophical school of the 18th and 19th centuries, whose main representatives were Jeremy Bentham and John Stuart Mill. Whereas the Confucians stressed family ties, the Mohists stressed universal love, the implementation of which they entrusted to the ruler. Thus, some consider Mo Di "the forerunner of socialism" (p. 36). One can readily see that Mohism also has much in common with the libertarian and social responsibility philosophies—a connection that escaped Siebert, Peterson, and Schramm (1956).

Yin-Yangjia

The Naturalists were the followers of Zou Yan (305?–240? BCE), who focused on the two universal forces—*yin* and *yang*—and the five elements of which all process and all substance was composed—water, fire, wood, metal, and earth.[8] They developed a philosophy of organic naturalism. The *yin* and *yang* characters were connected with darkness and light, respectively. Needham (1956) said the five elements were considered "five powerful forces in ever-flowing cyclical motion, and not passive motionless fundamental substances" (p. 244). Everything in the universe fitted into a fivefold arrangement in symbolic correlation associated with the five elements. Unlike the Daoists, the Naturalists "did not shun the life of courts and kings . . . [because] they confidently felt themselves to be in possession of certain facts about the universe which rulers could neglect only at their peril" (pp. 234–235). The Greeks' pre-Socratic school had also distinguished five elements—earth, fire, air, water, and the nonlimited—exhibiting certain similarities and striking differences with the Chinese version (p. 246). The *yin* and *yang* moved parallel to each other, but not along the same path because they met to operate as the controller of each other. Needham said,

> The implication was that the universe itself is a vast organism, with
> now one and now another component taking the lead—spontaneous
> and uncreated it is, with all the parts of it cooperating in mutual ser-
> vice which is perfect freedom, the larger and the smaller playing
> their parts according to their degree, "neither afore nor after other."
> (pp. 288–289)

The principle of the *yin-yang* complements, which demonstrates universal interconnections, provides the means to build a dynamic theory of
communication outlets and free expression—a theory that can provide
both explanation and probabilistic outcomes.

Mingjia

The Logicians, later identified as a school associated with Hui Shi
(380–305? BCE) and Gongsun Long (380–? BCE), were comparable to
the Greek Sophists. Needham (1956) saw a remarkable similarity
between the Logicians' paradoxes and those in Greek history associated
with Zeno of Elea. Both Mohists and Logicians, Needham said, "attempted to lay foundations upon which the world of natural sciences could
have been built. Perhaps the most significant thing about them is that
they show an unmistakable tendency towards dialectical rather than
Aristotelian logic, expressing it in paradox and antinomy, conscious of
entailed contradiction and kinetic reality" (p. 199). Dialectical logic,
which is common to both Eastern and Western philosophy, provides further muscle to build a dynamic theory of communication outlets and
free expression.

Chinese Philosophy and Communication

Li (1999) asserted that the "harmony model is at the core of the Chinese
culture" (p. 191), considering that most Chinese people follow a multiple
approach to life by following Daoism, Buddhism, and Confucianism at
the same time. Thus, although some core values of democracy may
seem incompatible with Confucianism, both can coexist in harmony—an
aspect most relevant to the conceptualization of social responsibility as
a cultural outcome of the interaction of the two extremes of libertarianism and authoritarianism. (However, as stated earlier, Confucianism
also embodied some of the essential elements of modern democratic
thought.) Li compared Western and Chinese philosophy in terms of
seven dimensions: being, truth, language, ethics, family, religion, and
justice.

Li (1999) pointed out that Chinese thinking follows Zhuangzi's *contextual perspective* ontology, whereas the Western world follows Aristotle's *substance* ontology that emphasizes individuality. The West, as evident in Heidegger's work, usually understands *truth* semantically, whereas the Chinese understand it as a matter of being a good person, as a way of life. In the West, *language* performs a solely semantic and logical function, whereas the Chinese see the social and pragmatic function of language as evident in the Confucian doctrine of "rectification of names" (p. 3). Important similarities exist between Confucian ethics and feminist ethics. On the issue of *family*, fundamental differences exist in relation to filial morality. In contrast to Western thinking, Confucianism states that people are "not atomistic, self-serving, rights-laden individuals coming to construct a society out of self-interest" (p. 138). As for *religion*, in contrast to Western orthodox monotheisms, the Chinese culture accepts multiple religious practices. Finally, as for *justice*, democracy as a "value system" can coexist with Confucianism even though the two systems are not fully compatible. These seven dimensions demonstrate that a purely Western definition of *social responsibility* is inadequate to capture the meaning of that term in East Asia or other non-Western cultures. A communication theory, therefore, must recognize different shades of social responsibility within different cultures.

Tu Weiming (1997) said that the Chinese thinkers, unlike their Western counterparts, were not all anthropocentric because a cosmological, as well as an anthropological, vision had inspired them. Thus, Chinese philosophy exhibited humanism—an emphasis on social relations, a strong commitment to the world, and the primacy of political order—from the outset. In building up her concept of intercultural personhood, Kim (2000) demonstrated how Eastern and Western traditions can rise above cultural differences—apparent in their worldviews on universe and nature, knowledge, time, and communication—to serve as complementary forces in the same fashion as the *yin* and *yang* are united under the all-encompassing *Dao*.

Tang (1991) saw Chinese philosophy as a threefold integration: the "integration of heaven with man," which inquires into the unity of the world; the "integration of knowledge with practice," the problem of an ethical norm; and the "integration of feeling with scenery," involving the creation and appreciation of artistic works (p. 6). Cheng (1987) expanded on these three integrations to derive six basic principles of Chinese philosophy most relevant to contemporary communication theory: the principle of part–whole interdetermination; the principle of dialectical completion of relative polarities—the *yin* and the *yang*; the principle of infinite interpretation; the principle of embodiment of reason in experience; the principle of epistemological-pragmatic unity; and the principle of symbolic reference. The theory of communication outlets and free expression developed in this book relies heavily on the first three principles.

HINDU PHILOSOPHY AND THEORY

The origin of Hindu philosophical ideas is associated with the Vedas, a body of texts—*Rigveda, Samaveda, Yajurveda*, and *Atharvaveda*—traced to some 2,000 years before Christ. Mohanty (2000) said that the Vedas provide "an exemplary spirit of inquiry into 'the one being' (*ekam sat*) that underlies the diversity of empirical phenomena, and into the origin of all things" (p. 1). More than 108 Upanishads, a group of texts dating from 1000 BCE to the time of Buddha, and other canonical texts, including the *Bhagavad-Gita*, gave Hindu thinking a more philosophical character with their attempt to reinterpret Vedic sacrifices and to defend one central philosophical thesis: the identity of *Brahman* (the source of all things) and *atman* (the self within each person). These ancient texts, as well as the epics *Ramayana* and *Mahabharata*, Kautilya's *Artha-shastra*, Buddha's *dharma*, Sukra's *niti*, and various literary works, provide the elements constituting the Indian philosophy of state, society, and law.

The notions of *samsara* (continuing reincarnations), *karma* (the fruit of past actions), and *moksa* (release or liberation) are central to nearly all varieties of Hinduism (Milner, 1993; Mohanty, 1998). Scholars list six orthodox schools of Hinduism that recognize the authority of the Vedas: *Nyaya*, which focuses on logic and reasoning; *Vaisesika*, which focuses on the nature of physical existence and is known for its theory of atomism; *Samkhya*, which explains the world of appearances (*maya*) in terms of its theory of evolution of existence and consciousness; *Yoga*, which focuses on the philosophy of yoga, as well as on yoga techniques and practice; *Mimamsa*, which is concerned with explaining and organizing the Vedic teachings on ritual and sacrifice; and *Vedanta*, which is concerned with the nature of Brahman and its relation to the world as described in the Vedas. The self or soul (*atman*) is what moves through *samsara*. The Hindu view of the individual and his or her relation to society, according to Radhakrishnan (1940), can best be brought out by a reference to the synthesis and gradation of the:

- fourfold object of life (*purusartha*): desire and enjoyment (*kama*), interest (*artha*), ethical living (*dharma*), and spiritual freedom (*moksa*);
- fourfold order of society (*vayna*): man of learning (*Brahmin*), of power (*Ksatriya*), of skilled productivity (*Vaisya*), and of service (*Sudra*); and

- fourfold succession of the stages of life (*asrama*): student (*brahmacari*), householder (*grihastha*), forest recluse (*vanaprastha*), and free supersocial man (*saññyasin*).

Within this threefold discipline, the Hindu attempts to reach his destiny.

Babbili (2001) stated that the Hindu concepts of *dharma* (construed as duty, righteousness, customs, traditions, law, nature, justice, virtue, merit, and morality) and *ahimsa* (nonviolence), a concept absorbed from anti-Vedic Jainism, form the basis of the entire superstructure of ethics in Hindu philosophy. *Dharma* takes three forms: virtues of the body (charity, helping the needy, and social service), virtues of speech (truthfulness, benevolence, and gentleness), and virtues of the mind (kindness, unworldliness, and piety). *Ahimsa* requires absolute harmlessness and friendliness toward all beings.

> Arguably, *dharma* is Hinduism's most fundamental concept. Hinduism itself is often referred to as *sanatana dharma*, the eternal dharma. . . . At its broadest level, it encompasses many other concepts including notions of salvation and liberation. But in its narrower and more concrete meanings, it refers to the rules governing day-to-day life. At the core of these are the norms that regulate a particular caste and distinguish it from other castes, that is, *svadharma*. Hence, to show the relationship between the key features of caste and the concepts of *samsara*, *karma*, and *moksa* is to relate these concept to dharma, at least in its narrowest meaning. (Milner, 1993, p. 304)

Weber ([1921]1958) surmised that two features hindered the rationalization of life in Hindu society to arrive at the "sprit of capitalism": the ritualistic and traditional inner relations anchored through the caste order to the *samsara* and *karma* teaching, and the religious anthropolatry of the laity against the naturally strong, traditionalistic, charismatic clergy of the *gurus*. Matilal (1989) explained that "karma or ethical rationalism emphasizes the 'merit-based' nature of the social order, while the caste-hierarchy emphasizes its 'heredity-based' nature" (p. 198). Matilal added that the caste hierarchy made the social system antirational and unfair, and the karma theodicy was introduced for the rationalization of the existing practice. Adams (2001), however, argued that, "contrary to Weber and his ofttimes closest allies," religious values or attitudes have little or no impact on the work habits or the work ethic in the Indian scene (p. 165).

Sarkar (1921) pointed out that the Hindu theory of the state emerged from an attempt to analytically define the state from the non-state or the state of nature. The Hindu thinkers associated the state of nature with the logic of the fish (i.e., the doctrine of matsya-nyaya). In the nonstate, people were "devouring one another like the stronger fishes preying upon the feebler," according to the *Mahabharata*; "the strong would devour the weak like fishes," according to the *Manu Samhita*; "people [would] ever devour one another like fishes," according to *Ramayana*; or "the child, the old, the sick, the ascetic, the priest, the woman and the widow would be preyed upon [based on] the logic of the fish," according to the *Matsya-Purana* (cited in Sarkar, 1921, p. 80). Kautilya (4th century BCE), who wrote the *Artha-shastra* (which is often compared with Sunzi's *The art of war* and Machiavelli's *The prince*),[9] asserted that the logic of the fish prevailed in the absence of the state. Kamandaka, who wrote the *Niti-shastra* in the fourth century after Christ, also said that the logic of the fish would operate in the absence of punishment (*danda*).

Sarkar (1921) stated that two "inseparable accidents" of the Hindu theory of state are the doctrine of *mamatva* or *svatva* (i.e., property), and the doctrine of *dharma* (i.e., law, justice, and duty). Lying behind these two is the doctrine of *danda* (i.e., punishment, restraint, or sanction). The Hindu philosophy of sovereignty is based on these three concepts. The absence of *danda* is tantamount to *matsya-nyaya* or the state of nature. "A state is a state because it can coerce, restrain, compel" (p. 84). Thus, the theory is based on two premises: 1. No *danda*, no state; and 2. No state, no *dharma* or property. In Hindu philosophy, the rationale for *danda* is the original nature of man as described by Kamandaka, Manu, and others. Sarkar explains, "The state is designed to correct human vices or restrain them and open up the avenues to a fuller and higher life" (p. 87).

The ruler in office is the *danda-dhara* (i.e., bearer of the torch of sovereignty). However, the ruler as a person is subject to *danda* as any other. *Danda* is a two-handed sword: It is a terror to the people and is a corrective of social abuses; it is also a most potent instrument of danger to the ruler himself. As Manu observes, *danda* would smite the king who deviated from his duty, as well as his relatives and possessions. Sarkar (1921) said herein lies "the logical check on the possible absolutism of the *danda-dhara* in the Hindu theory of sovereignty" (p. 90). In Kautilya's view, however, the king's authority is a matter of divine right, and no misgivings need be permitted to intrude themselves such as may weaken the ruler's will; and he must have no scruples, even when expediency compels him to be cruel (Gowen, 1929, p. 179).

Sarkar (1918a) says that every branch of Sanskrit literature provides accounts of Hindu political life and theory. The sources include some of the *Puranas* (legends), all the *Smriti-shastras* (treatises on human tradition), *Manu-samhita* (hymns of Manu), the epics *Mahabharata* and *Ramayana*, *Pancha-tantra*, *Raghu-vamsha*,

Hitopadesha, Dharma-sutras (aphorisms on Dharma), *Dharma-shastras* (treatises on Dharma), *Artha-shastras* (treatises on material gain), *Niti-shastras* (treatises on science of polity, particularly those of Kamandaka and Shukracharyya), *Dasha-kumaracharita, Dhanurveda* (a treatise on warfare), and King Bhoja's *Yukti-kalpa-taru* (requirements of the royal court). Sarkar asserted that the Hindu state was thoroughly secular, and never theocratic because of the absence of the concept of the divine right of kings.

Mohanty (1998) said the problems that the Hindu philosophers raised but escaped the attention of their Western counterparts include such matters as the origin and appreciation of truth. The problems that escaped Hindu philosophers "include the question of whether knowledge arises from experience or from reason and distinctions such as that between analytic and synthetic judgments or between contingent and necessary truths" (p. 191). Thus, he argues, knowledge of both Hindu philosophy and Western philosophy is beneficial to fill the gaps.

The Hindu theory is more akin to the benevolent despotism of Confucianism though it does not agree with Mencius' view of the "original goodness" of human nature. It agrees neither with the Daoists' faith in primitive agrarian collectivism nor with the extreme authoritarianism of the Legalists. It has similarities with the thinking of some early modern European philosophers as well. The Hindu theory favored monarchy whereas Buddhist theory "opposed monarchy and defended a sort of republican government" (Mohanty, 2000, p. 96) because change and impermanence were central to Buddhist philosophy. Buddhism, in its two sectarian forms, promoted individualism, as well as collective responsibility. It promoted democratic ideals with its disapproval of caste and class distinctions and its propagation of universal love. Mohanty clarifies that the Hindu concept of monarchy also involved compassion; therefore, it is not comparable to the concept of sovereignty in Western political thought because in India the concept of *dharma* maintained its superiority over the sovereignty of the king.

The Hindu description of the non-state was quite similar to the description of the state of nature by European philosophers such as Hooker, Hobbes, Spinoza, and Mill in the early modern period. They conceived the state of nature as a state of the right of might, a war of all against all, an anarchy of birds and beasts, or a regime of vultures and harpies. Mo Di, the Chinese philosopher, also painted a similar picture of the non-state although the Mohists' view of the non-state was sometimes consistent with that of Daoists.

Dissanayake (1987) pointed out eight guiding principles in Indian philosophy related to communication: oneness of things—the interlinking of all beings, events, and phenomena in a composite whole; intuition; transtemporality; nonindividuality; liberation (*moksa*); illusion (*maya*); idealism; and renunciation/nonattachment (p. 154). Despite the differentiation and separateness apparent in the caste system in this world, *moksa* emphasizes oneness with or connectedness to the divine other. The notion of totality is evident not only in Hindu philosophy but also throughout Indian culture. Godin (2000) asserted that India has developed an eschatology and a soteriology of totality looked upon in terms of extensive totality (*vishva*) and intensive totality (*sarva*). The whole expressed by sarva does not include everything. The Mundaka Upanishad says *Brahman* is everything. *Brahman*, therefore, is more or less similar to *Taiji* (Supreme Ultimate) in Chinese philosophy.

Several of the guiding principles of Hinduism show similarities to those of Chinese philosophy: The principle of part–whole interdetermination is related to the "karmic eschatology"—the tripartite *samsara-karma-moksa* mechanism—of Hinduism even though Chinese philosophy is not a soteriology. The Hindu principles of intuition and idealism fit in with the Chinese principle of infinite interpretation. The Chinese principle of the dialectical completion of relative polarities fits in with the Hindu principles of transtemporality, nonindividuality, and illusion because the meeting of *yin* and *yang* engenders the continual transformation of all things.

Weber ([1921]1958) pointed out that similar to the *yin* and *yang*, the early Upanishads refer to the *purusha* (the masculine spiritual principle) entangled with the *prakriti* (the feminine principle). Therein, the undeveloped, materially conceived psychic and mental powers of the empirical world are slumbering: These powers are the three basic substantive entities (*gunas*) of the soul—*satva* (intelligence or divine brightness and benevolence), *rajas* (energy or human striving and passions), and *tamas* (mass inertia or bestial darkness and stupidity). Srinivasiengar (1934) analyzed the *purusha-prakriti* interaction in terms of the Samkhya-Yoga doctrine, according to which the universe has sprung out of the primal cause, the *prakriti*, viz., the equilibrium of the three *gunas*, which together are responsible for the creation of the whole physical and mental world except the *purusha*. Evolution begins when the equilibrium of the triad of *gunas* is disturbed; and *karma* regulates the entire cosmic evolution in accordance with man's *dharma* (good/merit) and *adharma* (evil/demerit). The *Bhagavad-Gita*, the most typical expression of Hinduism as a whole, describes this phenomenon at length. It begins:

> Primal matter [*prakriti*] and spirit [*purusha*]—know them both to be beginningless. The modifications and the constituent properties—know them as originated from primal matter. (Embree, 1988, p. 293)

Siebert, Peterson, and Schramm (1956) excluded the insights of Hindu philosophy on the nature of man, the nature of society and the state, the relation of man to the state, and the nature of knowledge and truth—the beliefs and assumptions they used "to determine the true relationship of the press to the social system" (p. 2). They excluded all non-Western philosophy despite the thesis they claimed to underlie their volume: that "the press always takes on the form and coloration of the social and political structures within which it operates" (p. 1). Although they emphasized "that an understanding of these aspects of society is basic to any systematic understanding of the press" (p. 2), they developed their four theories solely based on West-centric experience. Thus, for instance, *dharma* and *ahimsa* did not enter their construct of social responsibility; the logic of the fish failed to ring a bell despite its resemblance to Hobbes' state of nature; and the different nuance of "sovereignty" in Hindu, as well as Buddhist, philosophy escaped them in their construct of authoritarianism. In short, they used—to borrow an expression from Hardt (2001)—"European history as the universal mediating term, the standard through which all other histories are understood" (p. 245).

BUDDHIST PHILOSOPHY AND THEORY

Siddhartha Gautama (c. 563-483 BCE) founded Buddhism in a revolt against Brahmanism and the monarchical state, which the Hindus glorified.[10] Buddhists split into sects long before written records came into being. However, Needham (1956) said, all sects and schools were united on certain fundamentals, including the pre-Buddhist theory of *karma*. The Buddhist "karmic eschatology"—*samsara, karma*, and *nirvana*— was not the same as that of Hinduism. The Buddhist version of *karma* differed from that of the Upanishads "in that the happiness or misery was regarded as being based only on moral or ethical grounds, and not on whether ritual or sacrificial acts had been performed" (p. 399). Hindu *samsara* (cycle of reincarnation) differed from Buddhist *samsara* (cycle of rebirth); and Hindu *moksa* (liberation, meaning oneness with or connectedness to the divine other) differed from Buddhist *nirvana* (cessation from the cycle of rebirth). Moreover, Buddhist *karma* was not associated with rigid caste groups (*jatis*).

The Buddhist *dharma* meant the doctrine based on the Four Noble Truths: That suffering exists; that the cause of suffering is thirst, craving, or desire; that a path exists to end suffering; that the Noble Eightfold Path is the path to end suffering. Described as the "middle way," it specifies the commitment to *sila* (right speech, action, and livelihood), *samadhi* (right effort, mindfulness, and concentration), and *panna* (right understanding and thoughts). The essence of the *dharma* is the chain of causation.

The Buddhist scriptures comprise three collections: the *suttas*, the *vinaya*, and the *abhidhamma*. The *vinaya* relates to the discipline of the monks, and the *suttas* relate to the doctrine. *Abhidhamma* relates to doctrinal matters mentioned in the *suttas* in greater depth (Dasgupta, 1922). Buddhism crystallized into the Hinayana (Lesser Vehicle) and Mahayana (Greater Vehicle) forms in the second century BCE The former advocated individual progress to *arhat*-ship and attainment of *nirvana*, while the latter advocated the salvation of everyone "by deliberate submission, if necessary, to a further series of rebirths, thus postponing the individual's attainment of *nirvana*" (Needham, 1956, p. 403). In the Mahayana view, the world was full of *bodhisattvas*, and "only the effort to save others could lead to the salvation of the self" (p. 404)—a paradox that the Daoists in China readily appropriated.

Mahayana Buddhism spread in East Asia from the second to the fifth century. In China, as Needham (1956) said, Buddhism "collided with Confucian skepticism and [Daoist] selflessness" (p. 410) because "Buddhism was a profound rejection of the world, a world which, each in their different ways, both Confucianism and [Daoism] accepted" (p. 430). Dasgupta (1922) pointed out that Buddhism encountered several ontological problems because of its thesis that everything was impermanent, so neither cause nor effect could abide; so no part-whole relationship could exist; so no universals could exist; so no substance, apart from its attributes, could exist; and no power-possessor separate from the power could exist (p. 165). Needham finds fault with Buddhism for turning away from Nature, thereby discouraging the development of science.[11] However, he asserts that Buddhism was a great civilizing force in Central Asia, and he credits Buddhism for introducing "that element of universal compassion which neither [Daoism] nor Confucianism, rooted as they were in family-ridden Chinese society, could produce" (p. 431).

De Bary (1958) draws attention to the few definite instructions on social and political life that Buddhist literature provides. Buddhism, as evident in *Sutta Nipata*, disapproved the extremer manifestations of social inequality in the system of class and caste; it "definitely discouraged the pretensions of kings to divine or semidivine status" and tended to mitigate the autocracy of the king (p. 128). The first king, according to the *Digha Nikaya* (the Discourse of the Great Passing-away), held office by virtue of a contract with his subjects—one of the oldest versions of the contractual theory of the state. The king was merely a leader chosen by the people to restrain crime and protect property. Buddhism encouraged deciding major issues after free discussion based on the practices of the tribal republics of the Buddha's day, for example, the republics of Sakiyas and Vajjians. (This calls into question the West-centric tendency to trace democracy to ancient Greece alone.) Moreover, as Goonatilake (2001) pointed out, personal experience and verification are central to Buddhist theory: "Buddhism is . . . experiential and experimental, built on individual perception and experiences, not necessarily on another's unverified word of his experience" (p. 16).

Konsky, Kapoor, Blue, and Kapoor (2000) attempted to extract the principles of communication related to Hinduism, Buddhism, and Christianity. They point out that Buddhism strongly upholds the "high ethical concepts of tolerance, non-violence, respect for the individual, love of animals and nature and a belief in the fundamental spiritual equality of all human beings" (p. 244). Chuang and Chen (2003) have analyzed how Buddhist teachings have influenced East Asian communication behaviors from five perspectives: ontological assumptions, communication ethics, communication behaviors, relationship development, and rhetorical communication. Ontologically, the Buddhist presumptions of holism, relationality, and mutual dependence are related to human communication. Ethically, the Noble Eightfold Path provides three basic guidelines on right speech, right action, and right livelihood. Behaviorally, the Buddhist emphasis on harmony, functional dependence, selflessness, compassion, and ethics have influenced the East Asian characteristics reflected in intuition, silence, empathy, emotional control, and non-aggressiveness. The Buddhist doctrine of dependent co-arising has played a critical role in the initiation, maintenance, and termination of human relationships. Buddhist preaching has influenced the rhetorical arts.

Siebert, Peterson, and Schramm (1956), in developing their theories, failed to examine the rich insights of Buddhist philosophy pertaining to sovereignty, democratic ideals, individual inquiry, ethical behavior, ontology, functional dependence, and so on, that would have enabled them to think of historical reality without the universal mediation of the history of Europe or, in the words of Chakrabarty (2000), by "provincializing Europe." Because these three authors developed their theories in the political context of the Cold War, they also failed to examine their theories in relation to the evolving right to communicate—a right that goes well beyond freedom of the press and includes responsibilities as well (Harms, 2003). Servaes (1999) pointed out that the right to communicate contains both the passive and active right of the receiver to inform and be informed whereas originally the concepts of freedom of expression and freedom of the press placed emphasis on "the active right of the so-called sender-communicator to supply information without externally imposed restrictions" (p. 143).

SUBALTERN VIEW VERSUS QUANTUM PHYSICS

Those who disagree with my identification of Daoism with libertarianism and Confucianism with social responsibility may also argue that these classical philosophies do not fit the conditions of contemporary "modernity." In my view, such objections arise from the semantic reification of "Enlightenment" concepts such as nation-state, democracy, rationality, freedom, equality, and pluralism. Tu Weiming (1997) would identify this as an "unintended negative consequence" of Enlightenment, which "marginalized the spiritual resources of the Chinese tradition, destroyed the core values of the Sinic world, and made the viability of the human species problematical" (p. 3). Postcolonial subaltern historiography (e.g., Chakrabarty, 2000) takes the view that although these concepts had European origins, they have gained universalism since the subjugated "non-Europe" used the self-same concepts to free themselves from the yoke of European imperialism. Tu also concedes that the Enlightenment mentality has become a defining characteristic of modernity.

The humanocentric approach to theory development adopted in this book has no conflict with the subaltern stand (Chakrabarty, 2000) that "Nativism" is no answer to West-centrism because the universals proposed by "Enlightenment" remain indispensable to any social critique that seeks to address issues of social justice and equity. The subaltern project of "provincializing Europe" entails a translation of existing worlds and their thought categories into the categories and self-understandings of capitalist modernity. Thus, the subaltern project involves globalizing[12] such thought by exploring how it may be renewed both for and from the margins. In my view, such a renewal is possible by establishing their connections to the classical philosophies of "non-Europe." I have pointed out elsewhere (Gunaratne, 2005a) that we cannot skip the past to enter the future. As Chakrabarty (2000) so elegantly puts it, "Pasts are there in taste, in practices of embodiment, in the cultural training the senses have received over generations" (p. 251).

The distinction that Chakrabarty (2000), in the fashion of Marx, makes between West-centric universal history (History 1) and the yet-to-emerge histories of the lifeworlds of the *hoi polloi* (History 2s) matters here. Whereas the dominant History 1 focuses on the global totality, History 2s would focus on the particular (e.g., the struggles of the postcolonial non-elites to cope with "modernity"). Provincializing "Europe" entails translating the West-centric universals to be congruent with the diverse lifeworlds of the common people—the grist for History 2s. If this interpretation is correct, the distinction between provincializing and glocalizing (without the bias of Robertson) disappears.

However, we should not hesitate to re-discover and highlight the universals inherent in Eastern philosophy rather than merely glocalizing Enlightenment thought. This is not "Nativism." The analysis in chapter 1 elucidated the point that liberal democracy, idealized by Enlightenment thinkers, is unlikely to wipe out other shades of democracy because such a concept cannot exist without its polar opposite. India's democracy cannot be the same as that of Britain, which made India a "nation-state" by virtue of which all Indians became "citizens" who have both "private" and "public" lives. Chakrabarty (2000) saw the fictive nature of the "public-private" life of the Indian "citizen" in comparison to the European citizen.

> This modern individual . . . is also supposed to have an interiorized "private" self that pours out incessantly in diaries, letters, autobiographies, novels, and, of course, in what we say to our analysts. The bourgeois citizen is not born until one discovers the pleasures of privacy. But this is a very special kind of "private self"—it is, in fact, a deferred "public" self, for this bourgeois private self, as Jürgen Habermas has reminded us, is "always already oriented to an audience [*Publikum*]." (Chakrabarty, 2000, p. 35)

Thus, Chakrabarty (2000) said, "Indian public life may mimic on paper the bourgeois legal fiction of citizenship" (p. 35), but the fiction of bourgeois private self fails to come through even in Indians' autobiographies. The ambiguity of the public-private distinction may appear to be another example of the "incompleteness" of bourgeois transformation of India. The metaphor of the sanctified and patriarchal extended family in India and elsewhere clearly does not fit the private-public dichotomy so central to Habermasian social theory. Tan (2003) clearly points out the need to reconstruct ancient Eastern wisdom, as well as Enlightenment concepts, to suit contemporary conditions in "non-Europe." For example, a Confucian democracy based on communitarian principles would have greater success in East Asian societies than a rights-based liberal democracy à la America that overemphasizes liberty, equality, and pluralism. Tan clarifies that liberalism and democracy are two separate concepts.

Moreover, some have drawn on the wisdom of the "nativistic" Buddhist precepts to bring fresh perspectives to once-intractable problems.

> The first precept, "not killing," has been applied to ethical dilemmas around food, land use, pesticides, pollution, and cultural economic invasion. The second precept, "not stealing," suggest examining the implications of global trade and corporate exploitation of resources.

"Not lying" brings up issues in advertising and consumerism. "Not engaging in abusive relations" covers a broad realm of cruelty and disrespect for nonhuman others. . . . [T]he precept of prohibiting drugs and alcohol [has been interpreted] to include the toxic addictions of television, video games, and junk magazines. Non-harming extends to all beings. . . . It also applies to environmental oppression of plants, animals, rivers, rocks, and mountains as well as to human oppression based on race, class, or gender discrimination. (Kaza, 2002, p. 300)

In contrast to the fear of reviving "Nativism," Capra ([1975]1999) sees a rethinking of Eastern philosophy by quantum physicists, cognitive scientists, and others. They see parallels between Eastern thinking and the revelations of modern physics, biology, psychology, and other sciences. Capra ([1975]1999) writes, "It is becoming ever more apparent that mysticism, or the 'perennial philosophy,' as it is sometimes called, provides a consistent philosophical background to our modern scientific theories" (p. 9). Capra ([1975]1999) points out the remarkable parallels between Eastern philosophy and modern science in regard to the concepts of the unity of all things, the unity of opposites, the illusory nature of space-time, the dynamism of the universe, the nature of the "physical vacuum," the quark symmetries of the subatomic world, the S-matrix theory on the interaction of hadrons, and interpenetration. The rationalism of "Enlightenment" thinkers failed to see through the extremely puzzling and seemingly illogical style of Laozi's *Daodejing* whereas today we can justifiably think of Laozi as an ancient physicist.

The emerging view of modern physics backs up the two basic elements of the Eastern world view—the unity and interrelation of all phenomena, and the intrinsically dynamic nature of the universe. Thus, these two elements are also vital for theory construction in the social sciences. A humanocentric theory of communication-outlets and free expression, just as much as a theory of democracy, should include them.

Although the focus of this book is on the Eastern world view, it is not intended to undervalue the congruence of some streams of Occidental "mysticism" with the new science of complexity. For example, Gordon (2002) pointed out that Kabbalah ("tradition")—a synthetic approach to Jewish mysticism, magic, and metaphysics that has evolved for more than 800 years—challenges the essence of Newtonian determinism by asserting the dialectical perspective of interdependent non-linearity. Kabbalah begins with the realization that creation is the immediate, ongoing process of continuous emergence. From the kabbalistic perspective, existence "is a self-organizing, self-creating system comprising self-organizing, self-creating subsystems" (p. 969). The unknowable God, *Ein Sof,* shapes creation in the same way that an attractor shapes a system. The sefirotic tree of life, the central metaphor for Kabbalah, expresses the dynamics of evolutionary emergence. *Keter* (Crown), the uppermost *sefirah* of the tree of life, is conceived as the primary generative force of the cosmos—an unknown and indescribable totality also called the *holomovement* beyond which is *Ein Sof*. The sefirotic tree creates itself both as a structurally coupled whole and as a differentiated autopoietic entity. This explanation makes it clear that the concept of *Keter* is very similar to the concept of *Brahman* in Hindu philosophy and the concept of *Taiji* in Chinese philosophy.

EXCURSUS: NEW CONFUCIAN HUMANISM

The main Eastern philosophies discussed in this chapter—Confucianism, Daoism, Buddhism, and Hinduism—have remained vibrant, despite quantum lapses, for more than two millennia because of the adaptability of their basic axiology to changes in the social environment. Tu Weiming (2001) asserted, "Today virtually all axial-age civilizations are going through their own distinctive forms of transformation in response to the multiple challenges of modernity" (p. 243). He clarified:

> Confucian modernity demonstrates that modernization is not, in essence, Westernization or Americanization. . . . What East Asian modernity signifies is pluralism rather than alternative monism. The success of Confucian East Asia in becoming fully modernized without being thoroughly Westernized clearly indicates that modernization may assume different cultural forms. (Tu Weiming, 2000, p. 207)

History shows that the Confucian tradition has undergone significant transformations from Classical Confucianism to Neo-Confucianism to New Confucianism. Classical Confucianism began with Confucius in the 6th century BCE and ended with the disintegration of the Han empire in the third century. The advent of Buddhism and the impact of Daoism had adverse effects on Confucianism. Neo-Confucianism, a rationalistic revival of Confucian philosophy, arose in the 11th century under the leadership of Zhou Dunyi, Zhu Xi, Shao Yong, Zhang Zai, and Cheng Yi. The reformed philosophy, which exercised profound influence on Chinese thought for the next 800 years, vigorously articulated the value of human life and morality (Wang, 2004). The next radical rethinking of Confucianism occurred with the social disintegration and domestic dissension that followed the sudden appearance of the Western powers in the mid-19th century. The Western presence spread the ideas of the Enlightenment project, which interpreted the Confucian ethic as "feudal" in Hegelian terms. The Evidential School of Han Learning argued that Buddhist thinking had diluted Confucianism reducing it to empty philosophical speculation unconnected with reality. The May Fourth (1919) intellectuals embarked on an iconoclastic attack on the Confucian tradition in an effort to find a "shortcut" materialist path to modernization.

> Unlike their Indian counterparts who maintained their native spirituality during centuries of colonization, Chinese intellectuals were prompted by their semicolonial status to reject all the spiritual traditions that defined China's soul. (Tu Weiming, 2000, p. 202)

Tu goes on to say that Enlightenment mentality, including secularization, rationalization, and development at any cost, and Talcott Parsons's three-pronged recipe for modernity—market economy, democratic polity, and individualism—loomed large in the intellectual discourse in China. Similar discourses had also occurred in Japan, and the four Mini-Dragons (viz. Hong Kong, Singapore, South Korea, and Taiwan). Thus, the impact of the West degraded Confucian humanism, which had largely defined political ideology, social ethics, and family values in East Asia.

Tu points out that two of the original New Confucians—Xiong Shili (1883–1968) and Liang Shuming (1893–1988)—had challenged the individualistic worldview and utilitarian ethics implicit in the Enlightenment vision. Both of these thinkers made critical contributions to the later ecological turn of the New Confucian Humanism. Xiong was an advocate of naturalistic vitalism while Liang was an advocate of the practice of moderation. However, their attempts to incorporate Confucian humanism into the modernist trajectory did not succeed.

Nevertheless, a New Confucian Humanism appears to be taking shape in East Asia spearheaded by three intellectuals—Qian Mu of Taiwan, Tang Junyi of Hong Kong, and Feng Youlan of Beijing. These three key figures have

> independently concluded that the most significant contribution the Confucian tradition can offer the global community is the idea of the "unity of Heaven and Humanity" (*tianrenheyi*), a unity that Confucians believe also embraced Earth. (Tu Weiming, 2001, p. 243)

The New Confucian Humanist trio have "signaled the movement toward both retrieval and re-appropriation of Confucian ideas" (p. 244). Four salient features make up the substance of the New Confucian ecological vision: fruitful interaction between self and community; a sustainable, harmonious relationship between the human species and nature; mutual responsiveness between the human heart-and-mind and the way of Heaven; and self-knowledge and cultivation to complete the triad (pp. 254–257).

With regard to the resilience of Confucianism, Tu Weiming (2000) argued that despite the powerful modernization forces, we see the continuous relevance of Confucian traditions in "ideas such as network capitalism, soft authoritarianism, group spirit, and consensual politics throughout the East Asian economy, polity, and society" (p. 204). He points out six salient features incorporating Confucian traditions in the East Asian social vision of modernity (pp. 205–206):

- Government leadership in a market economy is not only necessary but desirable. The government is perceived, in principle, as a positive force for social stability rather than as a necessary evil.
- Although law is the essential minimum requirement of social stability, "organic solidarity" can only result from human rites of interaction.
- Family as the basic unit of society is the locus from which core values are transmitted. The dyadic relationships within the family, differentiated by age, gender, authority, status, and hierarchy, provide a richly textured environment for learning the proper way of being human.
- Civil society flourishes not because it is an autonomous arena above the family and beyond the state. Its inner strength lies in its dynamic interplay between family and state.
- Education ought to be the civil religion of society. The primary purpose of education is character building.
- Since self-cultivation is the common root of the regulation of family, the governance of state, and peace under Heaven, the quality of life in a particular society depends on the level of self-cultivation of its members.

The New Confucian Humanism taking shape in modern Asian society illustrates the resilience of axial-age Eastern philosophy to the ideas and values embedded in antihumanistic currents of thought originating mostly in the West. Boron (1999) said that social theory must survive the "barbarism of the economicist reductionism characteristic of neoliberalism" and "the conservative nihilism of postmodernism—dressed up as 'progressivism' in some of its variants" (p. 60). The antihumanistic stance of postmodernist theorists such as Lyotard and Baudrillard (see Docherty, 1994) contrasts with the humanocentric theory developed in this book, which demonstrates how the interaction of antinomic forces (conceived as *yin* and *yang*) within the processes of autopoiesis and cognition engender socially responsible values appropriate to a given society.

NOTES

1. Serious scholars in the different strands of Eastern thought may criticize Capra for essentializing all Eastern philosophies. Capra has indeed underplayed the differences among the various schools of Buddhist, Hindu, and Chinese philosophies to derive a set of ontological platforms denoting Eastern thought. However, one may argue that Capra's purpose was to emphasize the unity (the *Dao*), rather than the diversity (the complement of unity), of Eastern traditions.

2. Bahm (1995) identified three major historical civilizations: the Chinese, the Indian, and the European. He drew attention to two main sets of different emphases among them. The first relates to *will*: The West idealized willfulness, India will-lessness, and China willingness. The second relates to *reason*: The West idealized definiteness, India indefiniteness, and China naturalistic analogy. This chapter attempts to capture the essence of the philosophical and political rationales of the Chinese and Indian civilizations. Space limitations prevent the elaboration of these complex philosophies in adequate detail. Siebert, Peterson, and Schramm (1956) presented the angle of the Western civilization, but with no reference to Judaism and Islam.

3. See Gunaratne (2002a) for a critique of the concept of "press freedom" in current parlance.

4. Some may disagree with the interpretation that *Fajia* was close to being fascist. They may equate the authoritarianism of *Fajia* with that of Plato or Hobbes because, although *Fajia* emphasized strong dictatorship, it assumed that the interest of the political leader embodied the state and the public interest. *Fajia* is also said to have applied Laozi's idea of nonassertion (*wuwei*) as a way of government that the ideal ruler should adopt (De Bary & Bloom, 1999). Having promulgated the laws, the ruler could no longer usurp them because then they would no longer be a guide to behavior.

5. The goal of Confucianism should not be confused with the misuse of the Confucian focus on harmony and cooperation by those in authority (e.g., the authoritarian-tending governments in the two Koreas and in China, particularly under Mao Zedong). In Japan, Confucianism enabled the emperor to command the intense loyalty of the people during World War II.

6. Disagreement exists on the interpretation of Confucianism. Li (1999) maintained that the value systems embedded in Confucianism and democracy are incompatible. First, democracy presupposes individual rights compared with the Confucian social ideal of *ren* with the family viewed as civil society. Second, democracy emphasizes liberty, where-

as Confucianism emphasizes duty. Third, democracy values equality, whereas Confucianism assigns unequal social roles to people. Fourth, democracy implies pluralism, whereas Confucianism implies harmony and unity. However, Li argued that these two value systems can coexist in Chinese culture as much as Buddhism and Daoism have coexisted with Confucianism for centuries. Other critics have argued that, because Rujia assigns different responsibilities for different role players, its concept of social responsibility differs in quality from the Western concept of social responsibility. This is exactly what I assert: Culture determines the meaning of *social responsibility*.

7.   Billington (1997) referred to a center of "realized Daoism"—a remote hermitage of Lei Gu Tail, located on top of a mountain, in Shenxi Province. He said that many Daoists who have moved into urban settings have found the ideas of Laozi relevant "even amid the essential artificiality of much that occurs in that setting" (p. 141).

8.   The Classic of Changes (*Yijing*) identifies the Supreme Ultimate (*Taiji*) as the source and union of the *yin* and *yang*. The *Taiji* generates and regulates the cycle of changes between *yin-yang* and the five elements that constitute the world. The Supreme Ultimate (or Supreme Polarity), which is similar to the Hindu concept of *Brahman* (see Babbili, 1997), is simply the principle of highest good. The 12th-century School of Principle identified *Taiji* with *li*, the rational principle ordering creation. Cheng (1988) illustrated the generative onto-cosmology of *yin-yang* in the *Yijing* formulation within which dialectical interaction leads toward both unity, embodied in *Taiji*, and diversity that occurs "through the generation of the basic forms or phenomena such as eight trigrams and 64 hexagrams" (p. 90).

9.   Gowen (1929) and Modelski (1964) compared the work of Kautilya and Machiavelli. Gowen described *Artha-shastra* as "the crown of all earlier Indian experiments in the exposition of political theory" (p. 178), whereas Modelski described it as "the finest, fullest, and most cogently reasoned Sanskrit treatise" on the science of polity (p. 549).

10. Pre-Buddhist philosophers who rejected Brahmanism and the authority of the Vedas included the Materialists (*Carvaka*), Samjaya, and the *Ajivikas* led by Makkhali Gosala. *Carvaka*, who denied the existence of transcendent or natural unity, were similar to Western empiricists; they believed that pleasure was the only thing desirable. Another rebel was Mahavira (599–527 BCE), founder of Jainism, who taught rigorous self-denial as the way to enlightenment, and asserted that all truths are relative to a standpoint. This chapter excludes these rebel philosophies because Hindu and Buddhist philosophies have the most contemporary relevance. Mohanty (1998, 2000) provided thumbnail sketches of these rebel schools, as well as of the six orthodox schools.

11. Buddhism has come under criticism for turning away from society rather than from nature. On the contrary, the adherents of the Zen tradition of Mahayana Buddhism, which incorporates Daoism, are known to love nature and help people in society.

12. A more appropriate term would be "glocalizing," which Robertson (1994) coined to signify the heterogenizing aspects of "globalizing"—"a process involving the increasing domination of one societal or regional culture over all others" (p. 33). However, Robertson's "spin" on globalization via glocalization has some serious flows from the point of view of non-Western contexts.

Three

Theory and Systems Thinking
Emerging Theory of Living Systems

As the world moves from the factory-based industrial to the computer-based information age, future communication scholarship will have to shift its emphasis from linear mechanics to nonlinear dynamics. Newtonian mechanics suited the environment of the top-down, command-and-control conditions of the Western industrial age. Order and equilibrium were its ideals. In contrast, the evolving nonlinear world of work—resulting from advances in computer technology, globalization and related factors—has accelerated disorder and nonequilibrium worldwide (Tetenbaum, 1998). The field of communication must recognize and reflect these changes.

Recognizing these changes, my attempt here is to build a dynamic humanocentric theory of communication outlets and free expression applicable to all social systems encompassing the world-system at large. I argue that the current normative "press theories" reflect a West-centric bias because they exclude the historical relationship between communication and community in the non-Western world. Splichal (2002) agrees, "The Western history of communication ideas is still extremely Eurocentric and completely neglects all 'non-Western' history" (p. 33).

Here, I have attempted to develop a theory of communication outlets and free expression based on the new complexity science of the
West and Eastern philosophy. In this chapter, I make the case for new
systems thinking, particularly the theory of living systems, as the most
suitable framework for constructing a dynamic theory. My aim is to
open up a new theoretical perspective so far overlooked by the mainstream communication scholars despite the ongoing debate on comparative communication theory (Carter, 1991; Dervin, 1991; Jacobson,
1991; Krippendorff, 1993; Pearce, 1991; Tehranian, 1991).

Donohew and Palmgreen (1989) observed, "A theory comes into
prominence when it is noticed and pursued by the scientific community,
and it passes into history when better explanations are found" (p. 31).
Kerlinger (1986) says a theory should achieve the twin purposes of
explanation and prediction. Kaplan (1964) suggested that a theory
should "appear as the device for interpreting, criticizing, and unifying
established laws, modifying them to fit data unanticipated in their formulation, and guiding the enterprise of discovering new and more powerful generalizations" (p. 295). Although these observations relate to the
classical reductionist Newtonian-Cartesian model, which the new science
of complexity has challenged, they remind us about the need to adjust
our theories and concepts to reflect the continuous changes occurring in
dissipative systems (viz. structures open to their environment).

Harvey and Reed (1994) explained that dissipative systems, grounded in the dynamics of deterministic chaos, are inherently historical, far-
from-equilibrium, boundary-testing, ontologically layered, and thermodynamically constituted configurations that evolve through mechanisms
of assisted bifurcations and symmetry-breaking processes. The asymptotic behavior of dissipative structures characteristically produces nonlinear outcomes. Nonlinearity, which can be functional or longitudinal,
reflects effects that are not invariantly proportional to their causes.

I contend that the incorporation of established concepts and "principles" particularly evident in non-Western philosophy will help build a
more realistic and dynamic theory of communication outlets and free
expression in comparison to the extant normative theories of the press
(e.g., Altschull, 1984; McQuail, 1984/1987; Merrill & Lowenstein, 1979;
Picard, 1985; Siebert, Peterson, & Schramm, 1956).[1] I assert that
Eastern philosophy, which for the most part is consistent with the systems thinking of nonlinear dynamics, enables us to develop a theory
that recognizes change, uncertainty, and far-from-equilibrium conditions in social systems.

The emerging theory of living systems[2] (Capra, 1996, p. 161) provides the framework to develop a dynamic explanation of how the systems of communication-outlets evolve. This framework incorporates the
theories of autopoiesis (Luhmann, 1992, 1995, 2000; Maturana &

Varela, 1980), cognition (Maturana, 2002; Maturana & Varela, 1980), and dissipative structures (Prigogine & Stengers, 1984). *Autopoiesis* reflects the pattern of organization of living systems, and *cognition* the process of life. These two fundamental phenomena are inherent to all dissipative structures, corresponding to supramolecular organizations. They are thermodynamic systems that interact with the outside world. Such interaction coupled with irreversibility of time produces increased entropy (disorder) and nonequilibrium conditions. Being nonlinear systems, they go through self-organization following periodic bifurcations resulting from the recursive effects of positive feedback (energy). Although they exhibit deterministic characteristics between bifurcations, they become extremely sensitive to random positive feedback engendered by the slightest perturbation at the threshold of bifurcation (Prigogine & Stengers, 1984).

The emerging theory of living systems offers an alternative to the Newtonian-Cartesian model, which has dominated empirical-analytic social science up to the present (Capra, 1996, 2002). Maturana (2002) stated that *living systems* are autopoietic molecular systems, which exist as singular entities that operate as totalities in interactions in the medium where each conserves its individual identity under the form of a unicellular or a multicellular organism. Living systems are invariably structure-determined molecular systems. Each living system operates as a *closed network* of molecular productions. (The molecules produced through their recursive interactions constitute the same network of molecular productions that produced them. Each system dynamically realizes its operational boundaries as a singular entity that operates as a totality in interactions in a molecular domain.) Each living system is constitutively open to the flow of molecules in the continuous realization of the recursive closed self-producing dynamics that creates it as a singular entity. Everything that makes up the history of living systems occurs through their realization as singular entities that exist as organisms while in interactions with the medium wherein they operate as totalities. Moreover, living systems exist in two domains: the domain in which they exist as *totalities* or *organisms* wherein they realize and conserve their identity as multicellular or unicellular singular beings; and the domain in which they operate as *molecular autopoietic systems* wherein they realize themselves as composite molecular entities.

Maturana (2002) identified human beings as living systems. They exist in structural coupling with all other living and non-living entities that compose the biosphere. Just like all living systems, human beings are both *autopoietic* and *dissipative*. Maturana's concept of structural coupling is congruent with the revelations of quantum physics and the Eastern philosophical concept of the interconnectedness of all things. Bell's mathematical theorem, which has been reformulated in several ways since the publication of its original version in 1964, clearly implies that, "at a deep and fundamental level, the 'separate parts' of the universe are connected in an intimate and immediate way" (Zukav, 1979, p. 298).[3] We can think of social networks—communities, nation-states, and the world-system—as the multidimensional manifestations of structurally coupled human beings.[4] Thus, from the perspective of the new paradigm, social systems are both autopoietic and dissipative because their component units are human beings.

Dissipative structures have the ability to (a) increase and store information in the form of increasing levels of internal structuration, and (b) export disorganization or entropy to their immediate environment. They are "information accumulating" and "information preserving" configurations in which communication plays a crucial role. The culture of a social system—the beliefs, attitudes, and values of its members—is the product of sharing information (the non-physical aspect of energy/matter) through communicative interaction. Socio-cultural characteristics determine the nature of a community's "public sphere," including the system of communication outlets. The theory of living systems belongs to what is called complexity science, which includes nonlinear dynamics, physics of nonequilibrium processes, and other new systems approaches. Complexity science presumes that change and disorder co-exist with short-term order in all social systems. Thus, a "press" theory developed from the perspective of complexity science must be dynamic, not static; and it must reflect the relation between the two aspects of reality—being and becoming.

The theory of dissipative structures asserts that interdependent open systems are prone to produce nonlinear outcomes that defy prediction (Prigogine & Stengers, 1984). (The exceptions are determinant regularities of the physical universe, biological evolution as a series of assisted bifurcations, ecological organization, and phenomena that occur in the short-time scales between bifurcations at lower ontological levels in the social system.) The best one could do is to estimate probabilistic outcomes. Moreover, because the arrow of time can only move forward and never backward, I take the view that retrodicting or applying reductionist "laws" or "quasi-laws" to the past is not a useful exercise. Kaplan (1964) reflected the Newtonian presumption of reversibility of time and linearity when he asserted that "a law is by no means restricted in its formulation to observational terms; it 'describes' the future as well as the past and present" (p. 90). Whereas Kerlinger claims that a theory should serve the twin requirements of explanation and prediction, I contend that only explanation and estimation of probable outcomes are possible beyond the lower levels of ontological complexity in the social system.

I also take a different view from Kaplan's (1964) on the usefulness of systems theory as a conceptual framework. Kaplan has doubts about the part-whole perspective of systems theory. He asserted, "From a methodological point of view, the most serious shortcoming of collective terms is the continuous temptation they hold out to commit the sin of reification" (p. 81). He says that the "whole" is not reducible to "the sum of its parts" in the sense that the collective term cannot be strictly defined as a theoretical one, or even as a construct with open meaning. Setting aside such objections, Luhmann (1995) took the view that systems-theoretical analysis has now moved away from part–whole concerns into *system-environment* concerns.

Systems theory in the social sciences takes two broad forms—the old and the new. Parsonsian structural-functionalism, its extension by early Luhmann, and its modification by Habermas (1987),[5] all of which presumed a structural-functional approach befitting the linear Newtonian approach, belong to the old form. The chaos theories, which saw the inability of Newtonian mechanics to deal with nonlinear dynamics of interdependent systems, particularly Prigogine's theory of dissipative structures, belong to the new form. The new systems approaches replaced Newton's timeless, machinelike universe[6] with a recursive universe, in which disorder, nonlinear complexity, and unpredictability are the rule (E. M. Knodt in Luhmann, 1995). These approaches reflect the recent theoretical developments in disciplines such as general systems theory, chemistry, physics, neurophysiology, cognitive science, and information theory.

Elsewhere, I have provided (Gunaratne, 2003c, 2005a) an overview of these systems approaches and of Habermas' (1987) quasi-systems theoretical approach (*deep hermeneutics*), which shows the dynamics of the interaction of a society's two system components—state and economy—with its lifeworld dimension. Herein, I go on to expand on the theory of living systems, emphasizing the properties of cognition, autopoiesis, and dissipative structure. I have chosen the sociobiological autopoietic model in preference to Luhmann's sociological autopoietic model because Luhmann's model of social systems is restricted to communication events. The Cartesian mind-matter divisibility is implicit in his theory. However, because Luhmann's emphasis is on communication and because he has analyzed mass media as a functional system, I examine his theory in some detail. The notion of autopoiesis, which Luhmann borrowed from Maturana and Varela, is not in question, although Luhmann's application of autopoiesis to communication events has raised doubts.

First, I introduce the theory of cognition from the perspective of cognitive science (Maturana, [1974]1999, 2002; Maturana & Varela, 1980). Then I deal with the theory of autopoiesis from the biological perspective (Maturana, 2002; Maturana & Varela, 1980) and the socio-logical perspective (Luhmann, 1995). Last, I take up the theory of dissi-pative structures (Prigogine & Stengers, 1984) from the perspective of thermodynamics. The combination of these three strands into a cohe-sive systemic whole would enable us to develop our dynamic theory, which is consistent with Eastern philosophy. I also introduce Capra's (2002) concept of *meaning* because social systems comprise both physi-cal and nonphysical aspects. For instance, culture is an outcome of meaning recursively produced from one generation to another.

COGNITION (COGNITIVE SCIENCE PERSPECTIVE)

In the computer model of cognition, one can define *information process-ing* as the process of knowing. Human intelligence, however, is utterly different from machine or artificial intelligence (AI) because human cog-nition is colored by emotion, not rationality alone. Cognition, the process of life, is inextricably linked to autopoiesis. "All living systems are cogni-tive systems, and cognition always implies the existence of an autopoiet-ic network" (Capra, 1996, p. 161). Cognition is the process of knowing in a living system. Cognition involves the entire process of life—including perception, emotion, and behavior. Mind is not a thing, but a process, according to the Santiago theory of cognition (Maturana & Varela, 1980). The entire dissipative structure of the organism participates in the process of cognition. A living system couples with its environment structurally. Thus, all living systems go through continual structural changes in response to the environment. However, the system specifies the extent of its cognitive domain by selecting the pertinent perturba-tions from the environment that would bring forth the changes. The interactions of a living organism with its environment are cognitive. Mind is manifest in social systems and ecosystems as well. Capra said that mind and consciousness have always been the primary objects of Buddhist contemplative investigations.

> Over the centuries, Buddhist scholars have formulated elaborate and sophisticated theories about many subtle aspects of conscious expe-rience, which are likely to be fertile sources of inspiration for scien-tists. The dialogue between cognitive science and Buddhist contem-plative traditions has already begun. (Capra, 2002, p. 48)

Ratanakul (2002) agreed that Buddhism can "contribute to the mod-ern quest for understanding the psychosomatic unity of the human being and the working of the mind" (p. 117). Furthermore, Capra (2002) pointed out that human consciousness is not only a biological, but also a social phenomenon because brains interact with other bodies and brains within communities of organisms. He added, "In these recurrent interactions, the living organisms change together through their mutual triggering of structural changes" (p. 53).

Maturana (2002) went on to explain that cognition is the capacity that a living system exhibits of operating in dynamic structural congruence with the medium in which it exists. He said that cognition can be instinctive or learned. The origin of instinctive cognition is phylogenic, whereas the origin of learned cognition is ontogenic. Structural coupling (viz. the sequential interactions of two plastic systems that engender sequential changes without loss of their respective identities) is the process that we distinguish as cognition. Living systems and their conditions of living exist in a network of continuous structural coupling. Thus, human beings are *potentially* interconnected (Goswami, 2000) or structurally coupled with all other living and nonliving entities in the biosphere. Human beings, as structure-determined systems, use language to live with each other in several domains of shared objects. They recursively live as self-conscious languaging beings.

AUTOPOIESIS (BIOLOGICAL PERSPECTIVE)

Maturana (1980) identified a biological autopoietic system as follows:

> A dynamic system that is defined as a composite unity as a network of productions of components that (a) through their interactions recursively regenerate the network of productions that produced them, and (b) realize this network as a unity in the space in which they exist by constituting and specifying its boundaries as surfaces of cleavage from the background through their preferential interactions within the network. (p. 29)

Autopoiesis, the pattern of life, means "self-making." Maturana (1980, [1974] 1999, 2002) hypothesized that the circular organization of the nervous system is the basic organization of all living systems, which are organized in a closed causal process that allows for evolutionary change. He also postulated that the nervous system is not only self-organizing, but also continually self-referring. Moreover, the process of circular organization is identical to cognition, the process of life. The *organization* of a living system is the set of relations among its components that characterize the system as belonging to a specific class. The system's organization is independent of the properties of its components.

The autopoietic organization of a living system includes the creation of a boundary that specifies the domain of the network's operation and defines the system as a unit (Capra, 1996). Because "all components of an autopoietic network are produced by other components of the network, the entire system is *operationally closed* even though it is open with regard to the flow of energy and matter" (p. 167). Capra (2002) further explained that all biological life consists of cells, each of which is a complex network of metabolic processes that enable self-maintenance (or autopoiesis). The cell's membrane is its boundary. All cellular structures exit far from thermodynamic equilibrium. When the energy flow increases, the structure may engender a "bifurcation point," at which point it may transform itself into an entirely new state (technically known as *emergence*).

Furthermore, Maturana (2002) explained that living systems exist as autonomous entities in the form of self-contained closed molecular dynamics of self-production, open to the flow of molecules through them. Such an autopoietic system has a singular existence. The molecular processes interconnect with each other so that a living system exists as a totality. What constitutes a dynamic system is its manner of composition, not the elements that compose it (e.g., tornado, social club). Biological evolution becomes a historical process because of the continuous conservation of autopoiesis and adaptation.

AUTOPOIESIS (LUHMANN'S SOCIOLOGICAL PERSPECTIVE)

Luhmann developed a theory of social autopoiesis in considerable detail. Stichweh (2000) said Luhmann's is "the first major sociological theory that opts for communication as the constitutive element of society and other social systems" (p. 5). However, Capra (2002) said that Luhmann "takes the curious position that social systems, while being autopoietic, are not living systems" (p. 82). According to Luhmann, the term *autopoiesis*

> refers to systems that reproduce all the elementary components out of which they arise by means of a network of these elements themselves and in this way distinguish themselves from an environment— whether this takes the form of life, consciousness or (in the case of social systems) communication. Autopoiesis is the mode of reproduction of these systems. (Luhmann, 1989, p. 143)

Thus, Luhmann's self-referential, autopoietic systems theory does not use the notion of autopoiesis in the same sense as in biology.

Whereas biological autopoiesis reproduces elements (e.g., molecules in cells) to stave off decay (entropy), Luhmann's social systems produce their own decay. Social systems maintain themselves not through the storing of patterns, but through producing elements. Moreover, in biological autopoietic systems, the terms *organization* and *structure* are used in an opposite sense than in Luhmann's sociology.

Luhmann's theory comprises two aspects: global/ontological and phenomenological/ontogenic. Within the former, Luhmann specifies three separate autopoietic systems: biological, psychological, and social. In Luhmann's view, each of these systems is autopoietic. An autopoietic system is one that self-reproduces (i.e., it produces the components that produce it). These three system types do not communicate with each other, although they do structurally couple. Luhmann used the concept of *coupling* to denote temporary interlocking of independent units. Structural coupling refers to the symmetrical interaction between society and its environment. Luhmann (1995) referred to three types of social systems: societies, organizations, and interactions. Both societies and interactions are operationally closed because communications within them take place only in relation to their internal context. However, the interaction systems are cognitively more open to the environment than society. Organizations, to which Luhmann paid little attention, lie in between these two polar types. Society is a composite of a number of specialized systems that differentiate themselves through binary coding involving a process of negation (e.g., the code legal/illegal determines the boundary of the legal system; Bausch, 2002).

Luhmann's ontogeny of social systems encompasses expectations, double contingency, and evolution of society. Luhmann said that all self-organizing (autopoietic) systems maintain themselves by means of expectations, which enable them to predict one another's behavior. Double contingency arises when ego tries to predict what alter will do and, in the process, finds out that alter is also trying to predict what ego will do. In this context, Luhmann considered "persons" to be social systems (Bausch, 2002). (Biologically and psychologically, human beings are self-organizing systems.) Evolution of society is reflected in both normative and risky behavior based on expectations. Luhmann's ontogeny of knowledge includes the concepts of asymmetries and redundancy. Asymmetries are hypotheses that are created outside the autopoietic circle but incorporated within it on confirmation. Redundancy occurs when hypotheses prove themselves repeatedly, thereby becoming facts and laws.

Luhmann (1995) interpreted his themes of the difference between system and environment, complexity, self-reference, and the temporal combination of irreversibility and reversibility (process and structure) "as an articulation of the problem of permanence . . . with the goal of opening up better and, above all, complex possibilities of analysis and comparison" (pp. 54–55). However, because Luhmann's model conceptualizes social systems as primarily meaning-processing systems of communication in the phenomenological sense, its reference to autopoiesis, as noted already, has no biological connotation. In Luhmann's view, society should *not* be considered a living system. He has "emphatically and repeatedly argued that society does not perform an evolutionary 'life'-cycle, since this system is not expected to be alive" (Leydesdorff, 2003, pp. 60–61).

Luhmann avoided thermodynamically derived concepts such as nonlinear dynamics, positive feedback, bifurcation, far from equilibrium, and so on, and he saw the relevance of irreversibility only to processes.[7] Luhmann brakes away from Parsonsian structural functionalism and with all versions of linguistic structuralism through his explicit subordination of structure to function. He created a distinction between social (or communicative) and psychic (or cognitive) systems, each of which is autopoietic and meaning-producing and serves as the environment for the other. He conceptualized society as a composite of autopoietic function systems—legal, political, economic, educational, mass media, fine arts, science, and so forth—each of which operates within its specific binary code for internal integration and external demarcation.

> Luhmann . . . provides a frame for a description of modern society as a complex system of communications that has differentiated itself horizontally into a network of interconnected social subsystems. Each of these systems reproduces itself recursively on the basis of its own, system-specific operations. Each of them observes itself and its environment, but whatever they observe is marked by their unique perspective, by the selectivity of the particular distinctions they use for their observations. (E. M. Knodt in Luhmann, 1995, p. xii)

Luhmann (1995) said that the distinction "between the *environment* of a system and *systems in the environment* of this system . . . blows apart the old thematic of domination/oppression" (p. 17). He said that, on the level of self-referential reproduction, "self-referential systems are *closed* systems, for they allow no other forms of processing in their self-determination" (p. 34). However, as noted earlier, all autopoietic systems are cognitively open to their environment.

It should be clear that Luhmann's theory of society is one confined to a system of autopoietic communication. His social systems are *communications*—or, more precisely, *communicative events* arising from the consummation of the *information —> utterance —> understanding* process—separated from conscious thoughts, behavior or actions, and living physical systems, all of which are placed in the environment (Mingers, 2002). Luhmann paid little attention to show the relationship between the social system of communication and the psychic systems of individual consciousness. Mingers (2002) pointed out the difficulty of accepting Luhmann's view "that communications are produced by other communications alone rather than by people within social interaction" (p. 291). Mingers added that Luhmann's model achieves "theoretical purity . . . at the expense of an incredibly abstract and reductive view of the social world" (p. 292).

Referring to Luhmann's view that social systems (i.e., communication systems) are autopoietic but nonliving, Hornung (2001) pointed out that Luhmann tries to apply the theory of autopoiesis, by definition a theory of the living, to nonliving systems. Hornung added that this appears to be a contradiction in itself, which does not become much clearer when one considers that large parts of Luhmann's writings on this topic at least sound as if he were writing about living systems.

Luhmann (2000) said that the mass media, just like other function systems, are "an *operationally* closed . . . autopoietic system" (p. 117), which, however, remain *cognitively* open from an empirical point of view. The distinction between information and noninformation makes up the binary code for the mass media system's "reproduction of communication from outcomes of communication" (p. 83). Luhmann identified mass media as a key cognitive system through which society constructs the illusion of its own reality. He said the mass media system selects its information (news) from its environment in accordance with its own criteria (e.g., surprise, conflicts, quantities, local relevance, norm violations, moral judgments, interest in particular people, topicality, expression of opinions, etc.) and communicates that information to society, thereby allowing society to process information without destabilizing social roles or overburdening social actors. The three programmatic strands produced by the mass media—news, advertising, and entertainment—generate different kinds of reality construction. They "increase the complexity of contexts of meaning in which society exposes itself to irritation through self-produced differences" (p. 82). The mass media form a reservoir (memory) of options for the future coordination of actions and provide parameters for the stabilization of political expectations. Thus, Luhmann's theory of the mass media is not normative or classificatory. It merely looks at the autopoietic process of the media system within his general theory of social systems, which "does not demand exclusivity for its truth claims in relation to the other, competing endeavors" (Luhmann, 1995, p. xvii).

We should note here that Luhmann and Habermas both made communication the centerpiece of their respective theories—Luhmann in his theory of autopoietic social systems, and Habermas in his theory of communicative action. Whereas Habermas saw rationality-based, intersubjective communication consensus as essential for social equilibrium and maintenance, Luhmann saw communication dissent as the dynamic ingredient that produces systemic autopoiesis (i.e., self-referential reproduction). They also differed on what they meant by communication.

DISSIPATIVE STRUCTURES (THERMODYNAMICS PERSPECTIVE)

The systems thinking associated with Prigogine's theory of dissipative structures fits in with the systems thinking associated with the theory of autopoiesis.[8] Prigogine's comprehensive theory of change sees fluctuations, instability, multiple choices, and limited predictability at all levels of observation. It asserts that irreversible processes (associated with the arrow of time common to all parts of the universe) lead to both order and disorder. It sees biological and social systems as open dissipative structures that exchange energy/matter with their environment. It says that entropy (in Greek, "evolution") distinguishes reversible (entropy-constant) from irreversible (entropy-producing) processes.[9] It illustrates how a bifurcation point or singular moment—engendered by random energy-flow fluctuations channeling themselves to positive feedback—can force a system to disintegrate or regenerate (self-organize). It asserts that Newtonian-type laws predicated on linear relations and *ceteris paribus* conditions cannot predict the nonlinear relations characterizing the far-from-equilibrium state of open systems.[10]

> [T]here exists in nature systems that behave reversibly and that may be fully described by the laws of classical or quantum mechanics. But most systems of interest to us, including all chemical systems and therefore all biological systems, are time-oriented on the macroscopic level. Far from being an "illusion," this expresses a broken time-symmetry on the microscopic level. Irreversibility is either true on all levels or on none. (Prigogine & Stengers, 1984, p. 285)

Prigogine and Stengers (1984) used the concept of *entropy* to distinguish between reversible and irreversible processes. Entropy increases only because of the irreversible movement of thermodynamic processes. Newtonian mechanics, by contrast, presumes a static (reversible) frame of analysis when studying dynamic systems, whereas Prigogine's paradigm takes the dynamic (irreversible or evolutionary) view. (Doubts about the presumptions of Newtonian mechanics became widespread following the 1927 Copenhagen Interpretation of quantum mechanics. See following discussion for a quantum mechanics critique of Newtonian mechanics.)

There can be no doubt that irreversibility exists on the macroscopic level and has an important constructive role . . . Therefore there must be something in the microscopic world of which macroscopic irreversibility is the manifestation. (p. 258)

Time flows in a single direction, from past to future. We cannot manipulate time, we cannot travel back to the past. (p. 277)

Prigogine derived his theory of dissipative structures by focusing on the second law of thermodynamics—the law of entropy—which introduced time and history into a universe that Newtonian physicists "had pictured as eternal" (Briggs & Peat, 1989, p. 135). The second law says that in a closed system disorder increases relentlessly until the system reaches equilibrium (or random dispersal of particles). Thus, the law implied that all the matter and energy in the universe would ultimately degrade to a state of tepid, inert uniformity (equilibrium) or heat death. Prigogine turned away from this negative view by identifying the universe as an open system where the disorder associated with a state of far from equilibrium would bring about order through spontaneous reorganization.

At all levels, be it the level of macroscopic physics, the level of fluctuations, or the microscopic level, nonequilibrium is the source of order. Nonequilibrium brings "order out of chaos." (Prigogine & Stengers, 1984, p. 287)

Prigogine made this intuitive leap from his observation of a phenomenon known as the *Benard Instability*. Tucker (1983) explained that Benard Instability

occurs when a liquid is heated from below. As heating intensifies, the mixture suddenly begins to "self-organize," taking on a striking spatial structure sometimes resembling miniature stained-glass cathedral windows, with ovals of brilliant colors arranging themselves in kaleidoscopic patterns. [These] . . . patterns resembled living cells, [and] within each cell, ordered molecular motion occurs.

Prigogine reasoned that if this were possible in fluid dynamics, it would also be possible in chemistry and biology. This self-organization of matter represented to him a critical link between animate and inanimate matter. It could even provide a clue to the spontaneous eruption of life's beginnings. Chemical processes known as the *Zhabotinsky Reactions* (named after a Russian biophysicist who discovered them) confirmed Prigogine's theory. Thermodynamically, Prigogine (1996) affirmed, "All arrows of time in nature have the same orientation: They all produce entropy in the same direction of time, which is by definition the future" (p. 102).

Prigogine's comprehensive theory of change, as Alvin Toffler out-lined in Prigogine and Stengers (1984), contains the following salient points:

- Although some parts of the universe may operate like machines, these are closed systems, which form only a small part of the physical universe. Most are open systems, exchanging energy/matter and information with their environment. Because biological and social systems are open, it is not possible to understand them in mechanistic terms. Most of reality is seething and bubbling with change, disorder, and process, and not orderly, stable, and equilibrial. Prigogine and his collaborators, who made a distinction between free energy and bound energy, saw three forms of thermodynamic systems: isolated, near to equilibrium, and dissipative. Equilibrated, steady-state systems such as crystals, minerals, and mechanical systems that cannot evolve internally belong to the isolated category. Systems that are organized around the principle of minimum entropy production, and therefore cannot evolve internally, such as chemical clocks, belong to the near-to-equilibrium category. Evolving systems found in enriched, free-energy environments, and whose far-from-quilibrium configurations are nonreplicable over time, belong to the dissipative category (Harvey & Reed, 1994). I identify the first two categories as closed systems.
- Fluctuations occur in an open dissipative structure when energy flows become too complex for the system to absorb. When a single such fluctuation or combination of them musters enough power through positive feedback, a singular moment or bifurcation point arises that forces the system to reorganize. Each reorganization produces greater complexity and greater likelihood of random fluctuations (viz. evolution). It is impossible to determine in advance the direction of the system change: whether it will disintegrate into chaos or give rise to a new, more differentiated, higher level of order.
- Nonlinear relationships prevail when a system is in a far-from-equilibrium state, whereon it becomes inordinately sensitive to external influences. A small perturbation or fluctuation can bring about startling, structure-breaking waves that replace the old with a new system (thereby bringing order out of chaos)—a finding that has analogical significance for the social sciences. In contrast, a system in equilibrium may have

reached maximum entropy where molecules are paralyzed or move around at random—the state toward which the universe is heading, according to the second law of thermodynamics. Nothing much happens in a near-to-equilibrium system as well because it is comparable to an energy well in which the system loses heat as fast as it gains heat.

Briggs and Peat (1989) explained that in a nonlinear equation, "a small change in one variable can have a disproportional, even catastrophic impact on other variables." A nonlinear solution tends "to be stubbornly individual and peculiar." Plots of nonlinear equations "show breaks, loops, recursions—all kinds of turbulence." Nonlinear equations have terms that "are repeatedly multiplied by themselves" to allow for feedback (p. 24). Gleick (1987) said that nonlinear systems "generally cannot be solved and cannot be added together" (pp. 23–24).

Raman (2003) explained that classical reductionism's success on explanation and prediction was confined to phenomena where the whole is equal to the sum of its parts—linear situations. Complexity asserts itself in the much more common nonlinear situations, where the total is much more than or very different from the simple sum of the components. Glaring complexity exists in the biological world, where life forms arise and act in utterly unpredictable ways because of the interconnecting principle known as *information*.

Thus, as Wallerstein (1999) put it, the science of complexity "sees instability, evolution, and fluctuation everywhere" (p. 165). It sees a narrative (rather than a geometrical) universe, in which the problem of time is the central problem. Probability is the only scientific truth. "Probability derives from the fact that there are always new statistical solutions of dynamic equations. Interactions within systems are continual, and this communication constitutes the irreversibility of the process, creating ever more numerous correlations" (p. 166). The holistic view of the dissipative structure is its *macroscale*. All its internal subsystems are known as the microscale. The interaction of macro- and microscales is fundamental to the dynamics of dissipative structures (Straussfogel, 2000).

Goonatilake (1999) saw the emergence of a metacommunicating system in the future that will "result in intense communication not only between machines and humans, but also with genetic systems so that information in the three realms of genes, culture and machines will result in one interacting whole" (p. 197). The strict functional differentiation associated with Luhmann's model—a result of combining autopoiesis and codified communication—may not be capable of accommodating such a vision so readily compatible with Buddhist philosophy in particular. However, a theory of living systems combining the elements of autopoiesis, cognition, and dissipative structures could readily accommodate such a vision. Such a combination would also accommodate better theory construction in social science, including communication.

At this point, it is pertinent to note the differences between quantum mechanics and the dissipative structures theory on the issue of irreversibility. Whereas irreversibility is fundamental to Prigogine's theory, quantum mechanics takes the view that certain processes in nature are reversible because "you cannot tell the direction of time by looking at these processes in time" (e.g., the motion of a pendulum; Goswami, 1993, p. 100). Schrödinger's equation, the wave equation for matter, is considered time-reversible. Quantum mechanics views time irreversibility, which exits *in potentia*, as an artifact of the measurement process. The second law of thermodynamics does not apply to conceptually isolated quantum objects because they are short-lived entities with no history. However, it does apply to molecules, cells, and people.

MEANING AS FOURTH PERSPECTIVE

Some may question the appropriateness of applying the concept of autopoiesis to social systems because of the simultaneous existence of social systems in two dimensions—the physical and the social. Capra (1996) pointed out that Maturana and Varela expressed somewhat different views on this issue:

> Maturana does not see human social systems as being autopoietic, but rather as the medium in which human beings realize their biological autopoiesis through "languaging." Varela argues that the concept of a network of production processes, which is at the very core of the definition of autopoiesis, may not be applicable beyond the physical domain, but that a broader concept of "organizational closure" can be defined for social systems. This broader concept is similar to that of autopoiesis but does not specify processes of production. (p. 212)

Luhmann (1995) appeared to have detached social systems (communication events) from psychic systems precisely because of these doubts. However, in achieving theoretical purity, Luhmann separated the essential link between autopoiesis and cognition. Capra (2002) attempted to resolve the issue by adding the perspective of *meaning* to the other three perspectives of life—life *process* (cognition), *form* (pattern of organization), and *matter* (material structure). Having introduced *meaning* as the fourth perspective, Capra went on to examine what a theory of living systems can extract from the two "most influential" (p. 77) integrative theories—Habermas' communicative action theory and Giddens' structuration theory:

> A social network, too, is a nonlinear pattern of organization; and concepts developed in complexity theory, such as feedback or emergence, are likely to be relevant in a social context as well. . . . Social networks are first and foremost networks of communication involving symbolic language, cultural constraints, relationship of power, and so on. (Capra, 2002, p. 82)

Capra (2002) asserted that a unified systemic framework for the understanding of biological and social phenomena emerge only when the concepts of nonlinear dynamics are combined with insights from social theory, philosophy, cognitive science, anthropology, and other disciplines. Social systems, he said, are living systems because they are simply networks of human beings who share language, consciousness, and culture. These attributes enable a social network to share ideas and contexts of meaning within its own boundary of expectations or social structure. Social networks can also generate material structures (e.g., Great Wall of China, geographical boundaries, etc.).

Capra (2002) said the *key point* is that the behavior of a living organism is constrained, but not determined by outside forces. They are not isolated from their environment, with which they interact continually. Therefore, they are self-organizing. A social network continually generates mental images, thoughts, and meanings (*semantic structures*) while continually coordinating the behavior of its members through the complex dynamics of its culture.

> Culture arises from a complex, highly nonlinear dynamic. It is created by a social network involving multiple feedback loops through which values, beliefs, and rules of conduct are continually communicated, modified, and sustained. . . . [T]he culture's values and beliefs affect its body of knowledge. . . . Cultural identity also reinforces the closure of the network by creating a boundary of meaning and expectations that limits the access of people and information to the network. (Capra, 2002, p. 87)

HUMANOCENTRIC FRAMEWORK

In summary, Capra's (1996, 2002) unified, systemic framework for the understanding of biological and social life adds a fourth perspective, *meaning*, to the three other perspectives he originally associated with the theory of living systems: *cognition* (process of life), *autopoiesis* (form or pattern of organization), and dissipative *structure* (matter). This framework, coupled with concepts extracted from Eastern philosophy and world-systems analysis, provides us with the theoretical tools to generate a humanocentric theory of communication outlets and free expression.

Byeon (1999) used the nonequilibrium thermodynamic perspective to develop a framework for the study of political systems. Using this perspective, I start with the presumption that the system of communication outlets is a dissipative *structure*. Because a dissipative structure is open, it is able to exchange energy/matter/information with its environment and is capable of managing its entropy function without violating the second law. That is, it can circumvent the movement toward a static equilibrium and maximum entropy associated with a closed system. These presumptions pertain not only to the macroscale, but also to the microscale. Thus, the component units (or entities) of the system of communication outlets also possess the characteristics of dissipative structures, which are invariably autopoietic systems. (Cell biology shows that each plant cell is an autopoietic system comprising some 500,000 production centers. The cell membrane constitutes the boundary of the cell.)

As already mentioned, *autopoiesis* reflects the pattern of organization of living systems and *cognition* the process of life. Each component unit is organizationally closed, but cognitively and structurally open to its environment. This merged theory incorporates Capra's systemic framework for the understanding of biological and social life. Luhmann's sociological model, which places function over structure, excludes cognition as the process of life. It is not a living system; therefore, it is devoid of cognition, the very process of life. Autopoiesis cannot occur if it is uncoupled from cognition.

I develop the theory of communications outlets and free expression by first connecting this model of living systems with the center-periphery notion of world-systems analysis (Wallerstein, 1974) on the basis that nation-states (or their emerging variants) are singular collectivities of structurally coupled human beings who have chosen to live within a geographical boundary because of specific sociocultural characteristics. The human beings within each nation-state compete for absorbing energy/matter/information (and managing the resulting entropy), with the human beings comprising other nation-states (or their variants). The world system, which is more than the composite of nation-states because of its emergent characteristics, is the macrosuperstructure of all human beings who are more loosely structurally coupled than at the nation-state level. The system of communication outlets has to be analyzed in the context of the nation-state (or its emerging variant) and the world system

To this broad model, which is more or less consistent with that of Baker (1993a, 1993b, 1994) I link the principle of the dialectical completion of relative polarities (denoting the unity of the opposites and the intrinsically dynamic nature of the universe) and the principle of part–whole interdetermination (denoting the potential unity and interrelation of all phenomena)—the two remarkable principles of Eastern philosophy now shown to be consistent with new physics—to derive a humanocentric theory of communication outlets and free expression.

> Some biologists believe that a single plant cell carries within it the capability to produce the entire plant. Similarly, the philosophical implication of quantum mechanics is that all of the things in our universe (including us) that appear to exist independently are actually parts of one all-encompassing organic pattern, and that no parts of that pattern are ever really separate from it or from each other. (Zukav, 1979, pp. 72–73)

Zukav (1979) concluded that the "new physics sounds very much like Eastern mysticism" (p. 96). Before I venture into the exercise of deriving a humanocentric theory, I draw attention to the philosophy of monistic idealism, which conjoins Eastern mysticism and quantum physics to provide an alternative paradigm of the universe. Then I use chapter 4 to elaborate on West-centrism in Western social science, and analyze the West-centric bias of the classical theories of the press. Because some may regard the works of Capra and Zukav as "unreliable guides to Eastern traditions of thought" (a point made by an anonymous reviewer of the draft version of this manuscript),[11] the ensuing excursus focuses on the work of a non-Western scientist who doubles as a practicing Eastern mystic.

EXCURSUS: MONISTIC IDEALISM

Goswami (1993, 2000), a physicist with a Hindu background, has drawn on quantum physics, Eastern philosophy, and cognitive psychology to develop a new scientific paradigm that introduces consciousness as the ground of being—an idea that has existed in psychology as transpersonal psychology. He identified this paradigm with the philosophy of *monistic idealism*.

> Positing consciousness as the ground of being calls forth a paradigm shift from a materialist science to a science based on the primacy of consciousness. In this science, matter has causal efficacy but only to the point of determining possibilities and probabilities. Consciousness

> ultimately creates reality because the choice of what is actualized, event to event, is always up to consciousness. . . . The world is *only seemingly* continuous, Newtonian, and material. In realty, it is discontinuous, quantum, and conscious. (Goswami, 2000, p. 16)

Whereas consciousness is an epiphenomenon of matter (the brain) in classical science, as well as in quantum physics, Goswami saw matter (the universe) as an epiphenomenon of consciousness. He saw consciousness as a transcendent phenomenon, which is beyond quantum physics, similar to the *Brahman* or the *Dao* or God. It is what Carl Jung called the *collective unconscious* which must operate outside space time. Applying the concepts of quantum physics, Goswami argued that the universe only existed as an abstract potential until life evolved to the point that a conscious, sentient being appeared. It was at that moment that the universe suddenly came into being, although scientific data give the universe a history of 15 billion years. This is what quantum physics refers to as *delayed choice*.

> There is no manifest cosmos—only possibilities, possible pathways of development—until a sentient being observes the universe. And with that "first" observation the entire pathway in possibility leading to the event manifests retroactively, going backward in time. (Goswami, 2000, p. 89)

Goswami (2000) then made a distinction between *consciousness* (God, the ground of being, the whole) and *awareness* (a subject–object split, implying an individual sentient being or quantum self). "Consciousness collapses the quantum wave function by choosing actuality from the superposition of possibilities, but only in the presence of brain-mind awareness" (p. 48). Goswami applied the Buddhist doctrine of dependent co-arising (*paticca samuppada*) to explain the paradox arising from the assertion that awareness is necessary for collapsing the quantum superposition while awareness implies a subject–object split. This apparent split occurs because of "our ability to see ourselves as separate from the objects we see" (p. 49) or *self-reference*. Yet this split is only appearance (*maya*) for "all the causal power of the quantum self resides in consciousness itself" (p. 50).

Thus, Goswami modified material quantum physics to accommodate the transcendent dimension of all religions. Goswami's perspective emphasizes downward causation while not refuting the relevance of upward causation. Downward causation, based on consciousness as the ground of all being, recognizes our free will, creativity, and causal power. Upward causation, the view of material science, assigns all causal power to elementary "particles," the interactions of which produce atoms, molecules, and cells that constitute all matter, including the brain. From the upward-causation perspective, our free will is only an epiphenomenon subservient to the causal power of matter.

Goswami (2000) explained the peculiarities of the *brain, mind,* and *consciousness* in one sentence: "The mind enables consciousness to see meaning, which the brain cannot process" (p. 152). Consciousness transcends both matter and mind, and mind is also distinct from the brain. The brain is the material structure that serves as a "symbol-processing machine" (p. 152). Furthermore, he asserted that consciousness does not obey quantum physics because it is not made of matter. If consciousness were an epiphenomenon of material elements, it would not be able to collapse its own wave function.

The Hindu doctrine of the five sheaths (*panchakoshas*) says that consciousness (Brahman) exists in a fivefold sheath. The outermost sheath is the physical body, followed in successive order by the vital body, mind, intellect, and the innermost bliss. This explains the unity of Brahman and our quantum self. With consciousness as the ground of being, downward causation sets in motion an involution from bliss to the physical body (matter) before upward causation or evolution could occur. Death ends the physical body, but not the other four. Moreover, Goswami drew on transpersonal psychology to clarify our two-self nature: the ego (which adheres to classical logic and reasoning) and quantum self (which adheres to quantum logic and creativity). The ego is continuous, determined, linear, local, and personal, whereas the *quantum self* is discontinuous, synchronistic, holistic, nonlocal, and transpersonal.

Thus, Goswami (2000) claimed that his *science within consciousness* has finally placed "science in the same class as the humanities and the arts, as a great vehicle with which to investigate ourselves" (p. 162) because the process of discovery requires creativity. He said the new paradigm accommodates both science (outer creativity associated with ego) and spirituality (inner creativity associated with quantum self). Extensive debates on the implications of quantum physics on religious beliefs have already taken place (e.g., Russell et al., 2001).

Goswami (2000) went on to assert that quantum physics has dismantled the fundamental principles of materialist-realist science: causal determinism, continuity, locality, strong objectivity, material monism and reductionism, and epiphenomenalism. He said, "In particular, continuity, determinism, and locality have been proven wrong" (p. 30). Goswami explained these principles and their faults in the following manner:

- *Causal determinism* asserts that every change or movement of an object is determined by the object's initial conditions (position and momentum) and the material forces that act on it. (Descartes, Newton, and Laplace enunciated this principle.) Quantum physics has indisputably established the uncertainty principle (associated with Heisenberg), according to which we cannot determine both position and momentum of "particles" (viz. "possibility waves") simultaneously with utmost accuracy. Goswami said, "Therefore, we can never determine those coveted initial values of Newtonian determinism" (p. 34). Thus, we cannot predict individual events. The most we can do is estimate the probability of a range of possibilities. Goswami added that even macroobjects are quantum possibility waves.
- *Continuity principle* asserts change or movement is continuous—the presumption that justifies the study of physics mathematically, objectively, and logically. Goswami said, "But quantum physics, from its very inception, has beaten the doctrine of continuity to a pulp" (p. 30). Quantum physics has established that the electron's quantum leaping ability originates from its wave nature. Electrons are waves of possibility. Bohr's complementarity principle has proved the wave-particle duality of light.
- *Locality principle* asserts that all causes, as well as their effects, are local. Einstein postulated that because material objects must obey the limitation of the speed of light, simultaneous action at a distance was not possible. However, the work of physicist Bohm and Bell backed the possible existence of nonlocally correlated quantum systems. Goswami said that the 1982 Aspect experiment "not only proved nonlocality but also confirmed the existence of a transcendent domain of reality beyond the material domain of space-time" (p. 37). Thus, correlated possibility waves positioned in two galaxies can instantaneously interact, defying the speed of light.

Goswami (2000) said that on the negation of the following three tenets of material realism (classical science), "quantum mechanics is strongly suggestive but not quite definitive (yet)" (p. 37).

- *Strong objectivity*, an idea that originated with Aristotle, asserts that the material world is independent of the observers (viz. consciousness).
- *Material monism and reductionism* claim that everything originates from matter (viz. atoms/molecules) and its corre-

lates (viz. energy and force fields). A related claim is that every phenomenon has a material origin to which it can be reduced.

- *Epiphenomenalism* claims that all subjective phenomena, including consciousness, are epiphenomena of matter. It justifies this claim on the basis of upward causation.

Authorities on both Eastern philosophy and quantum physics are rare. Physicist Capra (1999) wrote the first book drawing on the close parallels between quantum physics and Eastern philosophy. Zukav (1979) followed with a similar book. Goswami conceded that these two books have been important for the history of science. Although these two books were very good, Goswami said that both Capra and Zukav held onto a fundamentally material paradigm because they subscribed to the view that consciousness was an epiphenomenon of the brain. Goswami claimed that it was his good fortune to shift the paradigm by establishing consciousness as the ground of being. More recently, a volume edited by Wallace (2003) examined the complementarity of science and Buddhism.

Despite the optimism of Goswami and others about the laws of quantum physics and their applicability to other fields, pessimists tend to be cautious. Mosco (2004) questioned the applicability of the peculiar quantum laws of the subatomic domain—so dramatically different from those of traditional physics—to politics, economics, and other fields. He said that Becker (1991) produced a volume on "quantum politics" challenging Newtonianism, and that Slaton (1992) followed this perspective and applied quantum theory, "which she sees as positing the essential interconnectedness of seemingly unrelated events" (Mosco, 2004, p. 110). Mosco extended his sarcasm to dot.com entrepreneurs who went bust trying to apply quantum laws to economics.

Perhaps the first social scientist to interpret the parallels between quantum mechanics and the social sciences was William Bennett Munro, a Harvard professor. In an address to the American Political Association in 1927, the year of the Copenhagen Interpretation, he said:

> Political science should borrow by analogy from the new physics a determination to get rid of intellectual insincerities concerning the nature of sovereignty, the general will, natural rights and the freedom of the individual, the consent of the governed, majority rule, home rule, the rule of public opinion, state rights, laissez faire, checks and balances, the equality of men and nations, and a government of laws not of men. (p. 10)

> The new physics may well suggest the discarding of our atomic theory of ultimate, equal, and sovereign citizens in a free state. (p. 11)

Goswami's *monistic idealism*, which asserts that consciousness is the ground of being, brings back free will into quantum interpretation. This concept of free will, however, clashes with the concept of determinism in classical physics. Goswami (2000) said that scientists are bothered by Bell's theorem (the detailed theory behind the Aspect experiment), which proved quantum nonlocality.[12] Goswami explained the dilemma of the scientists thus:

> Once you see consciousness as the ground of all being, it is hard to carry on the often meaningless, materialist research programs that form the bulk of the academic, governmental, and industrial research. (Goswami, 2000, p. 75)

NOTES

1. Asante (1997) provides a summary of the improvements to the "four theories" that various scholars have suggested (pp. 16-21).
2. This is not a reference to Miller (1978) even though Miller's work on living systems also will lend further support to my theoretical framework.
3. Bell's theorem demolished the Einstein–Podolsky–Rosen argument (and the principle of local causes) published in 1935. The EPR thought experiment inadvertently showed an unexplainable relatedness between particles in two different places thereby creating the Pandora's box of modern physics: that communication of information can occur at superluminal (faster than light) speeds. But Einstein himself denied this possibility. The principle of local causes says that what transpires in one area has no connection to the control of variables by an experimenter in a distant space-like area.
4. Luksha (2001) proposed a much more elaborate model of society as a self-reproducing system. He sees society as a collectivity of social individuals with a social memory (languages, technologies, rituals, etc.) in individual neural systems. Society includes an internal artificial environment (means of production, objects of consumption, and non-economic material culture). External structures and objects (nature and other societies) make up a society's external environment.
5. Habermas' communicative-action theory, a merger of empirical-analytic and historical-hermeneutic approaches, represents a shift from action to communication. Habermas called it "deep hermeneutics" or emancipatory critical theory. His focus is the lifeworld, whose communicative action creates two system components, economy and state, which ultimately colonize the lifeworld through the media of money and power. The influence of Newtonian mechanics is obvious in Habermasian theory, which relies heavily on communication consensus, meaning social equilibrium—a hallmark of linear thinking.

6. However, Penrose (1989) identified Newtonian mechanics as a SUPERB physical theory because, "as applied to the motions of planets and moons, the observed accuracy of this theory is phenomenal—better than one part in ten million" (p. 152).

7. Occasionally, Luhmann (2000) used Prigogine's terminology to refer to recursivity in meaning production. Commenting on the entertainment strand of the mass media system, Luhmann said, "What goes on in each individual viewer, the non-linear causalities, dissipative structural developments, negative or positive feedback etc. triggered by such coincidental observations, can simply not be predicted" (p. 61).

8. Farazmand (2003) said that chaos and transformation theories, including Prigogine's theory, are not new concepts. He traced systems theory to Plato, Aristotle, Epicurus, Avicenna, Marx, and Engels. He said that Persian philosopher Avicenna "presented a grand 'synthesis' of the dialectical processes of change, including chaotic change, that follow a pattern of stability and order, and expected chaos or disorder" (p. 343). He added: "It is . . . astonishing to observe how ignorant, or reluctant at best, the modern Western scientific community has been about the dialectical nature of chaos and transformation theories" (p. 347).

9. In 1865, R. J. Clausius came up with the celebrated formulation: "The energy of the universe is constant. The entropy of the universe is increasing." Thus, Clausius provided the first evolutionary view of the universe: The increase in entropy is the result of irreversible processes in the universe. A. S. Eddington, therefore, called entropy the "arrow of time" (Prigogine, 1996, p. 19).

10. I have borrowed some of the material on dissipative structures from Gunaratne (2003c). Laszlo (1998) examined the patterns of history in light of general theories and concepts developed by Prigogine and other complexity theorists. Recently, several British scholars elaborated on the relevance of complexity theory to sociology (e.g., Cilliers, 1998; Medd, 2001; Urry, 2003; Walby, 2003).

11. Klostermaier (1991), who gave credit to Capra for establishing striking connections between modern physics and ancient Asian traditions, pointed out that Capra's presentation of Eastern mysticism fails to make an adequate distinction between the vastly different systems of Eastern thought and tends to blur the significant controversies among them. Klostermaier added that Capra's reliance on English translations of Eastern sources lets him draw conclusions not warranted by the texts (e.g., Capra's misinterpretation of the Upanishad phrase "Brahman is the void" to equate Brahman with the Buddhist concept of emptiness or *sunyata*). Mansfield (1976) observed that Capra, although reasonably accurate, "in his exuberance for making parallels occasionally makes comparisons between quite different levels of reality" (p. 56). White (1979) asserted that Capra's intellectual thesis—that Eastern traditions and quantum theory represent a similar view of the world—is "completely without merit or credibility" (p. 587). Bernstein (1979), in a sharp attack on Capra's work, said, "To hitch a religious

philosophy to a contemporary science is a sure route to its obsolescence" (p. 8).

12. Bell presented a mathematical proof in 1964 based on experimental results that indirectly demonstrated the existence of nonlocal influences. Bell used the same pair of hypothetical photons flying off in opposite directions as the Einstein–Podolsky–Rosen team did to demonstrate his point. However, Bell chose polarization, not position and momentum, as the particle characteristic to be studied. The particles maintained high correlations after they were separated and after experimental tampering to alter their correlation. Bell's inequality theorem received backup from Caluser's experimental test in 1972 and Aspect's experiment in 1982. The Aspect experiment confirmed that two entities separated by many meters and possessing no mechanism for communication with each other could nonetheless show striking correlations in their behavior (Overman, 1991).

Four

West-Centrism and Press Theories

NATURE OF WEST-CENTRISM

Enrique Dussel (2002) said that Weber and Hegel planted the first Eurocentrism (or West-centrism) in social science and philosophy, respectively. Each of them presumed the superiority of Europe—a superiority proved only by factors that were internal to that continent.

> Max Weber had the intuition that if Europe not been the region most prepared to carry out the Industrial Revolution, it would have been China or Hindustan. He thus devoted his sociological works, on a religious and ethical level, to showing why China and India did not give rise to capitalist society. His voluminous research produced the same answer time and again: China and Hindustan could not be capitalist because of their corporate property regime, because they had a bureaucracy that impeded competition, and so on. Conversely, studying the ethics of the prophets of Israel, Weber found that, as far back as this, the long road was being built that would lead to capitalist modernity; the last stage of this road would be the reform promoted by Calvinist ethics (the conditions for the realization of the capitalist system). Calvinist individualism, wealth considered as a

divine blessing, competition, private property, and the discipline of an austere subjectivity made the birth of capitalism possible, conditions not found in Chinese corporatism or in the magical quasi-feudalism of Hindustani Brahmanic culture. (Dussel, 2002, p. 226)

Eurocentrism, Dussel asserted, began at the end of the 18th century with the French and English "Enlightenment" and the German "Romantics," who reinterpreted all of world history, projecting Europe into the past and attempting to show that everything that happened before had led to Europe's becoming. Dussel went on to say that a second type of Eurocentrism (or West-centrism) is now superseding the first. This type, he said, still thinks from Europe, although it accepts that Europe established its dominion by means that came from outside (e.g., American precious metals). This outside allowed it to triumph in the competition that started in 1492 with the Islamic, African, and Asian worlds. The narrative descriptions always begin from Europe. Africa or Asia is the external world, far away and in the past.

In an extensive analysis of West-centrism, Balagangadhara (1994) presented the argument that the culture of the West believes (a) "that all cultures are constituted (partially) by religion," and (b) "that individuals and cultures require world views to orient and navigate themselves in the world" (p. 507). Balagangadhara challenged the claim that religion is a cultural universal. He asserted that because the constitution and identity of Western culture are tied to the dynamic of Christianity, it is possible to give a different description of non-Western cultures and religion than those prevalent in the West (e.g., Weber's views on the religions of China and India).

Buddhism, as the European savants viewed it, was a reaction against Brahmanism. In no time at all, Buddha became the Martin Luther of India rebelling against the "Roman Catholic" Brahmanic priestly caste. (Balagangadhara, 1994, p. 143)

King (1999) said the exclusion of non-Western theory is a reflection of the frequent claim in Western philosophical literature that "philosophy began with Thales" (p. 8).[1] Radhakrishnan (1952), however, pointed out that "philosophical speculations began earlier in India than in Greece" (p. 20) and that some of the earliest schools of Greek philosophy, especially the Orphic cult and the philosophy of Pythagoras (6th century BCE), show "a striking resemblance to Indian modes of thought" (p. 23). Pythagoras' view of the transmigration of the soul—that the soul exists as an immortal entity with the body simply as its temporary home; that on the death of one body it moves to another, and that through correct behavior the soul can move on to a happier existence (Freeman, 1996)—was quite similar to that of Indian philosophy. Goonatilake (1998) highlighted the resemblance between Buddhist thought and Aristotle's doctrine of the mean, as well as Heraclitus' belief that everything is in a state of flux. Heraclitus taught that all changes in the world arise from the dynamic and cyclic interplay of opposites, and he saw any pair of opposites as a unity. Tu Weiming (1997) said that the "humanistic splendor of Chinese civilization"—the Sinic worldview, cosmological thinking, benevolent despotism, and ethics—reached European intellectuals like Montesquieu, Voltaire, Quesnay, Diderot, and others through missionary reports. He added, "Ironically, the Enlightenment mentality, especially in its nineteenth century West-centric incarnation, has become the most devastating disputation that the Chinese mind has ever encountered" (p. 22).

Woelfel (1987) asserted that the extent to which Eastern and Western thinking merged during the early origins is still little known. The principles of Chinese philosophy often bore a striking resemblance to the views of pre-Socratic Greek philosophers. The philosophy of Heraclitus (540?–475? BCE), whose dictum that one could not step in the same river twice epitomized the idea of endless change and restlessness, came very close to the Chinese model. Woelfel wrote:

> Miletus, the largest city in the Greek world and the home of Thales, Aniximander, and Aniximines, was the largest commercial trading center of the Greek world and, as such, was in continuous contact with the East. Land travel to Mesopotamia was common, as was sea travel to Egypt, and there is good evidence that Thales himself traveled to Egypt at least once. (p. 300)

Radhakrishnan (1952) pointed out that various Greek philosophers traveled to the East in quest of knowledge (e.g., Democritus [460?–370 BCE] spent a long period in Egypt and Persia; Pythagoras traveled to Egypt, Solon [?–559? BCE] and Plato traveled extensively in the East.

King (1999) added that attempts to construct a linear history of (West-centric) philosophy are "misleading because they portray the development of Western intellectual thought in a manner [that] 'papers over the cracks' and avoid ruptures, heterogeneities and discontinuities of Western cultural history" (p. 9). Moreover, he said, "Philosophy has tended to function as the handmaiden of European colonial dominance" (p. 9). Lin, Rosemont, and Ames (1995) lamented the near exclusion of Chinese thinking from the discipline of philosophy in Western seats of learning. They said that "claims of total incommensurability, of impassable conceptual barriers, and of the other as wholly other" have become ready-made excuses "for Western philosophers to continue to ignore the belief systems of 75 percent of the human race" (p. 753). However,

Walter (1994) merged the approaches of the linear-minded West and the analog-style thinking of the East by showing that the genetic code and the *Yijing* (the *Classic of Changes*) function through the same chaos patterns. She translated mathematically the physical system of DNA into the psychic system of the *Yijing*.

The scholarship of the likes of Said (1978), Wolf (1982), and Amin (1989) has unraveled the distortions of West-centric discourse.[2] The discourse of the putative orientalists, according to Said, presents itself as a form of knowledge that is both different from and superior to the knowledge that the Orientals have of themselves. In Amin's view, West-centrism has been a systematic and important distortion "from which the majority of dominant social theories and ideologies suffer" (pp. vii–viii). Amin described West-centrism as a culturalist expansion of ongoing capitalist world expansion. It is the promotion of the Western mode of life, economy, and culture as the model for the rest of the world. It fits well with the ideologies of globalization (Fals-Borda & Mora-Osejo, 2003). Wolf drew our attention to the "conceptual shortcomings in our [Western] ways of looking at social and political phenomena" that bedevil "our [Western] thinking in the present" (p. 7), while Frank (1998) documented the tenuous foundations on which West-centric claims to universality rest. Inden (1990), who took a fresh look at the Indian intellectual traditions, pointed out that the Euro-American selves and Indian others have constituted one another dialectically.

WEST-CENTRISM IN COMMUNICATION THEORY

The field of communication accommodates both intercultural and international communication. Yet scholars have continually debated West-centrism in communication theory despite this accommodation (e.g., Carter, 1991; Dervin, 1991; Jacobson, 1991; Krippendorff, 1993; Pearce, 1991; Tehranian, 1991). Some have drawn attention to the similarities and differences between the East and West in interpersonal communication as well. For instance, contrary to the ethnocentric Western view that rhetoric does not exist in the hierarchical Japanese society, Ishii (1992) pointed out common features between the five canons of Western classical rhetoric and the Agui School's principles of Buddhist preaching. In contrast, Ishii (1988) said that in a high-context culture as Japan, "implicit nonverbal messages are of central importance" (p. 15). Therefore, "silences in communication settings are not empty and not to be filled with words, but they should be regarded as important nonverbal means of communication" (p. 4).

Jia, Lu, and Heisey (2002), as well as Lu, Jia, and Heisey (2002), pointed out West-centric biases related to Chinese communication in particular. Kim (2002) has asserted that "most current theories of human communication are rooted in Western philosophical presumptions about persons and in layers of practices and institutions that reflect and promote these presumptions" (pp. 27–28). In her view, "Communication theories must be freed from the confines of the pervasive Euro-American belief in the autonomous individual" (p. 3). Various other scholars, including Li (1999) and Paranjpe, Ho, and Rieber (1988), have analyzed the inaccuracies and shortcomings derived from West-centric interpretations of non-Western philosophy and psychology.

Tehranian (1991) wrote, "The challenge lies in developing comparative theories that consciously avoids . . . ethnocentric bias. We need to focus . . . on elements that appear to be both universal and immanent in most human societies" (p. 49). Wang and Shen (2000) asserted, "If theory-building is to be successful, all human histories, experiences, philosophies, cultural traditions and values relevant to theory formulation should be given due consideration in the process" (p. 29). Braman (2002) pointed out the need "to come up with an alternative typology of media systems that is comprehensive and complex enough to be able to cope with the great variety of media systems currently in existence and emerging" (p. 401).

Chen and Starosta (1996) drew attention to the need for more holistic theories reflecting the oneness of things. They said:

> Conceptually, scholars in the area of intercultural communication competence have been unable to provide a consistent framework for an understanding of the notion of interdependence and interconnectedness of the complex multicultural dynamics in the contemporary age. . . .
>
> Recent studies . . . have begun to examine communication competence from Chinese, Indian, Japanese, and Korean perspectives. . . . A coherent theme around which these researchers conceptualize communication competence is "harmony," which appears to be an element of most Asian cultures. (Chen & Starosta, 1996, pp. 370–371)

Chen and Starosta (1996) urged researchers "to try to discover more and different elements to account for intercultural communication competence from non-Western cultural perspectives" (p. 372). Five communication scholars—Collier, Hegde, Lee, Nakayama, and Yep—who engaged in a recent discussion on communication and culture, expressed concern over the prevalence of Eurocentrism among many scholars in their field (Collier et al., 2002). Yep contended that in terms of theory, research, and praxis, the field has remained "politically unconscious, ahistorical, disembodied, and Eurocentric during the past two decades (p. 235), In Yep's view, the current conceptualizations of culture as shared "is a lie that hides Eurocentric assumptions and historical truths" (p. 270); Hegde argued that the paradigms constituting communication theory have lost their explanatory reach because their Eurocentric tilt failed to even name certain realities. Lee saw the mainstream scholars in the field as constituting a Eurocentric empire that could "not see the subtleties and power of the fringe" (p. 246).

Dirlik (2000) clarified that "paradigms are not just innocuous models of explanation that guide intellectual work" because they are also "expressions of social ideologies" and power (p. 126). Thus, West-centric power and ideology associated with the dominant typologies or paradigms have prevailed over alternative explanations. As Servaes (1999) pointed out, empiricism and positivism were largely derived from Western thought. These concepts embodied the West's fundamental desire to change reality, which the West saw as something "concrete, measurable, and manipulable" (p. 20). The West absolutized these concepts and presumptions and intended them "to be transferred to the rest of the world" (p. 20).

WEST-CENTRISM IN MEDIA/PRESS THEORIES

McQuail (1984/1987) provided a media theory map identifying the main alternative approaches to the study of mass communication in the social sciences. First, he identified the (holistic and usually top down) macroapproaches: mass society theory; Marxist approaches and critical theory; theory of media structure and function; and normative theories of media. Second, he identified message-centered theory. Third, he identified the theory of audience and effect.

McQuail (1984/1987) explained that mass society theory "emphasizes the interdependence of institutions that exercise power and thus the integration of the media into the sources of social power and authority" (p. 58). The Marxist approaches include the political-economic media theory, the hegemony theory, Frankfurt School's critical theory, and the sociocultural approach. McQuail, however, fails to see any connection between the fundamental presumptions of Eastern philosophy—part–whole interaction; and unity and dynamism of all things—and the macrotheories he mentioned. In the present exercise, I excluded the microtheories because, from the standpoint of Eastern philosophy and systems thinking, parts cannot function outside of the whole. I also excluded functionalist social theories that connect normative principles with the mass media (e.g., Lasswell, 1948; Lazarsfeld & Merton, 1948) because they are not related to explaining the evolution of political/press philosophies or free expression. Lasswell saw three universal functions of communication outlets: surveillance of the environment, correlation of the parts of society, and transmission of social heritage. Lazarsfeld and Merton saw two social functions of communication outlets: status conferral and enforcement of social norms—in contrast to their narcotizing dysfunction. However, these norms are relevant to determining the different shades of social responsibility across the libertarian–authoritarian continuum.

The primary concern of this book is the construction of a theory of communication outlets and free expression within the framework of Eastern philosophy and the Western theory of living systems. It attempts to explain why and how different political/press philosophies emerge in the world system, rather than a single system preferred by one group or another. Although our theoretical framework is appropriate for reconceptualizing any of the macroapproaches that McQuail mentioned, the present endeavor is to use the framework to develop a more humanocentric theory that can replace the putative normative theories (viz. the *Four Theories* and the subsequent improvements). Yin (2003) called for a new paradigm in studying Asian media systems because it is hard to fit these systems into the existing normative theories.

> Asia is a politically and culturally diverse continent, where you can find reforming and developing communist countries next door to some of the most successful capitalist countries in the world. And no one or two religions dominate the continent. It is hard to lump sum Asia together in any kind of description and it is even harder to pigeonhole the vastly diverse Asian media systems into the existing press theories developed by Western media scholars and based on the analysis of Western media histories, operations and performances. (Yin, 2003, p. 1)

Four Theories of the Press

The normative theories of the press began with Siebert, Peterson, and Schramm's (1956) classic *Four Theories of the Press*, a static, deontic, or normative theory that ignored the dynamic diversity inherent in complex dissipative social systems. The pioneer mass communication gurus who formulated the original press theories were clearly influenced by Enlightenment thinking. Their theory was based entirely on the foundation of Western philosophy and history.

For Siebert, Peterson, and Schramm, *the press* meant "all the media of mass communication" (p. 1), which critical theorist Habermas (1989) subsequently identified as constituting the principal element of the public sphere.[3] Downing (2002), however, criticized the four theories model for heavily downplaying the media's entertainment function because of its obsession with the democratic functions of serious, quality media, "with their contribution to rational public debate and policy making" (p. 24).

The most elaborate critique of the *Four Theories* has come from eight scholars from the same institution where Siebert, Peterson, and Schramm (1956) produced their classic. These scholars—Berry, Braman, Christians, Guback, Helle, Liebovich, Nerone, and Rotzoll—asserted that *Four Theories* asked the wrong constitutive questions in the context of the historical circumstances of the mid-20th century. Thus, the book was driven not by ideas, but by history (Nerone, 1995). These scholars argued that freedom of the press made good sense as a natural right, but *Four Theories* postdated the demise of natural rights philosophy. Because the press was now understood to be an institution, the classical liberal notion of press freedom had ceased to make sense. Moreover, they argued that *Four Theories* did not offer four theories, Rather, it offered one theory—that in its structure, policy, and behavior, the communications system reflected the society in which it operated and that society could be categorically defined by a coherent philosophy—with four examples. They saw six flaws in *Four Theories*.

First, the four theories failed to have the same level of historical concreteness. Second, the four were not all theories in the same sense; authoritarianism, for example, was only a set of practices. Third, the scheme gave the incorrect impression that one coherent theory of the press was adequate to define any press system. Fourth, each of the theories, particularly the authoritarian and libertarian, was oversimplified. "Authoritarianism . . . has a notion of an incomplete human individual, a state that is an end in itself, knowledge that is difficult and available only to a few, and an absolute truth. Libertarianism has the opposite" (Nerone, 1995, p. 20). Fifth, the theories paid too little attention to concentration of power in the private sector, which they identified as the individual's realm of freedom, whereas they identified the public as the state's realm of control. Sixth, the *Four Theories* defined the four theories within one of the four theories—classical liberalism. Thus, the theories were oblivious to the controls imposed by "market forces and ownership ties and a host of other material bonds" (p. 22). These criticisms, however, failed to mention the West-centric bias of *Four Theories*.

C. J. Huang (2003) pointed out that normative media theories "lack the ability to adapt to changing social and media environments" (p. 454) because they are about "how media *ought* to be or are *expected* to operate" (McQuail, 1984/1987, p. 109). Huang agreed with McQuail that an "almost irresolvable conflict" exists between the normative concepts and the rapidly changing and expanding media systems in the real world. Therefore, Huang suggests a culturally open-minded, non-normative approach "that views human communication as a history of transition and makes change and adaptation its primary orientation" (p. 454)—an approach that presumes media change as a historical process that goes through both revolution and evolution.

> Whereas a normative media approach focuses on radical or evolutionary media changes in order to regroup media systems into various normative models, a transitional media approach pays attention to both revolutionary and evolutionary media change and treats both of them as a transitional process that is far more complex than certain normative press models are able to handle. (C. J. Huang, 2003, p. 455)

Although Siebert, Peterson, and Schramm (1956) claimed their book was "about the philosophical and political rationales or theories [that lay] behind the different kinds of press we have in the world today" (p. 2), their examination of those rationales or theories was vertical and separatist. Theirs was a cold war-era typology (Braman, 2002). They drew their concepts only from Western philosophers and theorists, and yet they tried to give the impression of universality to the theories they created as evident from their attempt to examine the degrees of press freedom in various non-Western countries. Had they followed what historian Fletcher (1985) termed the *horizontally integrative macrohistory* approach by examining human philosophies across space time, they would have found the concepts and laws to make their theories dynamic and more universally applicable.

To dissect the differences among the press systems (i.e., systems of communication outlets), Siebert, Peterson, and Schramm (1956) said one had to first examine the social systems in which the press (i.e., communication outlets) functioned. Furthermore, to determine the true relationship of the press to the social system, they said one had to look at certain basic beliefs and assumptions that the society held: the nature of man, the nature of society and the state, the relation of man to the state, and the nature of knowledge and truth. This meant, they argued, "in the last analysis the difference between press systems [was] one of philosophy" (p. 2). Then they followed the neo-Enlightenment path of West-centrism and omitted the philosophical and political theories of the non-Western world.

Siebert, Peterson, and Schramm (1956) anchored the four theories solely on Western philosophical and political theory. They traced the authoritarian theory to Plato (427–347 BCE), Machiavelli (1469–1527), Hobbes (1588–1679), Hegel (1770–1831), and Treitschke (1834–1896). They traced the libertarian theory to Milton (1608–1674), Locke (1632–1704), [Adam] Smith (1723–1790), Paine (1737–1809), Jefferson (1743–1826), Erskine (1750–1823), and Mill (1806–1873). They traced the social responsibility theory to the Commission on Freedom of the Press. They traced the Soviet communist theory of the press to Marx (1818-1883), Lenin (1870–1924), and Stalin (1879–1953). Thus, the four theories they created lacked the input of any non-Western philosophy.

Subsequent Improvements

Winfield, Mizuno, and Beaudoin (2000) criticized the critics of the four theories as well for looking at the world from a Western perspective without examining the historical philosophies of other civilizations. They pointed out that in the Far East "the philosophical tenets concerning the group, the hierarchy and truth" are indirectly linked with mass media and freedom of expression (p. 329). De Smaele (1999) goes on to show the inapplicability of Western media models even on the Russian media system, which exhibits both Western and Eastern/Asian characteristics.

The few scholars who subsequently attempted to improve on the *Four Theories* (see Asante, 1997; Lambeth, 1995) also failed to draw connections to Eastern philosophy. Nordenstreng (1997) said none of these revisions has gained "the same momentum as the original *Four Theories*," although the latter is already a museum piece (p. 97). Ostini and Fung (2002) pointed out that the theories of the press developed by Western scholars so far have focused on normative theories largely based on traditional media structures. They asserted, "Normative theories lack explanatory power in that they are based on how things should be and do not necessarily relate to how things are. . . . [T]he original *Four Theories* model was constrained by the ideology and historical circumstances of its inception" (p. 45).

Merrill and Lowenstein (1979) found fault with the four theories because they lacked the flexibility to describe all of the world's press systems. Lowenstein suggested a two-tiered typology that identified three types of press ownership—private, multiparty, and government—and five types of press philosophies—authoritarian, social authoritarian, libertarian, social libertarian, and social centralist. Although Lowenstein's formulation provided greater flexibility in classifying communities into specific slots, it too was a normative and static theory with no explanatory power. The Press Independence and Critical Ability (PICA) index that Lowenstein (1970) developed earlier was primarily based on government controls—laws, regulations and pressures. The

PICA presumptions evidently reflected the bias of the capitalist-libertarian philosophy.

Merrill (in Merrill & Lowenstein, 1979) conceptualized a continuum stretching from authoritarianism (A) at one end to libertarianism (L) at the other. Varying systems of communication outlets of the world community would occupy specific points along this continuum because "governments are designed on the philosophical base of these two basic orientations" (p. 154). Merrill's concept of the A to L continuum (i.e., the path stretching from libertarianism on one end to its antinomy authoritarianism on the other) is fundamental to the humanocentric model developed in this book. I borrowed this continuum from Merrill and have given it dynamic explanatory power by connecting it to Eastern philosophy and the theory of living systems.

Hachten (1981/1999) revised the four theories into five concepts: authoritarian, Western, communist, revolutionary, and developmental. He derived his Western concept by merging Siebert, Peterson, and Schramm's libertarian and social responsibility theories, although the latter arose as a reaction to the extremities of libertarianism. The social responsibility theory had become an uncomfortable thorn for the Western media during the New World Information and Communication Order debate that caused the United States' withdrawal from UNESCO in 1984. Thus, one can construe Hachten's merger of the two concepts as an ideological exercise. Hachten credited Lenin for providing the ideology and rationale for the revolutionary concept—the short-term use of illegal and subversive communication, such as *samizdat*, to overthrow a government. Hachten described the developmental concept as "an amorphous and curious mixture of ideas, rhetoric, influences, and grievances" (p. 31) that contained both authoritarian and social responsibility characteristics. Thus, Hachten's five concepts are not mutually exclusive. They constitute a mix of three normative concepts, a genre of journalism (developmental concept), and a short-term journalistic strategy (revolutionary concept). The criticisms of the *Four Theories* (Nerone, 1995) are equally, if not more, applicable to Hachten's five concepts.

In discussing normative theories of media structure and performance, McQuail (1987) too supplemented the four theories with two other types: the developmental media theory, which he tied to the ideas of the MacBride Commission, and the democratic participant media theory, which he associated "with the needs, interests and aspirations of the active 'receiver' in a political society" (p. 122). McQuail's development media theory emphasized collective ends, rather than individual ends, aimed at nation-building. Whereas Hachten embedded derogatory characteristics to his developmental concept, McQuail saw positive characteristics in his development media theory. McQuail described his democratic-participant theory, which subsumed Hachten's revolutionary concept, as a "reaction against the commercialization and monopolization of privately owned media and against the centralization and bureaucratization of public broadcasting institutions" (p. 122). These two theories respectively describe the environment conducive to the practice of developmental journalism and public/civic journalism. The democratic-participant media theory has much in common with the norms associated with Habermas' (1989) concept of the public sphere. A considerable overlap exists between the implicit characteristics of these two theories and those associated with the social responsibility theory. I have borrowed from McQuail's normative definitions of libertarianism and authoritarianism, which are philosophically balanced to a high degree, to construct my dynamic theory.

Picard (1985) developed a democratic socialist model of communication outlets based on the historical experience of Western Europe at the turn of the 20th century. He described nine flights of steps that communities must go through to establish press freedom: requisite technology, available audience, relative absence of economic restraints, relative absence of government restraint, media plurality, relative absence of social restraints, newsroom autonomy and democracy, public access, and social/public ownership. This has the evolutionary taint of the Parsonsian structural-functionalist development theory based on the universality of European modernity. It presumes the aporetic presuppositions of the Newtonian–Cartesian model, including the reversibility of time.

However, Altschull's (1984) threefold typology of the systems of communication outlets—market (First World), Marxist (Second World), and advancing (Third World)—is much less tainted although conceptually weak. His descriptors outline the ideology and, by implication, the associated behavior of each system. However, just like the *Four Theories* and all other improvements that followed, Altschull's typology fails to explain the dynamic interaction of the social structures constituting the world system that produces divergent media environments and philosophies. C. J. Huang (2003) pointed out that neither Schramm's Soviet theory nor Altschull's Marxist approach is adequate to conceptualize the significant changes that post-Mao Chinese journalism has gone through since the early 1990s. Huang asserted that each of these two models suffers from inner theoretical flaws as normative press theories. He said that ideological bias, as shown in Schramm's analysis of the Soviet communist press, has caused oversimplification.

> Altschull's three typologies appear to be a victim of his own critique of variations and complexities of the world's media systems and normative media theories' limited ability in conceptualizing those variations and complexities. He would have provided his readers more

critical wisdom to understand both the world's Marxist press in general and post-Mao Chinese journalism in particular had his analysis been more nonnormative and empirically oriented. (C. J. Huang, 2003, p. 153)

MODERN STATE-MEDIA INTERACTIONS

The recent analyses of the *modus operandi* of the global media system by scholars like Curran and Seaton (2003), McChesney (1999), and Price (2002) lead us to ask the question: Do the traditional normative media/press theories reflect the reality of state-media relations in the contemporary world?

Curran and Seaton (2003) exposed the frailties of the conventional libertarian theory and bluntly called for its revision. They said that the liberal conception of the press as independent watchdog is no longer accurate because, *inter alia*, the press is now organized into large corporations, whose profitability is affected by the policy outcomes of a greatly enlarged government. Thus, "calculations of mutual advantage" (p. 348) have submerged the four key functions of the liberal theory: informing the public, scrutinizing the government, staging a public debate, and expressing public opinion.

McChesney (1999) observed that commercial values have overwhelmed the vestiges of public service in the media. He asserted the global media system has turned out to be "one that advances corporate and commercial interests and values, and denigrates or ignores that which cannot be incorporated into its mission" (p. 103). He said the bogus nature of commercial journalism becomes clear when measured by any traditional notion of communication requirements necessary for a democracy (perhaps as evident in the libertarian and social responsibility "press" theories). McChesney, however, used the term democracy without examining the implications discussed in chapter 1.

Held (1995) put forth the view that the new global communication systems "operate in large measure independently of state control and are, accordingly, not easily amenable to direct political regulation" (p. 124). The growth of global communications, he said, has sharpened the interconnectedness of peoples and given people new ways of "seeing and participating" in global developments. Held explained that the globalization of the media has created a complicated set of processes that "can weaken the cultural hegemony of nation-states and stimulate the ethnic and cultural groups which compose them" (p. 126) as evident in the case of Los Angeles. Held added, "The cultural space of nation-states is being rearticulated by forces over which states have, at best, only limited leverage" (p. 126). The relevance of the classical four theories anchored to the concept of the sovereign nation-state becomes moot under these circumstances. To overcome the weaknesses of the nation-state, Held proposed the macroscopic concept of cosmopolitan democracy at the regional and global levels. This perspective calls for macroscopic theories of communication outlets as attempted in this book.

In a book that addresses state–media relations as they are actually empirically unfolding today, Price (2002) documented the changes that have occurred as a result of new technologies, political upheavals, and changing concepts of human rights. Having realized the inevitability of crossborder data flow would make the task of controlling information almost impossible or much too costly, nation-states are resorting to two categories of action: inward-directed efforts to protect the nation-state's own information space, and outward-directed efforts to influence or alter media space and media structures outside its borders. The latter type of action has not received much attention so far.

Whereas Held (1995, 1996) analyzed the weakening sovereignty of nation-states, Price (2002) asserted that nation-states are engaged in preserving their information sovereignty through regional or multilateral approaches to control the media. Price pointed out that media structures, media spaces, and information policies are increasingly negotiated—the product of subtle arrangements between states and multinational corporations, between international entities and states, and encompassing other vectors. Price saw the world as "a kind of force field where blazing technologies interact with gargantuan media entities, transforming geopolitical realities" (p. 228). A remapping process is occurring, with the concept of human rights being adjusted to the clash of national security with free speech standards. Price went on to say that the principles of freedom of speech and of the press, the latter in particular, "deconstruct as technological change and commercial realities wreak havoc with existing categories of 'news,' 'journalists,' and the very institutions of media that have claimed the mantle of the fourth estate" (p. 248).

Only a macrotheory approach can analyze the contemporary scenario of state–media relations that Price and Held documented in much greater detail. Freedom House's method of determining press freedom within nation-states or the use of normative theories as exemplars for nation-states now stands to be challenged. I have already pointed this out elsewhere (Gunaratne, 2002a, 2003a, in press). Price's taxonomy of media–state relations requires the analysis of both unilateral and consensual actions (technology, law, force, negotiation) that nation-states adopt to alter external markets and protect internal markets. Price also mentioned seven main factors as determinants of a nation-state's approach to media: sensitivity to international speech norms, national security concerns, tradition of private versus state media, availability of new technology, protectionism versus free trade, nature and history of regime structure, and isolation versus vulnerability to power realignments.

The state–media relations that Price documented can be analyzed within the system-theoretical framework developed in this book (chapters 3, 5, and 6). We take up this matter in chapter 7 after we grasp the sense of the entire theoretical framework.

EXCURSUS: BUDDHISM AND SCIENCE

The Enlightenment vision caused the West to skip the timeless knowledge of the East and seek universal truth through Newtonian science and Occidental rationality. However, this vision did not go unchallenged. Theosophist Olcott (1885) pointed out the parallels between Buddhism (law of *karma*) and science (law of motion). Olcott said that both Buddhism and science taught evolutionism. Subsequently, at the 1893 World Parliament of Religions in Chicago, Anagarika Dharmapala, a Sri Lankan Buddhist leader, claimed that it was Buddhism, not Christianity, that could heal the breach between religion and science (Cabezon, 2003).

Since the Copenhagen Interpretation of quantum mechanics and the advent of systems thinking, the potential links between science and Eastern philosophy have caught the attention of more scholars. The arrogance of instrumental-utilitarian rationalism, which misled the likes of Weber to denigrate or downplay the insights of Eastern thought, hit a roadblock with the appearance of authoritative treatises such as the *Early Buddhist Theory of Knowledge* by philosopher K. N. Jayatilleke (1963) and the more popular work of Capra, Zukav, and others.

Robinson (1969) described Jayatilleke's treatise as "a masterpiece of Indology and of history of philosophy [that] deals superbly with the questions of authority, reason and experience in the Pali Canon" (p. 380). Robinson wrote an 11-page review of the book because "the contents are so rich and exposition is so tightly woven that a summary can no more do it justice than a prose digest can express the meaning of a poem. . . . [It is] by any standard a masterpiece" (p. 390).

The treatise, *inter alia*, discusses Buddhist logic and truth, paying particular attention to the controversial fourfold (*catuskoti*) form, which figures prominently in the Pali Canon: the relation among truth-value, utility, and pleasantness; truth, correspondence, and coherence; truth and verification; and the theory of double truth (conventional and absolute). The Pali Cannon offers rich insights on the Buddhist attitude to authority and reason, as well as on analysis and meaning—all of which could have helped produce a more global philosophy had the post-Enlightenment scholarship opened up to the East. Habermas, for example, could have developed a much more inclusive theory of communicative action had he made an attempt to delve into the Pali Canon via the Jayatilleke treatise, which has persuasively shown that Buddha's theory of knowledge was empiricist (Gunaratne, 2005a).

German scholar Paul Dahlke (1913) also made an early attempt to draw the parallels between Buddhism and science. Using Buddhism as a working hypothesis, Dahlke analyzed the problems of physics, physiology, biology, cosmology, and thought. Long before Wallerstein, Dahlke called for "a world-theory and therewith a world-conception . . . to comprehend adequate causes" (p. 7). Long before Prigogine, Dahlke noted that "the idea of reversible processes has practical and theoretical possibility only in an absolutely closed system" (p. 17). In the world of actuality, he said, all things stood in relation to one another as Buddhists believed.

Max Weber (1864–1920) was writing his essays on Protestant ethic and the Protestant sects—sociological concepts having the epistemological and ontological status of ideal types in relation to the *Geist* of modern capitalism—between 1904 and 1906. Therefore, it is highly unlikely that Dahlke's work had any chance of coming to the attention of Weber, whose ideas about Buddhism, as revealed in the English translations released in the 1930s, were highly orientalist. Weber's intent was to build a materialistic theory of instrumental rationality based on the Protestant-ethic thesis. Although Habermas (1987) was better situated to enrich his deep hermeneutics with Eastern thought, he too chose the vertical West-centric path.

Jayatilleke (1984) followed his treatise with further explorations into Buddhist philosophy, including an essay on the parallels between Buddhism and the scientific revolution. In this short essay, he asserted that Early Buddhism offered "a self-consistent scientific hypothesis touching matters of religion and morality [that] each person can verify for himself" (p. 15). Jayatilleke's work, coupled with earlier work of Dahlke, could provide the catalyst for humanocentric theory building in communication studies and other sciences.

The most recent work on the subject is an edited volume by Wallace (2003). One part of the book examines the parallels between Buddhism and the cognitive sciences while another part examines the parallels between Buddhism and the physical sciences. Introducing the book, Wallace critically examines the fundamental presumptions of the dogma of scientific materialism: objectivism, reductionism, monism, physicalism, and the closure principle. Wallace asserted that it is "misleading to categorize Buddhism as a religion to the exclusion of its scientific and philosophical elements" (p. 20). Writing on the nature of the dialogue, one contributor to the volume explained:

Science is concerned with the exterior world, Buddhism with the interior one. Science deals with matter, Buddhism with mind. Science is the hardware, Buddhism the software. Science is rationalist, Buddhism is experiential. Science is quantitative, Buddhism qualitative. Science is conventional, Buddhism contemplative. Science advances us materially, Buddhism spiritually. But whether the difference is identified principally in terms of content, of method, or of goal, the perceived problem—diagnosed in terms of overemphasizing one of the two elements—is overcome by a balance when the two parts are brought together harmoniously. Unlike conflict/ambivalence as a mode, the logic of complementarity eschews the kind of triumphalism in which one of the two spheres emerges as victorious over the other. Unlike identity/compatibility as a mode, by holding firmly to the notion of irreconcilable differences it refuses to allow either Buddhism or science to be reduced to the other. (Cabezon, 2003, p. 50)

Sheth (2004), a Catholic Indologist, asserted that Buddhism and science show complementarity rather than similarity. Sheth said that parallels between Buddhism and science exist both in *method* and *content*. Buddhism's emphasis on personal verification, rather than on authority, matches the scientific method, and the fundamental Buddhist doctrine of dependent co-arising (*paticca samuppada*) matches the principal of universal causation in science. With regard to content, parallels between Buddhism and science exist on cosmology and evolution. Sheth went on to illustrate the similarities between quantum mechanics and the Buddhist doctrine of emptiness; between evolutionary biology/development psychology and the Buddhist understanding of "no-self"; between cognitive sciences and the Buddhist concept of mind; and between the mathematical concept of zero and the Buddhist idea of emptiness.

The Buddhist distinction between *absolute* truth (*paramattha-sacca*) and *conventional* truth (*sammuti-sacca*) needs an explanation.[4] According to Sheth (2004), the Theravada school believes that sentient beings are not unitary substances or souls, but impersonal mental or physical phenomena—a series of succeeding moments that give the false impression of a substance. This false impression is what is called *conventional truth*. In reality, every sentient being is a series of momentary aggregates of the five khandhas (material shape, feelings, perceptions, habitual tendencies, and consciousness). This is the absolute (or ultimate) truth (Sheth, 2004).

The Mahayana school (Madhyamika sect) believes that the only reality that exists is the Body of Essence (*Dharmakaya*) or the First Buddha. The absolute reality is also called Emptiness (*Sunyata*), meaning that it is empty of the imperfections of the unreal world that exists at the practical or conventional level. The unreal world is also empty because it lacks intrinsic nature inasmuch as things in the unreal world are not absolute, but dependent on other things (as evident in dependent co-arising). However, this conventional existence is merely a mirage. Thus, *absolute* truth and *conventional* truth do not have identical meanings within the two schools (Sheth, 2004).

Bell's theorem in quantum mechanics parallels the doctrine of dependent co-arising. Quantum mechanics confirms emptiness that becomes reality only when an observer subjectively collapses a possibility wave into an object. In this sense, objectivity is an oxymoron.

Buddhism also has parallels with systems theory. For example, Buddhism approaches a human being holistically. Sivaraksa (2002), a Thai social scientist, pointed out that Buddhist approaches can provide solutions to the injustices and environmental degradation engendered by the contemporary economic reality, widely known as *neoliberal capitalism*, which "places the accumulation of profits over human well-being and environmental sustainability" (p. 47). Sivaraksa believed that it is possible to achieve human freedom in community when the individual's interests are in harmony with those of the whole, and that liberating and sustainable lifestyles are possible when people live in small communities. To illustrate the Buddhist view, Sivaraksa (2002) quoted Buddhadasa Bhikku:

> The entire cosmos is a cooperative. The sun, the moon, and the stars live together as a cooperative. The same is true for humans and animals, trees and soil. Our bodily parts function as a cooperative. When we realize that the world is a mutual, interdependent, cooperative enterprise, that human beings are all mutual friends in the process of birth, old age, suffering, and death, then we can build a noble, even heavenly environment. If our lives are not based in this truth, then we shall all perish. (p. 58)

NOTES

1. Thales of Miletus (624–546 BCE) was reputedly the first to explain the world in nonmythological terms. He believed that one original substance (water) formed all other substances in the world. He described the Earth as a flat disk floating in water.

2. Goonatilake (2001) wrote: "The two grand theorists in sociology, Marx and Weber, both saw Asia as backward and static, as illustrated by Marx's residual category, the Asiatic mode of production, and Weber's rise of capitalism through Protestantism" (p. 5).

3. Hannah Arendt's political philosophy and the critical theory of Jürgen Habermas saw the *public sphere* as a specifically political space (distinct from the state and the economy) that was home to citizen debate, deliberation, agreement, and action. A democratic political theory based on European experience, it has come under sharp attack by postmodern theorists, including Foucault, Lyotard, and Baudrillard, who question its basic presuppositions (Charney, 1998; Villa, 1992). Public/civic journalism advocates, however, tie their philosophy to the concept of the public sphere, which provides another approach to study communication outlets vis-à-vis civil society (Rosen, 1999). Postmodernism, cultural studies, postcolonial studies, feminist studies, and so on, emerged as a reaction to Newtonianism. This, however, does not mean that these approaches necessarily agree with the "new" systems thinking.

4. Jayatilleke (1963) asserted that the Pali Canon makes no clear-cut distinction between these two kinds of truth. He added, "What we do find is a distinction between two types of Suttas (Discourses), which seems to have provided a basis for the later emergence of the doctrine of the two kinds of truth in medieval times; but even this latter theory, which appears in the commentaries, must be distinguished from the doctrine as understood by modern orthodoxy" (p. 361).

Five

Unity and Dynamism of Universe
Linking Eastern Philosophy With Western Science

BRIDGING EAST–WEST GAP

The world philosophies outlined earlier contain elements appropriate for constructing nonseparatist, universally applicable theories. Radhakrishnan (1952) asserted that the "fragmentation of philosophy into different compartments has prevented the survey of philosophical problems from a truly universal point of view" (p. 26). He called for studies that cover philosophical developments of all climes and ages.

Both Chinese and Hindu philosophy (and, depending on interpretation, Buddhist philosophy as well)[1] share the principle of part–whole interdetermination or system–environment interdependence. Mote (1989) pointed out that the "genuine Chinese cosmogony is that of organismic process, meaning that all parts of the entire cosmos belong to one organic whole and that they all interact as participants in one spontaneously self-generating life process" (p. 15). Oliver (1971) said that in Indian philosophy the world and all its creatures are "individual particles that possess essentially a primordial unity" so that "everything . . . is actually akin to everything else" (p. 15). Thus, one can see similarities between the fundamental philosophical principles of Eastern philosophy and the fundamental presumptions of modern physics and deep ecology (Capra, 1999, 1996, 2002). They are also congruent with the premises of the emerging theory of living systems incorporating autopoiesis, cognition, and dissipative structures. Eastern philosophy has much in common with the post-Parsonsian systems approaches, including world-systems analysis.

This holistic view, however, is not confined to Eastern philosophies alone. Soteriology of West Asia also speaks to the principle of unity of the universe. Speaking of Islam, Mowlana (1996) asserted: "The first and most fundamental outlook regarding man and universe in Islam is the theory of *tawhid*, which implies the unity, coherence, and harmony of all parts of the universe" (p. 119).

If the whole is more than the sum of its parts, the analysis of the world as a single unit should precede the analysis of its atomistic units, such as regions, or nation-states, or communities (Gunaratne, 2002a, 2002b). Dissecting a system into isolated elements destroys systemic properties. Because contemporary system theories have adopted the system–environment interaction approach, we can conceptualize the world as a dissipative structure divided into networks of a multitude of autopoietic systems, which are organizationally closed, but structurally and cognitively open.

Using the theory of living systems and world-systems analysis as guides, as well as quantum mechanics where appropriate, we can also conceptualize the world as a far-from-equilibrium dissipative structure divided into three layers—a center, a semiperiphery, and a periphery. Each layer comprises a number of autopoietic systems (nation-states of human beings who are autopoietic and dissipative), some of which belong to cooperative networks of systems along the same layer or across the layers. The world system serves as the superstructural environment for each of its autopoietic substructural unities (e.g., nation-states or human beings), which may use their cooperative networks of other substructural unities as their immediate environment. Although every living and nonliving entity in the world system is (potentially) structurally coupled, substructural organisms (or unities) like the nation-states will pay closer attention (be cognitively open) to other substructural organisms with which they have closer cultural, economic, political, or military connections. Baker (1993a) said that social phenomena associated with these substructures "exhibit both a degree of self-determination and a degree of dependency" (p. 132)—features that are intrinsically related. This is true of the superstructure as well because every living system, as Maturana (2002) pointed out, exists in two domains.

Periodic bifurcations of the superstructure (world system) produce self-organization within and across its layers. Because parts do not have systemic properties of the superstructural unity, they cannot effectively function outside the unity of the superstructure. Substructures (at the level of nation-states or individual human beings in our example) are also subject to periodic bifurcations. Each organism uses its own boundary (viz. the borders of the nation-state or the structure of the individual human being) for self-reference. This basic model incorporates the pattern of autopoiesis and the process of cognition within a dissipative structure. It is consistent with the systems thinking of Eastern philosophy—cosmos as "one organismic whole" or "primordial unity" of the world.

The principle of the dialectical completion of relative polarities (i.e., the *yin-yang* complements, which the Japanese adopted as the *in-yo*) offers the conceptual tool we need to explain the dynamics within the basic model we have derived. It is a conceptual tool that the so-called Orient has used for more than two millennia. If one were to consider the Hindu *purusha-prakriti* interaction as another version of *yin-yang* thinking, its universality becomes more apparent. In quantum mechanics, the interaction of elementary particles (possibility waves)—the clash of each particle (lepton, meson, or baryon) with its antiparticle in a perpetual dance of recreating themselves—illustrates the *yin-yang* dialectic.[2] In my view (Gunaratne, 2002a), the *yin-yang* dialectic will serve well to derive a theory of communication outlets and free expression at the world-system level and at the level of each of its three layers—center, semiperiphery, and periphery, or, conceived differently, at the three main levels of the world system—the world as a single unit (or superstructural unity), the nation-state (substructural unity), and the individual (primordial substructural unity). Therefore, a detailed explanation of the principle of the dialectical completion of relative polarities is in order.

DYNAMISM AND UNITY

In *Daodejing*, Laozi interconnects the Supreme Reality (*Dao*) with all beings through the harmony of *yin* and *yang*:

> Dao gives birth to one,
> One gives birth to two,
> Two give birth to three,
> Three give birth to ten thousand beings.
> Ten thousand beings carry *yin* on their backs and embrace *yang* in their front,
> Blending these two vital breaths (*qi)* to attain harmony (*he*). [3]

As procreative agents representing Heaven and Earth, *yin* and *yang* are dynamic airs of breaths (*chong qi*) blending harmoniously to become all beings (E. M. Chen, 1989). In the Daoist cosmology, the Absolute (the nameless) created the universe of energy/matter/information (or what quantum mechanics identifies as possibility waves). The Dao is the way that everything in the universe changes and evolves; it accounts for the behavior of the physical laws that conjoin energy and matter (possibility waves of various magnitude) into everything and direct their evolution (Rhee, 1997). It moves through the world smoothing and harmonizing everything. (Monistic idealism may see the Dao as *consciousness*, the ground of all being.) Complementarity or polarity[4] is the underlying principle in Daoist philosophy. Thus, every action engenders a reaction. The Absolute stands outside the universe and space time it created.

> The Dao produced the One: temporal/spatial reality. The One produced the Two: the opposite charges of positive and negative (*yin* and *yang*). The Two produced the Three: matter, energy, and the physical laws that bind them together. From these three came the existence of all things in the universe. All things are interconnected and interdependent, and from this concept comes the behavior of polarity. (Rhee, 1997)

Zhou Dunyi, the 11th-century Chinese philosopher who came to be known as the founding ancestor of the Neo-Confucian Cheng-Zhu School, wrote the following in his "Explanation of the Diagram of the Supreme Polarity":

> Non-Polar (*wuji*) and yet Supreme Polarity (*Taiji*). The Supreme Polarity in activity generates *yang*; yet at the limit of activity it is still. In stillness it generates *yin*; yet at the limit of stillness it is also active. Activity and stillness alternate; each is the basis of the other. In distinguishing *yin* and *yang*, the Two Modes are thereby established.

> The alternation and combination of *yang* and *yin* generate water, fire, wood, metal, and earth. With these Five [Phases of] *qi* harmoniously arranged, the Four Seasons proceed through them. The Five Phases are simply *yin* and *yang*; *yin* and *yang* are simply the Supreme Polarity; the Supreme Polarity is fundamentally Non-Polar. [Yet] in the generation of the Five Phases, each one has its nature.

> The reality of the Non-Polar and the essence of the Two [Modes] and Five [Phases] mysteriously combine and coalesce. "The Way of *qian* becomes the male; the Way of *kun* becomes the female; the two *qi* stimulate each other, transforming and generating the myriad things. The myriad things generate and regenerate, alternating and transforming without end.

Only humans receive the finest and most spiritually efficacious [*qi*]. Once formed, they are born; when spirit (*shen*) is manifested, they have intelligence; when their fivefold natures are stimulated into activity, good and evil are distinguished and the myriad affairs ensue. (De Bary & Bloom, 1999, pp. 673–675)

How do we explain the *Dao* in relation to the Non-Polar (*Wuji*) and Supreme Polarity (*Taiji*)? Cheng (1997) explained that the two concepts of *Taiji* and *Dao* characterize the ultimate reality of human experience, according to the *Xici Commentary* on the Book of Changes (*Zhouyi*). This cosmogonic and cosmographical way of thinking viewed reality as (a) inexhaustible origination, (b) a polar-generative process, (c) a multi-interactive harmony, (d) virtual hierarchization, (e) recursive but limitless regenerativity, and (f) an organismic totality. The interpretation of Zhou Dunyi implies that *Wuji* gives rise to *Taiji*, but the whole world is always the unity of *Taiji,* which is no more than the beginning state of *Wuji.* Thus, from an ontological point of view, Cheng (1997) said, "one could regard *Wuji* and *Taiji* as two alternating states of the Dao which exists at the same time and form a mutually defining unity" (p. 193).

These explanations make it abundantly clear that Eastern philosophical concepts, which the Enlightenment thinkers downgraded as "myths," can lead modern scientific thinking. Chang (2003) pointed out that connectionism (as established by Bell's theorem, which I have already explained in chap. 3) can be best understood in terms of Laozi's philosophy of emergence. Laozi maintains that every form of existence in the universe and the universe itself are products of interaction (or connection) between *yin* and *yang*—two properties or two sets of properties which, although differing from and even conflicting with each other, can interact/connect in various ways to generate one or more new forms. Now, compare this view with that of quantum physics:

The universe is made of both particles and anti-particles. Our part of it, however, is made almost entirely of regular particles which combine into regular atoms to make regular molecules which make regular matter which is what we are made of. (Zukav, 1979, p. 229)

The *yin* and *yang*, which the Chinese use in a cosmological sense (Lai, 2002), are parallel to particle and anti-particle. (They are also close to the philosophical concepts of *thesis* and *antithesis* popularly attributed to Hegel.[5] This dialectic goes back to Heraclitus whose cosmo-ontological view was similar to Laozi's.) In Chang's view, Laozi would perceive the molecule as originating from interaction/connection between a nucleus (with *yang*) and one or more electrons (with *yin*), and a business firm as emerging out of interaction/connection between capital (with *yang*) and labor (with *yin*). Furthermore, every type of *yang* has the potential to be connected with numerous types of *yin* (and vice versa) and thus to give rise to an infinite number of new forms of existence (both novel and reproductive). Before a certain connection between *yin* and *yang* is materialized, it is called *wu* (nonexistence, i.e., existing only in potential or possibility). Once the connection is materialized, it is called *you* (materialized existence).

We already know that the *yin* (conceived as earth, female, dark, negative, receptive, passive, and absconding) and *yang* (conceived as heaven, male, light, positive, creative, active, and penetrating) are complementary universal forces. They represent both the physical and the nonphysical. Materialist physics—both classical and quantum—sees the mind as an epiphenomenon of matter. Monistic idealism sees matter as an epiphenomenon of consciousness, the transcendental dimension of existence and the ground of all being. In either case, we have to look at human concepts as subatomic wave packets whose reality depends on the measurement method of the observer. That is to say, the reality of the concept (object) that the observer (subject) derives through collapsing the wave packet cannot possess Newtonian objectivity. This is because of Heisenberg's uncertainty principle: The path of the electron comes into existence only when we observe it. It is impossible to measure accurately both the position and momentum (velocity) of particles (or wavicles), which can propagate themselves elsewhere at superluminal speed. Because our mental constructs cannot have objective reality, social sciences cannot aspire to go beyond ideal type models.

We can theorize that the far left and the far right of the sociopolitical spectrum worldwide are two complementary universal forces. In China, the Daoists represented the far left, and the Legalists represented the far right. The Daoists were extreme libertarians who believed in an undifferentiated natural condition of life devoid of sociopolitical shackles. They had faith in the nature of man in a state of nature where man could pursue the unsullied, simple, and genuine life of the universe. They did not have faith in the nature of society and the state, both of which placed fetters of false duties and obligations on man. For them social knowledge was false, and truth emerged only from knowledge of nature. Although the Daoists were not interested in social knowledge, including what we call *news* (in the context of *Daodejing's* call on people to abandon language and return "once more to the use of knotted ropes" that we discussed in chap. 2), they were unlikely to endorse any shackles on free expression, including press freedom, because that would mean endorsing social shackles. The Legalists were extreme authoritarians who believed in subjugating the masses through codified sociopolitical shackles. They had little faith in the nature of man. They promoted codified law aimed primarily at punishment to bring order out of what Hobbes called the *state of war* with other men or what Hindu philosophy identified as *matsya-nyaya*. They believed that man was subservient to the interests of the feudal bureaucratic state, which was best served by keeping man away from knowledge and truth.

Obvious links exist between the emergent theory of living systems originating in the West and the onto-cosmological concept of part–whole interdetermination of Eastern philosophy. The oneness of things linked to Supreme Polarity (*Taiji*) in Chinese thought or *Brahman* (the source of all things) in Hindu thought illustrates this point. A resemblance also exists between the Chinese *yin-yang* antinomy (regulated by *Taiji*) and the *purusha* (the masculine spiritual principle) entangled with the *prakriti* (the feminine principle) in the early Upanishads (Weber, [1921]1958). The three *gunas* in *prakriti* were originally in a state of equilibrium, which was disturbed by contact with *purusha*, the self. Following this disturbance, the evolution of nature began in progressive heterogeneity, in unequal distribution of the three components (compared with the five components in *yin-yang*). Freedom (*moksha*) arises from the knowledge that the self (*purusha*) is different from nature.

The *yin-yang* phenomenon, as mentioned earlier, also has some resemblance to the West's thesis–antithesis dialectic. The classical Greek thinkers' concept of the dialectic evolved into different forms in early modern Europe. One form was the thesis–antithesis dialectic, which Marx misinterpreted as Hegel's dialectic while formulating Marx's own dialectical materialism. (This method of dialectical reasoning was based on the premise that every idea or concept [thesis] generated its opposite [antithesis], and the two working against each other produced a new concept [synthesis]. Those who used this dialectic believed that world history followed this triad.)[6] The *yin* and *yang* traveled along parallel but separate paths acting as a control mechanism on each other at their meeting point. Similarly, the clash of the thesis and antithesis produced a synthesis in a continuing cycle of the dialectic. Both approaches lead us to conclude that the interaction of two complements (*yin-yang*) or opposites (thesis–antithesis) usually prevents the occurrence of extremes. More often than not the two polarities bring about what Buddhists conceive to be the "middle path."[7] In China, Confucianism (*Rujia*)—a conservative stabilizing force associated with benevolent despotism—represented the middle path between Daoism (*Daojia*) and Legalism (*Fajia*). Social responsibility, a concept that the East and West may understand differently, represents the middle path between the extremes of libertarianism and authoritarianism.

My humanocentric approach is an attempt to merge the systems approach of Western science with Eastern philosophy. As developed in this revision, it is much more than my original attempt in 2001 to draw on the similarities between the *yin-yang* polarity and the thesis–antithesis dialectic. Marx, Hegel's most prominent interpreter, believed the chief implication of the dialectic was violent revolution—an interpretation that conflicts with the Chinese interpretation of the two polarities as controlling mechanisms. However, *yang* (conceived as positive feedback) has the potential to muster accelerated speed over *yin* (negative feedback) to bring about the complete reorganization of a dissipative structure at crucial bifurcation points. (In terms of quantum mechanics, we can explain these revolutionary shifts as extraordinary quantum jumps of the *yin-yang* "wavicles" around their nuclei.) The idea of fluctuations as the basis of order is one of the major themes in Daoist physics. Interpreting *Daodejing* in this regard, Rhee (1997) said:

> The Dao acts through polarity, a physical law that governs cause and effect. The law of polarity changes and evolves all things by acting upon extremes. Extremes are overcharged and begin moving in their opposite direction. (chap. 40)

The movements of the Dao follow the laws of the physical forces. Jones and Culliney (1999) attempted to interpret chaos theory with Daoism in relation to the following: the Daoist notion of *wu-wei* as perfect congruence, *yin* and *yang* at the edge of chaos, the emergent nature of the myriad things, and a Daoist warning against fractal disconnections in the world.

SYSTEM–ENVIRONMENT INTERACTION

System–environment interaction (or what used to be called *part–whole interdependence*) is also evident in the *karmic eschatology*—the tripartite *samsara-karma-moksa/nirvana* mechanism—of Hinduism and Buddhism. This mechanism illustrates how the individual is tied to the perpetual cycle of existence until achieving *moksa* or *nirvana*. The core Buddhist doctrine of *paticca samuppada* (dependent co-arising) explains all physical, psychological, moral, and spiritual phenomena in the following concise way:

> When this is present, that comes to be;
> From the arising of this, that arises.
> When this is absent, that does not come to be;
> On the cessation of this, that ceases.

The Buddhist belief in impermanence (*anicca*) does not mean an absence of system-environment interaction (see chap. 4 excursus for the Buddhist view of being).

Thus, although the Chinese explain the unity of all things through the nonpolar, the Dao, and the field forces of *yin-yang*, the Hindus explain it through the Brahman, the *purusha-prakriti* phenomenon, and the karmic eschatology; and the Buddhists explain it through the doctrine of *paticca samuppada* and their own version of karmic eschatology. Here a qualification is in order with regard to Hinduism: The Samkhya-Yoga-Vedanta systems look at reality from the top–down perspective of the whole, whereas the Vaisesika-Nyaya-Mimamsa systems look at reality from the bottom–up perspective of the parts (Larson, 1998).

Marx turned Hegel's dialectic into the philosophy of dialectical materialism, which asserts that things are in continual change because they are made up of conflicting elements and because all things are interconnected—a notion that goes well with Eastern philosophy if the term *complementary* is substituted for *conflicting*. Hegel's followers and adversaries interpreted the Hegelian dialectic in different ways. A single interpretation of semantics does not prevail, according to the receiver-centered principle of infinite interpretation in Chinese philosophy and the related principles of intuition and idealism in Hindu philosophy. The dialectical polarities, whether in the Eastern or Western sense, can produce the recursive outcomes associated with dissipative structures.

The concepts of impermanence (*anicca*) in Buddhist philosophy and illusion (*maya*) in Hindu philosophy—that everything is in a state of flux—enables us to grasp the constantly changing nature of the world system. The theory of dissipative structures, which asserts the irreversibility of time, backs up the concept of *impermanence*. The center-periphery structure keeps on changing just like every element in the unfathomable universe. Theories we develop to explain phenomena are also impermanent. It follows that the applicability of those theories to the whole and its component units also is impermanent. The meeting of the complementary forces of the *yin* and *yang* will produce different effects on the whole and its component parts over time and space. Because ongoing change is inherent in social systems, the best we can do is analyze presumed linear relations of deterministic processes between bifurcations because we know that dissipative systems display two fundamentally different types of behavior: deterministic, predictable motion in the short-time scales; and random, unpredictable motion in the long-time scales. This refers to an aspect of the correspondence principle, which justifies the application of Newtonian mechanics "in the realm of most (but not all) bulk matter as a special case of the new physics" (Goswami, 1993, p. 43).

LINKING THE CONCEPTS

Thus, we can attempt to develop a broad classification of communication-outlet systems valid in the short-time scale using the authoritarian–libertarian antinomy as the obvious starting point. In some ways, this antinomy resembles the binary codes that Luhmann used to define his abstract social systems. Reality has two sides. In Luhmann's autopoietic systems, this duality is at the heart of self reference. (Whether nonliving social systems can be autopoietic is another question we have to answer.) The binary code Luhmann used to define the mass media system is information/noninformation. This binary code helps identify the boundary of a system of media outlets, but not its philosophy. If we were to follow Luhmann, we would have to use another set of binary codes (e.g., libertarian/nonlibertarian, authoritarian/nonauthoritarian, etc.) within his mass media system to identify its philosophy. The libertarian/authoritarian code enables us to identify how autopoietic communication-outlet systems move back and forth between the two polarities over or beyond spacetime. The principle of irreversibility of time, which is integral to the theory of dissipative structures, prevents a reversal back to a previous superposition. (In quantum mechanics, however, time reversibility exists *in potentia*; i.e., while the particles are represented by propagating wave functions. Zukav [1979] clarified the second law of thermodynamics, which establishes the irreversibility of time; it is not considered applicable to conceptually isolated, short-lived entities in the subatomic domain.)

From the perspective of quantum mechanics, neither the space–time continuum nor our construct of the libertarian–authoritarian continuum can be linear or two dimensional. We have to presume that our concepts exist as wave packets within which the *wavicles* can shift to random trajectories around their nuclei in quantum jumps skipping some intervening trajectories within the libertarian–authoritarian continuum. Because wave packets possess superluminal properties, we can superimpose this continuum over the space–time continuum, which cannot defy the speed of light.

Our approach presumes that the system of communication outlets is operationally coupled[8] with the political system. The apparent reality is that the freedom of opinion outlets depends on the nature of the political system. The political system also moves back and forth along random trajectories around their nuclei between the two polarities along the libertarian–authoritarian continuum. This allows for the possibility of a libertarian system turning into an authoritarian one in one quantum jump, bringing about a similar shift in the system of communication outlets and free expression.

The perspective of *meaning* becomes relevant because our focus is on philosophical concepts—the nonphysical outcomes of the consciousness of a network of human beings. The unity of all things in Eastern philosophy means the clear rejection of the Cartesian separation of mind and matter. Thus, the *yin-yang* forces (wavicles or possibility waves with opposite charges) operate on both the physical and nonphysical aspects of the universe at the same time. In terms of monistic idealism, consciousness, guided by the quantum self's mind or awareness, collapses the *yin-yang* possibility waves constituting these concepts. The observer (viz. the quantum self) subjectively determines the nature of the objects (the concepts).

Baker's Model

Before proceeding any further, I outline the exploratory model developed by Baker (1993a, 1993b, 1994) to link the dissipative structure theory with world-systems analysis.[9] He started with the premise that human behavior embodies the dual dimension of *idergy*—a neologism Francis (1983) coined to mean *idergetic* (culture and information) and energetic (material energy) exchanges. Discernible within these idergetic exchanges is a pattern akin to the twin features of autopoiesis and dissipation associated with the dual domains of a living system. This pattern is the *centriphery* (center–periphery) holon—the dynamic *attractor* that creates the turbulence and re-creates the order in social life. It is a holon because, as Baker (1993a) explained, "insofar as the center creates the periphery, part of the center is in the periphery, and vice versa" (p. 136).

Thus, Baker (1993a) viewed the world system as a product of the ongoing process of centering and peripheralizing:

> Individuals, families, communities, villages, companies, and societies attempt to center their world and control the flow of energy and information through it. Centering involves both access to and use of resources and the know-how and the ideological justification for this. . . . Peripheralization is a counter phenomenon. It involves a loss of control. . . . Centering creates both the center and the periphery. This dynamic holon . . . is the "attractor" around which social relations are formed. (p. 136)

Baker (1993a) said that the Western world became a center through the peripheralization of the non-Western world. Within each center, the city that peripheralized the rural hinterland became the megalopolis. Relating this model of the world-system to the notion of entropy, Baker said that entropy measures the loss of energy/information during energy/information transformation. Thus, entropy implies randomness, disorder, noise, and pollution. It is entropy that essentially gives time its arrow and history its direction. Baker (1993b) asserted, "The loss of energy means that the processes of energy transformation are not reversible and ensures that there can never be a return to the original state" (p. 415).

Furthermore, according to Baker's model, human beings, individually and collectively, use various centripetal activities to bring the world into their orbit of control. However, the world never capitulates because of the counteractivities of the centrifugal forces. Baker (1993a) stated, "When key sociological concepts are considered from this centriphery perspective what is accentuated is the interplay of autopoietic and dissipative elements in social life" (p. 139). Baker (1994) applied this model to interpret the prehistory and history of Dominica.

Merged Model

Baker's model easily fits in with what we described as the theory of living systems. It provides an epistemic explanation of how the center–semiperiphery–periphery structure of the world system dynamically evolves. It also fits in with the Eastern philosophical concepts already discussed. Inasmuch as the forces of *yin-yang* are comparable to those of *idergy* and *entropy*, the interplay of those forces would not only give rise to the center–periphery structure of the nation-states within the world system, but also to the system of communication outlets and free expression. Whereas the *centriphery* (*yin* = periphery, *yang* = center) attractor gives rise to a far-from-equilibrium distribution of nation-states, the *libertarian–authoritarian* attractor gives rise to far-from-equilibrium distribution of communication outlet systems within the world system and within each nation-state. The individual human being's right to communicate also shows a far-from-equilibrium state.

A classification of the world system and its component nation-states on the proposed lines as *ideal type models* can be used for historically, culturally, and politically sensitive analysis of change and be subject to change. However, in studying the higher ontological levels—norms, values, idiographic or historical phenomena—of dissipative structures, researchers run the risk of reifying those phenomena should they use predictive, statistical, or iconological models. They should use such models primarily to investigate the lower ontological levels that represent determinant regularities, biological and ecological organization, facilities, and roles (Gunaratne, 2003c, 2004).

Leydesdorff (2003) argued that we need a mathematical (i.e., probabilistic), but a nonphysical (i.e., nonthermodynamic) interpretation of self-organization because, in his view, social systems are different from biological and psychological systems, including human beings. Leydesdorff agreed with Luhmann that "society should no longer be considered as composed of human beings but as consisting of communications" (p. 19). This approach deviates from my objective of linking Eastern philosophy with the theory of *living* systems. I contend that, because sociological concepts (related to higher ontological levels) lack universality in operational definitions, it makes sense to work within the deep realm of realist philosophy of the social sciences (Baert, 1998).

Saher (1970) pointed out that in Western philosophy, an idea is *not accepted* unless proved to be correct. What is *not proved* is to be treated as false. In Eastern philosophy an idea is *not rejected* unless proved to be false. What is *not proved* may be accepted as true until proved to be false. Thus, Eastern philosophy concedes both the inability and unsuitability of nomothetic empiricism to analyze natural phenomena at the higher ontological levels of dissipative structures, whereas Western philosophy, in general, expresses faith in reductionism—the ability to apply universal laws to explain phenomena at all ontological levels.

I concede that reductionism has been greatly reduced in the Western scholarship since Karl Popper's (1962) *Conjectures and Refutations*. Other pragmatists ranging from Dewey (1948) to Rorty (1983), as well as later Wittgenstein (1953), have argued against naive naturalistic formulation in philosophy as well as science. Although much of social science remains reductionistic, a great many social theorists and philosophers, including Habermas (1987), Luhmann (1995), and Giddens (1984), have worked against naive naturalism or nomothetic empiricism. Neverless, Kamhawi and Weaver (2003) documented the dominance of the reductionistic approach in mass communication studies: During the 20-year period of 1980 to 1999, almost 72% of the studies published in the field's major journals used the quantitative approach.

As mentioned earlier, a humanocentric theory of communication outlets and free expression requires the incorporation of Western science and Eastern philosophical concepts. It is not a claim for the superiority of Eastern philosophy, but an attempt to show its relevance to explain how nature works. Because *yin* and *yang* represent energy/matter/information, we can analyze the interplay of any two psychophysical antinomies in *yin-yang* terms.

We first take up the three-layer model of the world system (Fig. 5.1)—the whole, the nation-state, and the individual. The cognition of the substructural unities is structurally coupled with the superstructural cognition of the world system. As Zhou Dunyi explains, the reality of the non-

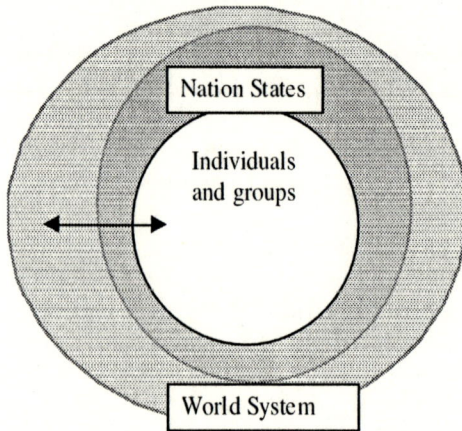

Fig. 5.1. Three main levels of the world system

polar and the essence of the two modes (*yin* and *yang*) and five phases (energy/matter/information denoted by earth, water, wood, fire, and metal) combine and coalesce to form and continually evolve the whole (world system) and its component parts, including the nation-states and the individual human beings. The two *qi*—male (the Way of *qian*) and female (the Way of *kun*)—stimulate each other, transforming and generating the myriad things that, in turn, recursively regenerate, alternate, and transform without end. Human beings receive the finest *qi* (psychophysical energy). Once they stimulate their fivefold natures into activity, their intelligence enables them to differentiate between good and evil.

As we see, the two modes have produced an interconnected whole (a far-from-equilibrium dissipative superstructure) through cognition—the process that enables the autopoietic pattern of each substructural organism encompassing the superstructural unity. The continual interplay of chaos (*yin*) and order (*yang*) gives this structure a dynamic balance. The structure is far from equilibrium because a thermodynamic equilibrium of *idergy* (*yang*) and *entropy* (*yin*) will stop the flux and flow of change and cause its collapse. Whereas negative feedback (*yin*) will bring about some stability to the structure in the short run through cancellation of effects, positive feedback (*yang*) can force the structure to reorganize itself into a more complex structure at periodic bifurcation points. Thus, one can examine the different facets of a dissipative structure through the *yin-yang* perspective.

The two modes are also active at the level of the substructural components. Communities, cultures, societies, nation-states, supranational networks, and so on, emerge as a result of human intelligence, which manifests itself in both emotional and rational actions. Autopoiesis is the *modus operandi* of these components. At the nation-state level, each substructure (nation-state) is autopoietic in the sense that it is organizationally closed even though cognitively and structurally open to its environment. The two modes—*yin* (libertarianism) and *yang* (authoritarianism)—autopoietically produce the political system and its operationally coupled system of opinion outlets befitting a nation-state. (Because mind and matter are inseparable, the two modes are capable of moving back and forth between the physical and the non-physical.) They do so in the context of the related subsystem characteristics they have created—social (integration), cultural (pattern maintenance), personality (goal attainment), and behavioral organism (adaptation) in Parsonsian terms (Parsons, 1971), or lifeworld (combining culture, society, and personality), economy, and state in Habermasian terms (Habermas, 1987). the two modes also take cognition of the immediate environment (the substructure's network of partners—cultural, commercial, political, military, etc.) and the world system as they reproduce, alternate, and transform these functional social systems.

The individual human being (as a system) is also organizationally closed but cognitively open to the environment in going through self-organization through the mediation of the two modes. They autopoietically adjust the degree of free expression (or the elements encompassing the right to communicate) available to the individual along the libertarian-authoritarian (*yin-yang*) continuum by assessing his or her personality, culture, and society, as well as other systems in the environment. The individual in the East is more network–bound than his counterpart in the West.

The world system of communication outlets and free expression is more than the sum of its component parts of nation-states and individuals. The whole has emergent characteristics that the components lack. Examples of such emergent characteristics are evident in what is commonly called *globalization*: global currency flow, global trade, global media conglomerates, global competitiveness, satellite broadcasting, international division of labor, and so on. These characteristics reflect cognition, the process of life of the world system. It is inextricably linked to the autopoietic patterns of its constituent parts—the nation-states and the individuals who inhabit them. The outcomes of the patterns of autopoiesis (*yin-yang* interactions) regulated by the Supreme Ultimate (*Taiji*) via cognition, the process of life, is a far-from-equilibrium dissipative structure, which we call the world system. Thus, superstructural cognition, which interconnects all parts of the world system, is an emergent characteristic of the whole.

As the superstructural unity, the world system of communication outlets does not have similar systems in its environment, although it is cognitively and structurally open to receive communication signals from the biosphere and beyond. Stichweh (1998), a systems theorist of the Luhmann school, pointed out that, on the basis of communications, society as one worldwide system is operationally closed. This "means there is no system in the environment of society that can introduce communications into society," which cannot "pretend to communicate with its extrasocietal environment" (p. 304).

In summary, in the foregoing discussion, I theorized on the forces that create the world system and its components, together with the concomitant political systems and systems of communication outlets using the combined ontology and epistemology of Chinese cosmology, quantum mechanics, complexity science (incorporating the theory of living systems), and world-systems analysis. Quantum mechanics and the chaos principles of complexity science are remarkably similar despite the presumption of irreversibility *in potentia* by the former in comparison to the latter's strong assertion on irreversibility. Chaos and order coexist in the subatomic domain, and the nonlinear behavior of wave packets is quite similar to the asymptotic behavior of attractors in far-from-equilibrium dissipative structures. From the perspective of quantum physics, we use our consciousness/mind, an epiphenomenon of our material brain, to see the manifest world created by the interaction of elementary particles. From the perspective of monistic idealism, we determine the reality of the universe creatively in diverse ways—à la Wallerstein, Prigogine, Habermas, Luhmann, Parsons, Weber, Marx, or any other observer—through transcendental consciousness (the union of the quantum self with the Dao, Dharmakaya, Brahman, Allah, or God), the ground of all being.

In chapter 6, I apply the same ontology and epistemology to outline my humanocentric theory of communication outlets and free expression relying heavily on the correspondence principle mentioned earlier.

EXCURSUS: THEORETICAL DIFFERENCES

We have used the work of several Western theorists to build our theoretical framework. In this Excursus, I point out the epistemological tensions among four of the theorists—Luhmann, Habermas, Wallerstein, and Prigogine. Although all four of them made use of systems thinking, their approaches were distinctly different. Of the four, Luhmann (1927–1998) became the first full-fledged systems theorist in sociology. Wallerstein (1930–present), who followed the path of historical social science, developed the approach of world-systems analysis to explain the dynamic of intercapitalist geopolitical competition. Prigogine (1917–2003), the chemist and physicist, developed his macrotheory of dissipative structures, which served as a bridge between natural and social sciences. Habermas (1929–present), the critical theorist and philosopher, integrated numerous theories to derive his theory of communicative action.

Whereas Wallerstein and Prigogine consider their theories to be complementary, this is not the case between Luhmann and Habermas, who have engaged in a public debate on their differences. Habermas is a quasi-systems theorist in comparison with Luhmann, who originally followed the footsteps of Parsons, but broke away to create a shift in sociological systems theory to the extent of placing function over system. Habermas rejected a full-fledged systems theory that deemphasized individualism and rationality.

Bakker (2003) pointed out that both Luhmann and Habermas treated the social sciences no differently from the hard sciences in their theoretical disagreements. Thus, they made a priori presumptions about ontology in a sociological context, where the epistemology was not a matter of exact science. In contrast to Weber, who formulated the notion of an ideal type epistemology for his concept of Protestant ethic, Luhmann and Habermas were arguing about the empirical reality of their epistemology pertaining to the concept of society. Wallerstein advocated the dismantling of the artificial barriers that separated the so-called *disciplines* within the social sciences—economics, sociology, and political science. Just like Prigogine, Wallerstein also believed that the time had come to collapse the hard sciences, social sciences, and humanities into a single epistemology because these false partitions were created by the Newtonian–Cartesian model, which no longer commanded much credence. Prigogine backed Wallerstein in the call for a single epistemology. Prigogine even cited Chinese cosmology to ridicule reductionism in Newtonian physics.

Bausch (1997) pointed out that the Luhmann–Habermas debate focused on three areas: meaning, technocracy, and norms. Luhmann held that *meanings* were a construction of past selections made in the course of a system's survival. Habermas held that meanings were created through interpersonal communication or intersubjectivity, and that they rested on interpersonally accepted norms. Luhmann argued that one's actions had meaning because of a history of selections in complex situations (Bausch, 1997).

Habermas held that Luhmann's concept of meaning reduced all values to the *technocratic* one of how to make the existing social system function better; moreover, it ignored the legitimate claims of people who are victims of technological systems. Luhmann argued that the modern world had become too complex for Habermas' ideal speech situation to ever happen, and that under such complexity rationality has ceased to be a means of communication (Bausch, 1997). On this theme, Luhmann clearly projected himself as an antihumanist.

Habermas argued that human communication would be impossible without the acceptance of *norms*, particularly the three basic norms of propositional truth, rightfulness, and sincerity (or authenticity). Luhmann countered that cognitive expectations would be easily modified in the face of contrary experience, whereas normative (or value) expectations would not be modified by contrary facts because the latter demanded conformity. Moreover, Luhmann said, normative expectations tended to blind us to the differences existing in situations (Bausch, 1997).

I have elucidated the complementarity between Wallerstein's world-systems analysis and Prigogine's theory of dissipative structures elsewhere (Gunaratne, 2005b). Inden (1990) said the

> holism of Wallerstein has much to commend it as a corrective to the atomism of many classical or liberal economists and modernization theorists who have looked on "nations" or "societies" as enlarged versions of the "individual" agents . . . presupposed in their theories, each competing with the other on an even footing. (p. 30)

Nevertheless, Inden asserted that Wallerstein "remains committed to the materialist teleology that provides history with a purposive agent and requires that a system persist until exhausted by its inner contradictions" (p. 31).

The world-systems analysis places supreme emphasis on ceaseless accumulation of capital. Frank and Gills (1993) developed a humanocentric version of world-system analysis going back 5,000 years, in comparison with Wallerstein's "Eurocentric" version, which limits the world system only to the last 500 years.

NOTES

1.   King (1999) said that the predominant emphasis in Buddhist philosophy is on the reduction of "wholes" into their constituent factors (*dharmas*). Two basic Buddhist principles reflect this emphasis: (a) Wholes do not ultimately exist if they are capable of reduction into their constituent parts, and (b) the whole is no more than the sum of its parts. In contrast, Goonatilake (1998) said that the Buddhist theory of "dependent co-arising"—*paticca samuppada*—links Buddhism and systems theory, which sees the whole as greater than its constituents.

Co-dependent origination occurs because of karma, the totality of both good and evil thoughts that carries the body through the cycle of rebirths. However, no permanent self exists. The Buddhist continuity across births occurs through a stream of becoming interconnected with the external environment in which it operates.

2. Every "particle" has a counterpart ("antiparticle"), which is exactly like it but opposite in several major respects. A few "particles" are their own "antiparticles" (e.g., photon). The meeting of these opposites (called an *event* in the subatomic domain) is what constitutes the unceasing dance of annihilation and creation. Zukav (1979) explained that every subatomic event is marked by the annihilation of the initial particles and the creation of new ones (as illustrated in what are called *Feynman diagrams*).

3. *Daodejing* is a short book of just 5,000 pictograms comprising 81 short chapters. Tradition attributes its authorship to Laozi in the 6th century BCE. Some scholars believe that the book brings together the accumulation of ideas about *dao* and *de* over some two centuries (Billington, 1997).

4. In quantum physics, *complementarity* refers to the wave-particle duality of subatomic particles and not simply their opposite polarities. Bohr established that electrons are neither waves nor particles. When an observer attempts to measure (i.e., collapse) a quantum possibility wave, it invariably takes the illusion of a "particle." Lai (2002) said that, although similarities exist between the complementarity principle and the *yin-yang* philosophy, significant differences also exist between the two. For example, *yin-yang* is used in a cosmological sense, rather than in an epistemological sense.

5. Mueller (1958) claimed that the continual evolution of phenomena through the thesis–antithesis–synthesis dialectic is a legend spread by Marx "whose interpretation of Hegel is distorted" (p. 413).

6. The dialectical method had its origins in Stoic philosophy, a product of Greek and Oriental thought, traced to Zeno (c. 333–261 BCE). Stoicism viewed the world as a changing conflagration limited and ordered by the creative force of *logos* (world reason). Jaspers (1981/1993), however, identified Heraclitus as "the most ancient philosopher of dialectical thought," and Plato as "the originator of dialectic as method" (p. 287). Murti (in Radhakrishnan, 1952) pointed out that dialectic is also the soul of the Madhyamika system of Buddhist thought systematized by Nagarjuna in the second century. Dilworth (1989) credited Hegel for tracing "the movement of philosophy from East to West, for reasons connected with the dialectical movement of his thought," and for Hegel's enlarged vision reflecting "reconstructive classicism" (p. 4). Ironically, as Jung (1999) pointed out, Hegel was a totalizing West-centric who displaced Oriental philosophy "in the marginalized periphery of truth" (p. 287).

7. Strictly speaking, the last of the Four Noble Truths (viz. adherence to the Noble Eightfold Path) represents the Hinayana Buddhist notion of the "middle path." In a practical sense, it also implies avoidance of the

extremes. However, as Hoffmann (1978) pointed out, Nagarjuna's Madhyamika (middle doctrine) School, which furnished the philosophical background of Zen Buddhism, viewed the nature of everything as a mystery: It was neither *atman* (being) nor *anatman* (nonbeing or becoming) nor a synthesis of both, but *sunya* (emptiness or void). According to Nagarjuna's dialectic, experience was a succession of interrelated momentary states. According to Hegel's dialectic, the synthesis of *atman* and *anatman* is not only possible, but also necessary.

8. I owe this terminology to Leydesdorff (2003), who said that, "given the differences in the coupling mechanisms, it makes sense to use two different words—'structural' and 'operational coupling'—for the two different concepts which are covered by the original concept of 'interpenetration'" (p. 27).

9. Wallerstein (1974) identified two types of totality—*world empires* and *world economies*—as world systems. "They are distinguished from *mini-systems* in that they involve multiple cultures, and from one another in the essential fact that the former has a single political center while the latter has multiple centers of differing strength" (Goldfrank, 2000, p. 166). Wallerstein drew the center-periphery notion from dependency theory. Other concepts associated with world-systems analysis are unequal exchange, capital accumulation, division of labor, and international state system (denoting imperialism, hegemony, and class struggle).

Six

Theory of Communication Outlets and Free Expression

Egotistical Desire tries to force the round peg into the square hole and the square peg into the round hole. Cleverness tries to devise craftier ways of making pegs fit where they don't belong. Knowledge tries to figure out why round pegs fit round holes, but not square holes. *Wu Wei* doesn't try. It doesn't think about it. It just does it.
—*The Dao of Pooh* (Hoff, 1982, p. 75)

THE FRAMEWORK

So far we have attempted to link Eastern philosophy with a Western systems theoretical framework, combining the aspects of autopoiesis, cognition, and dissipative-structure models (encompassing aspects of quantum mechanics) and world-systems analysis. We have also introduced the perspective of meaning and snatched the system components of the Parsonian structural functionalist theory and the Habermasian critical theory as reference points for *yin-yang* (particle-antiparticle) interactions or autopoietic recursivity. We have merged Baker's model by identifying its *idergy-entropy* interaction with *yin-yang* interaction. We can also incorporate Price's perspective of the massive changes in state-press relations resulting from the technological revolution and globalization. Price (2002) implicitly confirmed that state–press relations have to be viewed within the framework of unity and dynamism of the world. Presuming that bulk matter retains some deterministic characteristics in the short term, as conceded in Bohr's correspondence principle (Goswami, 1993), I now lay out the following theoretical presumptions and propositions:

- The world system, which exchanges energy and matter with its environment, is thermodynamically a *far-from-equilibrium* dissipative structure, which spontaneously goes through self-organization at bifurcations. The whole (viz. the world system as the superstructure) is more than the sum of its parts because of its emergent characteristics resulting from energy flow and superstructural cognition, the process of life, which enables all its substructural totalities to be structurally coupled. (This combines the theories of cognition and dissipative structures with a fundamental principle of Eastern philosophy—the oneness of all things. This is also consistent with Bell's theorem and the Aspect experiment on quantum nonlocality.)
- The world system evolves into a triadized—center–semiperiphery–periphery—structure because of the inherent tendency of human collectivities (e.g., nation-states or their emerging variants) to vie for the exchange of *idergy*. The resulting entropy creates the semiperiphery and periphery, with the successful center dominating the world system. The *centriphery* attractor is an emergent characteristic of the world-system superstructure, which maintains a dynamic balance. The *idergy-entropy* interaction is another aspect of the *yin-yang* dialectical operation. (This combines Baker's model with Eastern philosophy.)
- The *centriphery* holon, the attractor that centers and peripheralizes the living systems of human beings, is a manifestation of the *samsaric* cycle that implements the law of *karma*—a fundamental facet of Buddhist, Hindu, and Jain philosophy. It is also the invisible *Dao*, which gave rise to "ten thousand beings," or the *Brahman*, the indivisible reality that manifests in all things and of which all things are parts. (This connects the Indian philosophical concept of karma with the *centriphery* process of world-system analysis and the theory of living systems.)
- It follows that the *yin-yang* interaction is the progenitor of all individuals, their grouping into nation-states, and the super-

structural totality of the world system—the three levels pertinent to building a theory of communication outlets and free
expression. At each of these three levels, the autopoietic operation of the authoritarian–libertarian antinomy (the dialectical
completion of relative polarities *yin* and *yang*) produces a
range of sociopolitical possibilities spanning the authoritarian–libertarian continuum. The political systems and systems
of communication outlets and free expression at each level
across space time are reflections of these outcomes.
Thermodynamically, each level shows a far-from-quilibrium
system in a state of dynamic balance. (This combines the
West's emerging theory of living systems with the Eastern
philosophical concepts of universal dynamism and unity of
opposites. It is also consistent with the scientific [material
realism] explanation of the bottom–up creation of matter—
from elementary particles to atoms, molecules, and cells—and
its epiphenomena, which include human mental constructs
such as authoritarianism and libertarianism.)

- At the first two levels, these outcomes represent political systems and systems of communication outlets of varying shades
of self-referential social responsibility, which one may classify
into broad categories for comparative purposes in the short-
time scale. At the level of the individual (or the individual-in-
network context of the East), these outcomes denote the
extent of freedom of expression (or the right to communicate)
that people enjoy both within the macroscopic world system
and the microscopic nation-state. (This takes into account the
parallel Eastern and Western concept of interpenetration,
which is also known as structural or operational coupling.
The political and communication outlet systems are *operationally* coupled.)

- These broad outcomes (coherent superpositions) represent,
for the most part, systems of social responsibility determined
by the *yin-yang* autopoietic process through cognition of other
relevant systems (e.g., culture, society, economy, and personality) within the nation-state's boundary, as well as those in
the external environment (e.g., trading partners, global pressure groups, etc.). The *meaning* of social responsibility
derived through this cognitive process by the political and
communication outlet systems of a nation-state will reflect the
spiritual, moral, cultural, economic, and other attributes relevant to a particular system, including ethics based on the middle path (in Buddhist systems), the five constants (in
Confucian systems), the *Dharma-Ahimsa* principles (in Hindu

systems), and so on. (Here we concede Parsons' recognition of the importance of the cultural system for pattern maintenance. The operationally closed pattern of autopoiesis is a natural defense against total globalization, which in current usage is a euphemism for Westernization.)

- Because the *centriphery* holon produces a powerful center, the nation-states constituting the center over space time will dominate the political and communication outlet systems at the level of the world-system totality. The structural coupling of all living systems facilitates the phenomenon of peripheralization. Thus, the center becomes the beneficiary of the world system's emergent characteristics—global media, global financial flow, global trade, and so on. (In ontocosmological terms, the *Taiji* or the *Brahman* regulates the dialectical process [e.g., rich–poor, weak–powerful, libertarian–authoritarian, etc.] by letting it follow the law of *karma* vis-à-vis individuals and communities [Gunaratne, 2003b].) The nation-states in the periphery have limited access to *idergy*. Therefore, the center determines the meaning of social responsibility (pertaining to communication outlets and politics) at the world-system level.
- Except for the short-time scale, as well as determinant regularities at the lower ontological levels, the theory described here claims neither predictive nor retrodictive power (of individual events) because of its presumptions—asymptotic behavior of dissipative systems and their irreversibility. (Heisenberg's uncertainty principle states that a quantum object's position and momentum can never be measured simultaneously with complete accuracy. Because everything is "made" of quantum objects, including our mental constructs, this principle applies to everything whose initial conditions can never be determined.)

CONCEPTUAL CLARIFICATIONS

System of Communicatio Outlets

In the preceding framework, the term *system of communication outlets* (as explained previously) is an expanded substitute for the traditional term *press system*. It encompasses all forms of public communication transmitted through methods appropriate to each stage of historical progress—methods technically identified today as hard copy, airwaves, cables, and cyberspace.[1] The "spread of printing in the western world" is the starting point of the *Four Theories* (Siebert, Peterson, & Schramm, 1956, p. 9). A theory of communication outlets and free expression cannot be confined to the post-Gutenberg period. Block printing was widespread in the East for centuries before Gutenberg (Gunaratne, 2001). The right to communicate, which encompasses information rights, can trace its origins well beyond the invention of printing.

We can look at the world system as the center–semiperiphery –periphery structure of nation-states or clusters thereof reflecting their economic, political, cultural, military, and communication power relationships. Within that structure, the communication outlets at the world-system level refer to those outlets concerned with transmitting information to reach audiences across geographical boundaries. The communication outlets at the nation-state level refer to those outlets concerned with transmitting information for domestic consumption. (Price [2002] documented the two-pronged efforts of nation-states, mostly those constituting the center, to focus both outward [e.g., negotiation with global media players and other related actors] and inward [e.g., use of force or passing laws to punish users] to control the information flow.) Individual freedom of expression at the world-system or nation-state levels refers to the extent to which an individual or an individual-in-group can claim the information rights (to inform, to be informed, and to inquire) specified in Article 19 of the Universal Declaration of Human Rights. (Again, Price has documented the efforts of nation-states to change the sense of human rights to fit the needs of national security in the milieu of global terrorism.) An option would be to assess the individual's right to communicate, which includes the association (assembly, speech, and participation) and global (privacy, choice, and cultural) rights as well (see Harms, 2003).

Authoritarian-Libertarian Continuum

Merrill (in Merrill & Lowenstein, 1979) introduced the idea of an authoritarian–libertarian continuum. Authoritarianism and libertarianism refer to the two extremes of the continuum of the distribution of communication outlets reflecting the relative degree of autonomy enjoyed by each. Thus, the meaning of these two concepts (as elucidated in the principle of infinite interpretation in Chinese philosophy and the principles of illusion and intuition in Indian philosophy) may not be the same from the frame of reference of every observer spread across space time.

In keeping with Einstein's special theory of relativity, which presumes frames of reference that move uniformly relative to one another, we can visualize a four-dimensional space-time continuum.[2] Time is the fourth dimension that conjoins the three-dimensional space (width, height, and depth) to constitute the space-time continuum. Within this universal continuum, we can conceptualize an authoritarian–libertarian continuum on our planet that makes sense to its human inhabitants. In this continuum, the position of the observer (frame of reference) determines what he or she sees as authoritarian (*yang*), libertarian (*yin*), or socially responsible (varying combinations of *yin-yang* or what physicists call *coherent superposition*). Because particle physics tells us that pure energy is the ultimate stuff of the universe, "the world is fundamentally dancing energy" (Zukav, 1979, p. 212). The yin and yang are nothing but dancing energies that react to each other to produce photons, leptons, mesons, or baryons, all of which can metaphorically represent our mental creations or concepts pertinent to the present discussion.

The definitions that Siebert attached to the concepts of authoritarianism and libertarianism reflected the Enlightenment-backed liberal-capitalist view pertinent to the 1950s. As we saw in chapter 4, the term *libertarian press* has taken a different meaning within the frame of reference of conglomerate media—a meaning that reflects their commercial interests. Within the frame of reference of the founding fathers who crafted the First Amendment to the U.S. constitution, the meaning of *freedom of the press* (or the equivalent *libertarian press*) had nothing to do with the commercial interests of the media owners. Meanings and definitions vary according to the position of the observer in the authoritarian–libertarian continuum. Dissipative structures, which operate within the space-time continuum comprising the universe, embody irreversible processes that produce entropy (disorder) and ongoing change resulting in "fluctuations, instability, multiple choices, and limited predictability at all levels of observation" (Prigogine, 1996, p. 4). Entropy is constant only in reversible processes.

(Thus, although subaltern scholars [e.g., Chakrabarty, 2000] may rightly see the virtues of universalizing the Enlightenment version of *liberalism*, the arrow of time changes all things to reflect the space-time context. In terms of subaltern historiography, this means that we retain the usefulness of the concept by defining [or glocalizing] it to suit a system's sociocultural values. Subaltern scholars may find it hard to agree with the modern meanings attached to *liberalism*, *social responsibility*, and *freedom of the press* by the Western media conglomerates and their patrons in government. One cannot bring back the past. Normative definitions require adjustments to reflect the ongoing autopoietic processes of social systems.)

However, in tracing the evolutionary history of normative concepts, one must discard the vertical approach of focusing on one civilization and seek the relevant roots in all civilizations. In this sense, we need to de-Westernize Siebert's authoritarian and libertarian theories, and Peterson's social responsibility theory—the three theories that demarcate the extremes and the middle. The history of the authoritarian theory of the press must concede the different interpretations of sovereignty in Eastern philosophy, particularly in the light of Siebert's assertion that the authoritarian theory "has been the basic doctrine for large areas of the globe . . . consciously or unconsciously adopted in modern times by . . . diverse national units" (Siebert, Peterson, & Schramm, 1956, p. 9). The authoritarian theory, Siebert said, grew out of the philosophy of absolute power of monarch, his government, or both—a philosophy reflected in the divine right of kings, which is largely discredited in Eastern thought. (See chap. 2 to get a glimpse of the Hindu and Buddhist perspectives on the limits of sovereignty. Some argue that even legalism in China assigned a passive role to the ruler in favor of a strong bureaucracy. Mencius had no doubts about the supremacy of the people over the ruler.) Although Siebert pointed out that a basic assumption of the authoritarian theory is that "the group took on an importance greater than that of the individual since only through the group could an individual accomplish his purposes" (p. 11), he failed to show its connection to Eastern thought.

We can identify the two ends of the authoritarian–libertarian continuum with relative, culture-balanced characteristics good for the short-time scale. Lowenstein (1970) operationally defined a *completely controlled* press (i.e., the authoritarian extreme) as "one with no independence or critical ability. Under it, newspapers, periodicals, books, news agencies, radio and television are completely controlled directly and indirectly by government, self-regulatory bodies or concentrated ownership" (p. 131). This definition would project the contemporary global media system, as well as the media systems in the United States and other center countries, as more or less authoritarian because of concentrated ownership as documented by McChesney (1999) and others. It implicitly exposes the ideological bias of Freedom House rankings of press freedom. However, Lowenstein's definition excludes the Internet and the pre-Gutenberg avenues of free expression, such as rock inscriptions (as in the Maurya Empire), theatrical performances (e.g., *wayang kulit* in Indonesia), or other elements encompassing the right to communicate.

McQuail (1984/1987) asserted that Siebert's term *authoritarian* remains an appropriate one, but the name can "also refer to a much larger set of contemporary press arrangements, ranging from those in which support or neutrality is expected from the press in respect of government and state, to those in which press is deliberately and directly used as a vehicle for repressive state power" (p. 111). Price (2002) documented the widespread use of these arrangements by contemporary nation-states. As with Lowenstein, McQuail identified "the lack of any true independence for journalists" as the fundamental characteristic of the authoritarian theory. Merging these viewpoints with Eastern thought, we can apply the following characteristics to derive an *ideal type* model of authoritarian theory:

- No communication outlet or any mode of public expression can criticize the political machinery or officials in power. (This agrees with the *Fajia* position.)
- All communication outlets, as well as any public expression of views, are always subordinate to established authority (the *danda-dhara* in Hindu philosophy). Discipline and subservience are vital.
- Communication outlets, as well as any public expression of views, should not offend the majority, or the dominant moral and political values, such as the five constants in Confucian cultures, *Dharma* in Hindu cultures, and the middle path precepts in Buddhist cultures. The group takes precedence over the individual.
- Censorship, rewards, and punishment (*danda*) are all justified means to enforce these principles. Moral and religious sanctions are not relevant.
- Unacceptable attacks on authority (*danda-dhara*), deviations from official policy or offenses against moral codes should be criminal offenses.
- Professionals who work for communication outlets or are otherwise engaged in public expression of views have no independence.
- Communication outlets are completely controlled directly or indirectly by government, self-regulatory bodies, or concentrated ownership.

Lowenstein (1970) operationally defined a *completely free* press (i.e., the libertarian extreme) as "one in which newspapers, periodicals, news agencies, books, radio and television have absolute independence and critical ability, except for minimum libel and obscenity laws. The press has no concentrated ownership, marginal economic units or organized self-regulation" (p. 131). Except for the exclusion of some communication outlets referred to earlier, Lowenstein's definition avoids a major drawback in Siebert's libertarian theory, which states that market-dependent, privately owned communication outlets alone represent the fullest freedom of expression. Siebert (in Siebert, Peterson, & Schramm, 1956) said the chief purpose of the libertarian communication outlets is to inform, entertain, and sell while helping to discover truth and acting as a check on government. According to Siebert's formulation of the libertarian theory, the "sales or advertising function" (p. 51) is what ensures financial independence of communication outlets—a condition that reflects a West-centric capitalist bias. Cannot publicly funded communication outlets (e.g., noncommercial broadcasting operated by independent bodies) fit equally well into libertarianism?

McQuail (1987) pointed out that, in its most basic form, the underlying values and principles of the *free press* theory are identical to those of the liberal democratic state—"a belief in the supremacy of the individual, in reason, truth and progress, and ultimately, the sovereignty of the popular will" (p. 113). Subaltern scholars would probably see the universality of this concept with some modification because the Indian press used it in the struggle against British imperialism. However, as we saw in chapter 1, "belief in the supremacy of the individual" is incongruent with Eastern philosophy, although "sovereignty of popular will" is not. Price's (2002) analysis of intra- and interterritorial actions and negotiations intended to control media input and output shows that the libertarian extreme is nothing but a mere ideal. McQuail argued that under contemporary conditions it is absurd to argue that private ownership will guarantee the individual's right to publish. McQuail (1987) also said the free press theory has been "most frequently formulated to protect the owners of media" (p. 115).

Despite the many problems and inconsistencies associated with the libertarian theory, particularly with Siebert's West-centric version, we can derive a culture-balanced set of characteristics on the lines suggested by McQuail and Lowenstein with a slight touch of Daoist input to derive an *ideal type* model of libertarianism:

- Prior censorship is inapplicable to communication outlets and public expression of views.
- No person or group needs permits or licenses for "public" expression of views or for publishing and distributing communication outlets in any form.
- No person or group can be punished for criticism of government, political parties, or officials, although public criticism of private individuals, as well as treason and breaches of security, may be punishable.
- No authority can compel a person or group to publish anything. (Possibly in line with Daoist thinking), communication outlets are free from obligations and duties.)
- In matters of opinion and belief, protection extends to publication of error as much as truth.
- No restrictions are applicable on the collection, by legal means, of information for publication.
- No restrictions are applicable on export or import or sending or receiving messages across national boundaries. (Literal application of Article 19 of UDHR at the individual level.)

- Those working for various communication outlets enjoy professional autonomy and freedom.
- Communication outlets are free of concentrated ownership, marginal economic units, or organized self-regulation.

Before exploring the range of social responsibility (or middle path) systems, one should acknowledge the contribution of both East and West to the development of the main theoretical concepts of authoritarianism and libertarianism. Siebert, Peterson and Schramm (1956) identified only the Western contributors to these two theories. As principal contributors to the authoritarian theory, we can add the *Fajia* (Legalist) advocates Shang Yang, Shen Bui-hai, and Shen Dao; Sunzi, who wrote "The Art of War"; and Kautilya, the so-called "Indian Machiavelli" (although it is far more accurate to identify Machiavelli as the "Italian Kautilya"). The paradox is that, even though the West appears to see the East as the more authoritarian, Eastern philosophy overall reflects a high degree of humanism and universal love. As principal contributors to the libertarian political philosophy, we can also add the *Daojia* and its leaders Laozi and Zhuangzi, and Gautama, the founder of Buddhism. The Daoists were extreme libertarians who wanted no social shackles. (Some may express doubts about the Daoists' support for a libertarian press in the light of *Daodejing*'s call on people to abandon language and return "once more to the use of knotted ropes.") Gautama, a moderate libertarian, preferred republican government to monarchy, thereby sowing the seeds of democracy (Fig. 6.1).

Social Responsibility

Although culture-balanced characteristics can broadly define the libertarian and authoritarian extremes, the same is not true of the social responsibility concept. As explained in the theoretical framework at the beginning of this chapter, the pattern of autopoiesis and the process of cognition determine the nature of social responsibility relevant to each society or nation-state. Thus, we can provide a dynamic explanation of the range of socially responsible systems of communication outlets and free expression spanning Merrill's A–L continuum. Although Merrill (1970) did not analyze the dynamic forces that produced the *operationally* coupled political and communication outlet systems, his observations on the different shades of social responsibility and their connection to political systems are remarkably congruent with the presumptions underlying our theory:

Extreme Libertarianism ← → Social Responsibility → Extreme Authoritarianism

| Libertarianism | | | | Authoritarianism | |

EAST

Dao Jia
Laozi
Zhuangzi

Mo Jia
Modi

Ming Jia
Hui Shi
Gongsung Long

Yin-yang Jia
Zou Yan

Ru Jia
Confucius
Mencius

Fa Jia
Shang Yang
Shen Buhai
Shen Dao

Sunzi

Buddhism
Gautama

Hinduism

Kautilya

WEST

CFP
Milton   Hutchins
Locke   Hocking
Smith
Paine
Jefferson
Erskine
Mill

Plato
Hobbes
Hegel
Treitschke
Marx

Machiavelli

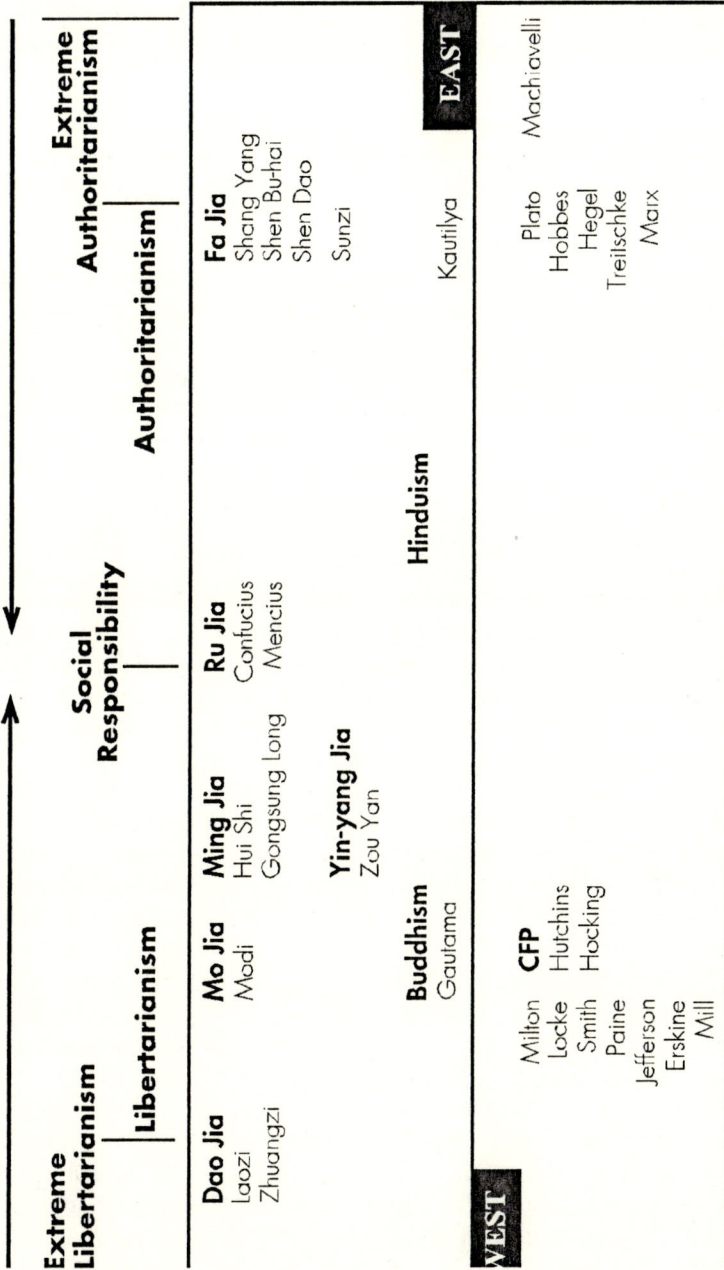

Figure 6.1. Theories of communication outlets with supporting philosophers and philosophies

> Assuming that a nation's socio-political philosophy determines its
> press system, and undoubtedly it does, then it follows that every
> nation's press system is socially responsible. . . . [The press of a
> nation] reflects the governmental philosophy and fits into the theo-
> retical structure of its society. If it does not, then the politico-social
> structure of the country is in flux. . . . Responsibility and irresponsi-
> bility are not only relative to the particular national society under
> consideration, but even within an individual society the terms have a
> multitude of meanings depending on the degree of pluralism pre-
> sent. (Merrill, 1970, pp. 17–18)

Peterson's formulation of the social responsibility theory based on
the Hutchins Commission report has a strong American flavor with
West-centrism writ large. Subaltern scholars might value its universalistic features to the extent they can be adapted in nation-states heading
toward greater modernity. The way of the Dao lets the polarities evolve
all features of the micro autopoietically within its boundary while keeping it cognitively open to other systems constituting the macro. Thus, the
West-centric norms of social responsibility may not necessarily reflect
the norms of social responsibility in many nation-states outside of so-
called "Europe."

Let me illustrate this for clarity. For example, take the communication outlet system in Singapore, South Korea, or Taiwan. Each will
autopoietically determine its concept of social responsibility, but do so in
keeping with the autopoiesis of the political system with which it is *operationally* coupled. Both systems will absorb much from all other systems
to which they are closely *structurally* coupled (mostly within the nation-
state) and/or cognitively open (mostly outside the nation-state)—the entities that Parsons and Habermas place in the categories of lifeworld (culture [e.g., Confucian philosophy], society [e.g., education], personality
[e.g., disposition of people], economy [e.g., agricultural, industrial or
informational], and state/law). Because autopoiesis is inextricably connected with macro-systemic cognition, the process of life that interconnects the world system, both systems will also absorb inputs from all
relevant systems in the environment (e.g., global economic, political,
military, trading, financial, media, and other systems) according to its
needs to derive its own pragmatic sense of social responsibility.

In the three nation-states in our example, New Confucian humanism largely defines the socially responsible behavior of individuals
toward family members, the community, and the rulers. However, the
meaning of social responsibility as it relates to the political or communication outlets systems will go beyond its Confucian value framework
because of the multifarious influences of the world system. In our example, Singapore's political and communication outlets systems appear to

have evolved a sense of social responsibility somewhat different from their counterparts in South Korea and Taiwan. This is because of the autopoietic process that allows a system to be more or less cognitively open to the various systems in its environment. This theoretical framework can also explain the contemporary multilateral approaches to control communication outlets (Price, 2002).

Autopoiesis allows nation-states to avoid potential cultural annihilation because of the push toward globalization. Globalization occurs because of cognition. Because cultures tend to defend themselves against globalization, we can conclude that the *yin-yang* interaction (autopoiesis) enables systems (within nation-states) to dynamically preserve their own notions of social responsibility. Thus, as Merrill (1970) contended, it is unrealistic to attempt a universally valid concept of social responsibility. Shuter (2000a) pointed out that, although social responsibility is an important value both in Islamic and Western societies, from the Islamic perspective of Saudi Arabia, "social responsibility is synonymous with compliance to the Koran" (p. 188). For the United States, such an interpretation would violate the essence of social responsibility that requires volition and choice. Keeping this in mind, let us look at the following characteristics that McQuail (1987) used to identify the social responsibility theory of communication outlets and consider how they can give rise to culturally valid objections (in parentheses):

- Professionals working for communication outlets are accountable to society as well as to employers and the market. (Eastern thought places less emphasis on accountability to the market, an artifact of West-centric capitalism. However, an erosion of Confucian humanism occurred in China since the arrival of Western powers in the 19th century. Japan and the Four Dragons also paid less attention to Confucian values because they embraced advanced capitalism. But see chap. 2 on the New-Confucian humanism that is emerging in these countries.)
- Communication outlets should accept and fulfill certain obligations to society by setting high professional standards on truth, accuracy, objectivity, and balance. (Whereas the West interprets *truth* semantically, the Chinese understand it socially and pragmatically as a matter of being a good person, as a way of life. Similarly, the West's semantic interpretation of *objectivity* and *balance* may differ from that of the East, where meanings are subject to infinite interpretation and intuition. Quantum theory questions the attainability of strong objectivity.)
- To fulfill these obligations, communication outlets should be self-regulating within the framework of law and established institutions. (Two West-centric notions are implicit in this cri-

terion: a capitalist economy oriented toward advertising, and distrust of government. First, poor economies lack an adequate advertising base to support communication outlets. Second, East has less distrust of government than the West because, as in the Confucian view, the state is responsible for "the happiness of all people.")

- Communication outlets should avoid whatever might lead to crime, violence, or civil disorder or give offense to minority groups.
- Communication outlets as a whole should be pluralist and reflect the diversity of their society, giving access to various points of view and to rights of reply. (Although pluralism is desirable, harmony is much more important in Eastern thought.)
- Society and the public have a right to expect high standards of performance. Intervention can be justified to secure public good. (What is understood as *high standards* in the West may have different connotations in the East.)

The preceding characteristics may fit a West-centric *ideal type* model of social responsibility. A humanocentric view of the concept would require culturally adjusted criteria that recognize the role, *inter alia*, of the five constants in Confucian cultures, *Dharma* in Hindu cultures, and the middle path in Buddhist cultures. We can universalize the social responsibility theory by implanting relevant ideas from Confucian, Hindu, Buddhist, Islamic, and other philosophies. In this regard, Shuter (2000b) observed that the main ethical concerns (related to social responsibility) in both Confucianism and Hinduism are "fundamentally incompatible with Western communication ethics" (p. 448) because neither treats reason as the touchstone for determining value or truth. Shuter calls on the Western and U.S. cultural ethicists "to admit that their research has an intracultural bias" (p. 448) and to focus more on studying "communication ethics in societies outside the United States" (p. 449) and the West.

Confucianism holds that man is born for uprightness, and that people's goodwill is essential for good government in the context of an intellectual democracy headed by a benevolent ruler. Referring to Confucianism, Mote (1989) pointed out "its strong ethical sense, its *social responsibility*, and its constructive, rational approach to immediate problems" (p. 31). Mohists represented a shade of social responsibility somewhat to the left of Confucianism. The Naturalists, who saw "perfect freedom" in the harmony of the social organism, also reflected another shade of social responsibility.

Hindu philosophy appears to agree with the social responsibility concept somewhat to the right of Confucianism. Hinduism's association with the caste system contrasts with Confucianism's advocacy of education for all and demolition of social barriers. However, Hinduism's doctrine of *dharma* and *danda* discouraged authoritarianism in favor of a benevolent monarchy reflecting democratic ideals. Hindu theory of sovereignty is not the same as the Western theory of sovereignty. Because social responsibility is a reflection of these core cultural values, they are applicable to the performance standards of communication outlets as well. From the Eastern point of view, the following characteristics, which reflect much of human rights, are relevant to an *ideal type* model of social responsibility:

- (From the Confucian perspective) Promotion of harmony and goodwill among individuals and their families and community in the context of the five constants: *ren, yi, li, zhi,* and *xin* (humanity, righteousness, decorum, wisdom, and trust, respectively).
- (From the Confucian perspective) Serving as vehicles of education and knowledge conducive to maintenance of (an intellectual) democracy.
- (From the Hindu perspective) Applying the principles of *dharma* and *ahimsa*—duty, law, justice, and nonviolence, as well as righteousness, customs, traditions, virtue, merit, and morality.
- (From the Hindu perspective) Assisting the state to control or restrain human vices (evident in the *matsya-nyaya*) and "open up the avenues to a fuller and higher life" (through, *inter alia*, the practice of developmental/public journalism).
- (From the Hindu perspective) Serving as "a logical check on the possible absolutism of the *danda-dhara*" (i.e., ruler or government).
- (From the Buddhist perspective) Interpreting and analyzing news and information from the perspective of the middle path: *sila* (right speech, action, and livelihood), *samadhi* (right effort, mindfulness, and concentration), and *panna* (right understanding and thoughts).
- (From the Buddhist perspective) Serving as a vehicle to fight inequality based on race, creed, economic class, or gender; promote free discussion and democratic practice to ensure freedom of religion and conscience, freedom to select the government, freedom from cruel and unusual punishment, and freedom from want; and uphold rights related to education, clean environment, just compensation, and equal treatment under the law (Peek, 1995).

Our theory leads us to speculate that the interaction of the *yin-yang* complements or the operation of the principle of the dialectic would produce a communication outlet system of varying shades of sociocul-turally defined social responsibility. The part–whole interaction of the world system, which is a dialectic, would ensure some common standards of social responsibility across cultures, in addition to the cultural-ly specific standards that each component attempts to maintain through autopoiesis.

Applying the thermodynamic aspect of our theory of living systems, we can presume a far-from-equilibrium system of communication outlets and free expression befitting different sociocultural definitions of *social responsibility* along the A-L continuum at all three levels of the world system. Statistically, adhering to the correspondence principle, this would resemble a more or less positively or negatively skewed distribution. Order derives spontaneously from chaos because "nature is spontaneous harmony" (Prigogine, 1996, pp. 12–13)—a fundamental concept of Chinese philosophy. The meeting of the *yin* and *yang* comple-ments (or the clash of the thesis–antithesis antinomy) results in the gradual rearrangement of the skewed distribution of communication outlets in the short-time scale. At a bifurcation point, positive feed-back—nonlinear effects triggered by a singular movement—can pro-duce spectacular changes in the system of communication outlets spon-taneously creating order out of chaos. One can view the East–West clash during the debate on the New World Information and Communication Order in the 1970s and the 1980s as an example of the asymptotic behavior of the world system that resulted in a major self-organization at the point of bifurcation. It virtually wiped out the communist version of socially responsible communication outlets and, *inter alia*, caused the emergence of giant capitalist media conglomerates at the world-system level that demarcated a new *far-from-equilibrium* condition.

Some may argue that incorporating Chinese, Hindu, or Buddhist philosophical concepts to construct press theories would be pointless without showing how these philosophies work in Chinese, Indian, Sri Lankan, or any other press in reality. In this regard, it is important to note that the media in countries that emerged from European imperial-ism operate at two levels of the so-called *public sphere*. These countries have an indigenous press for the nonelite majority and a global-lan-guage press for the elite minority of modernized citizens. Mass commu-nication researchers rarely analyze the content of the indigenous media, which generally adhere to the Hindu or Buddhist values of their audi-ence. The Sinhalese-language newspapers in Sri Lanka, or the vernacu-lar-language newspapers in India, Bangladesh, and Pakistan, are much more sensitive to indigenous cultural norms than their English-language counterparts. The mainland newspapers in China have followed the social responsibility philosophy of the communist party, and they may be in the process of moving along the A–L continuum toward New-Confucian humanistic values rather than Western values, despite some intellectuals' infatuation with the Habermasian concept of rationality (Gunaratne, 2005a). As we theorized, the autopoiesis of the system of communication outlets and free expression is operationally coupled with the political system. The *yin-yang* interaction occurs in the cognitive context of all systems constituting society.

In this chapter, we used a composite theoretical framework to hypothesize how elementary particles—the *yin-yang* interactions—create the *transcendent* (conceptual) and *immanent* (material) reality of the world system, its subsystems, and their political and communication ideologies. What I, the observer, have done is use the creative genius of several scholars to creatively design my particular view of the manifest world. I did so by using my awareness to create a distinction between me, the subject, and the world system, the object. My awareness sprang from the agency of my mind-consciousness complex, the putative epiphenomenon of my material self (brain). I succumbed to Cartesian dualism. But can I claim objectivity for my vision of the manifest world when I am an integral part of it? The Buddhist view is that I and all other sentient beings are aggregates of successive moments bearing the illusion of physical form. Biologists assert that all sentient beings are aggregates of cells, molecules, and atoms, all of which originate in the empty subatomic domain, which may or may not be part of the space-time continuum. Therefore, is this book ultimately the product of a dense cluster of superluminal wavicles?[3]

Goswami (1993, 2000) provided a creative answer to these quantum-mechanics paradoxes, which bear an uncanny resemblance to Zen Buddhist *koans*. Goswami's "monistic-idealism" interpretation of quantum physics would see all these concepts as creations of our *consciousness*, the transcendent domain of reality—the ground of all being. (Goswami asserts that the 1982 Aspect experiment has proved the existence of a transcendent reality outside of the space-time continuum.) From the perspective of monistic idealism, all forms of material reality, including concepts, are manifestations of downward causation from the ground of consciousness. Goswami says "monistic idealism" coexists with the upward causation of material reality originating with quantum wavicles, which are not things, but "tendencies to exist." These appear as particles or waves depending on the measuring technique used by an observer.

Goswami points out that whenever we measure a quantum object, it appears as a particle at some single place. But when we are not measuring it, the quantum object spreads like a wavicle and exists in more than one place simultaneously through quantum jumps that no observer can see. Heisenberg's uncertainty principle tells us that no observer can measure both the position and momentum of any particle accurately. We can only derive approximations and probabilities. Whether we think of concepts as creations of consciousness or quantum particles, the intervention of the observer will affect their identification and measurement. The uncertainty principle is applicable to all sentient concepts.

SUMMARY

Our humanocentric theory of communication outlets and free expression (derived from combining Eastern philosophy, theory of living systems [encompassing the relevant aspects of quantum physics], Western dialectic, aspects of world-system theory, and social systems identified by Parsons and Habermas) contains four broad elements. These four elements comprise two complementary or antonymic variables (*libertarianism* and *authoritarianism*), the dialectical interaction of which produces a synthesized variable (*social responsibility*) in the context of an intervening variable (*socilcultural values*). [This refers to the *meaning* perspective of the theory of living systems.] Sociocultural values dynamically evolve from the close structural coupling of systems within a nation-state (or its emerging variant), which is more or less cognitively open to its environment (i.e., all other systems comprising the world system). The communication outlet system and political systems (representing the rulers) at the nation-state level are *operationally* coupled. At the level of superstructural unity (world system), the global media outlet system is *operationally* coupled with the political system of the center nations, which dominate the global communication outlets system. Although it is also structurally coupled with other nations involved with global information transmission, peripheralization diminishes the value of this connection.

Applying the physics of nonequilibrium processes, libertarianism (*yin*) and authoritarianism (*yang*) occupy the two tails of a (probable) skewed distribution of a far from-equilibrium system of communication outlets and free expression denoting varying shades of social responsibility (coherent superposition). Thermodynamically, chaos (i.e., disorder or entropy) spontaneously produces order. Because of the inevitability of change in dissipative systems, the processes related to which are irreversible, the elements denoting the *yin* and *yang potentially* change over space time. (However, if the *yin* and *yang* are indeed superluminal, they are not subject to the rules of quantum physics.)

This model is applicable to all three levels of the world system: the world system the nation-state, and the individual (in the West) or the individual-in-network (in the East). The model also explains the dynamics of the far-from-equilibrium distribution of power—economic, political, cultural, communication, and military—relevant to each of the three levels of the world system. The dialectical process of part–whole interaction and the clash of antinomies recursively produce unequal distributions of power, as well as systems of communication–outlets and free expression.

It should be clear that the principle of the *yin-yang* complements[4] has more explanatory power than the putative Hegelian dialectic because the former allows for nonlinear dynamics. As Cheng (1987) explained, everything in reality is not only regarded as generated from the interactions between *yin* and *yang* forces but everything is composed of these two forces. In this sense, Cheng says, everything is a synthetic unity of *yin* and *yang* in various stages of their functioning, and this dialectical change of things forces us to understand them realistically.

> Change relativizes the standards of evaluation, because it generates new interests, new relationships, and new values. . . . [But] one must bear in mind the distinction between relativization in an absolute sense and relativization in a relative sense. In an absolute sense, relativization is the essential principle for the change and transformation of a thing and a situation. [R]elativization in a relative sense consists in seeing and placing things in a different light and at different angles without necessarily requiring a change in time. (Cheng, 1987, pp. 34–35)

The mysteries associated with phenomena in the subatomic domain of quantum physics are quite similar to the mysticism associated with the world of Eastern philosophy. The remarkable similarity of *yin-yang* interaction to particle–antiparticle interaction, which creates all material and nonmaterial manifestations of an interconnected universe (Dao), shows the folly of the separation of philosophy and science. Quantum mechanics has proved that objectivity so highly valued in nomothetic empiricism is an oxymoron. The very attempt to measure a quantum object changes the nature of that object. The claim of objectivity for operationally defined concepts (e.g., social responsibility) at the higher, more abstract ontological levels of dissipative structures needs to be challenged. Subjectivity is inherent in all research.

Chinese philosophy established the *yin-yang* phenomenon with the Supreme Ultimate (*Taiji*), the principle of highest good, as its source and regulator. In this sense, the cosmological operation of this phenomenon is similar to that of the Buddhist-Hindu-Jain concept of *karma* in the samsaric cycle. As Prigogine (1996) explained:

The concept of a passive nature subject to deterministic laws is quite specific to the Western world. In China and Japan, nature means "what is by itself". . . . For [Chinese], the idea that nature is governed by simple, knowable laws seemed to be a perfect example of anthropocentric foolishness. According to Chinese tradition, nature is spontaneous harmony; speaking about "laws of nature" would thus subject nature to some external authority. (pp. 12–13)

EXCURSUS: INTERCULTURAL ASIACENTRICITY

Reacting to the pervasive and persistent Eurocentrism in the field of intercultural communication, just as in the field of international communication, Yoshitaka Miike (2003a, 2003b) worked on developing an Asiacentric paradigm, which aims to be grounded entirely on Asian philosophy and culture. Influenced by the scholarship of Satoshi Ishii (1984, 1988, 1992, 1998), Miike's aim is to move away from Eurocentrism, which appears to manifest itself in three spheres: theoretical concepts and constructs, research material and methodology, and "otherization" in theory and research.

Miike (2003a) said scholars should not always count on "U.S.-derived, English-language, pseudoetic concepts to compare and contrast cultural patterns of communication" (p. 246). Because theory construction is not independent of methodology, Miike suggested not to prioritize "Eurocentric theoretical perspectives over indigenous theoretical standpoints" (p. 247) by focusing on research methodology of U.S. origin. On *otherization*, Miike said scholars should use different mirrors that enable them "to capture intracultural/intercultural communication from diverse vintage points" (p. 248).

Miike (2003a) conceded that *Asia* is a highly abstract and ambiguous label. However, he justified the use of the term on three grounds: It signifies a certain geographical location, it designates a political entity against Western imperialism, and it implies the shared heritage of diverse Asian cultures. A common core of Asian beliefs, values and worldviews has emerged from the religions and philosophies of Buddhism, Confucianism, Daoism, and Hinduism in particular. Miike definds *Asiacentricity* as "the theoretical notion that insists on placing Asian values and ideals at the center of inquiry"; and *Asiacentric approach* as "the theoretical position that views Asian phenomena from the standpoint of Asians as subjects rather than objects" (p. 251). Three themes—relationality, circularity, and harmony—underlie the Asiacentric idea.

Thus, Miike (2003a) said, the Asiacentric paradigm would be based on the following philosophical assumptions:

- Everyone and everything are interrelated across space and time (*ontological* assumption).
- Everyone and everything become meaningful in relation to others (*epistemological* assumption).
- Harmony is vital to the survival of everyone and everything (*axiological* assumption).

Chen and Starosta (2003) added a *methodological* assumption to this list: Transforming process of the universe does not proceed onward in a linear way—the nonlinear cyclic approach of reasoning.

Miike (2003a) argued that Eastern cultures emphasize interrelatedness and interdependence much more than Western cultures. Based on this emphasis, Asian philosophies insist that no individual thing can be determined and evaluated without reference to the whole to which it belongs. The emphasis in the Buddhist concept of dependent co-arising (*paticca samuppada*) is on functional dependence, rather than mutual dependence. Harmony is the cardinal tenet of the axial-age Asian philosophies. In this context, it is noteworthy that the multiplicity paradigm (Servaes, 1999) presumes that all nations, in one way or the other, are dependent on one another.

Furthermore, the Asiacentric paradigm would be based on the following communicative assumptions:

- Intracultural/intercultural communication takes place in contexts of multiple relationships across space and time.
- Intracultural/intercultural communicator is perceptually and behaviorally active and passive in a variety of contexts.
- Mutual adaptation is of central importance in harmonious intracultural/intercultural communication processes.

Miike pointed out that Asian communication contexts contain both transpersonal and transtemporal dimensions as evident in the Buddhist concept of *en* (predestined connection) relevant to Ishii's (1998) Japanese model of communication. Moreover, contrary to the Eurocentric view that Asians are "passive communicators," they are, in fact, extremely active on the sense-making level when they accept or reject various communication contexts such as *en*-belief systems. Ishii's (1984) *enryo-sasshi* model demonstrates how the speaker and listener adjust their messages to maintain interpersonal and situational harmony.

Referring to the potential of his Asiacentric paradigm, Miike (2003a) proposed three initial lines of future inquiry:

- to generate more and more emic conceptualizations in Asian languages as they relate to culture and communication;

- to compare, without Eurocentric "otherization" mirrors, Asian indigenous concepts that Asiacentric researchers have already examined to various aspects of cultural communication activities;
- to pay due attention to the rich intercultural histories of Asian nations and peoples.

In a subsequent essay, Miike (2003b), added five objectives for Asiacentric research:

- to critique misleading Eurocentric studies of Asian communication behaviors;
- to preserve Asian cultural values and modes of communication;
- to explore spiritual liberation through communication;
- to depict multiple visions of harmony among complex relationships; and
- to examine (inter)cultural communication needs and problems seen through Asian eyes.

Miike (2003a) also mentioned three challenges: the dilemma between the great traditions (the axial religions and philosophies) and the little traditions (the common people's values, beliefs, and ways of life), observability in real life, and the paradox of cultural specificity and universal relevance.

> The basic task of Asiacentric interculturalists is not to completely ignore Eurocentric studies of intracultural/intercultural communication, but to address their minds to Eastern religions, philosophies, and histories to assess cultural values and communicative practices in Asia more accurately, critique Eurocentric models and modules according to such Asiacentric assessments, and formulate authoritative theories of intracultural/intercultural communication. (Miike, 2003a, p. 264)

Dissanayake (2003), a pioneer advocate of Asiacentricity, specified four areas that merit closer study to develop Asian communication theory: investigation into classical texts, exploration of the vast storehouse of concepts from classical traditions and current cultural practices, examination of the arena of rituals and performances (folk plays, folk dances, ballads, rituals, and ceremonies), and studying the day-to-day communication behaviors to dissect how they have been understood and discursively enframed by traditional cultures. Dissanayake argued that Asiacentric scholars should creatively and critically examine Western theories, thereby engaging in a profitable dialogue. For example, phenomenology, which emphasizes intuition and intersubjectivity, "has much in common with Asian traditions of thought" (p. 25). Moreover, he said, Asiacentric scholars must also be alert to criticisms and answer them persuasively. The criticism based on cultural essentialism shows the need "to historicize . . . concepts within their respective and evolving traditions" (p. 28). Scholars must also respond to other criticisms of Asiacentricity, such as East–West binarism, deep concern with humanism, and lack of historical/cultural locations for Asian concepts.

The philosophical assumptions of the Asiacentric model—as evident from my assessment of the new physics, complexity science, world-systems analysis, and the theory of living systems—are highly congruent with the emerging alternatives to Newtonian science in the Western world. The new systems thinking in the West, in its non-Luhmanian humanistic form, implicitly owes much to the East's wisdom on interconnectedness and functional dependence. The quantum principle of nonlocality resonates with the Asiacentric paradigm's assumption on transpersonal and transtemporal communication. Most intracultural/intercultural and international communication studies in the West are grounded on the Newtonian model despite its faulty assumptions. Thus, in my view, the Asiacentric paradigm is poised for a quantum leap. The philosophy of monistic idealism, which implants a transcendental dimension to materialist quantum mechanics, provides another boost for the new paradigm's take-off. However, the Asiacentric paradigm stands to violate its own fundamental assumption on interconnectedness and functional dependence if it were to isolate itself radically by "unthinking" Eurocentric theory and methodology to escape domination. Such an isolationist approach may not meet the guiding principles of subaltern scholars as well.

Asian approaches to human communication have received significant attention in the new millennium. In 2003, a special issue of *Intercultural Communication Research* (Vol. 12, No. 4) published 12 articles examining various dimensions of the topic. It included a selected bibliography compiled by Miike and Chen (2003).

NOTES

1. Thus, it takes into account the pre-Gutenberg communication outlets such as *Acta Diurna*, which appeared in 59 BCE when Julius Caesar led the Roman republic; and *Di/Jing Bao* distributed in China from 618 to 1911.

2. The special theory preferred to view the space-time continuum as a static phenomenon, wherein everything that appears to "unfold before us with the passing of time, already exists *in toto*, painted, as it were, on the fabric of space-time" (Zukav, 1979, p. 172). This mathematical proposition is not in accord with the basic presumption of complexity science that we cannot go back in time.

3. Siu (1957) explains: "To a physicist, [a human being] is a mass of whirling protons, electrons, and other nuclear particles undergoing continuous exchange with the surroundings. To a biologist, [a human being] is a succession of biological transformations and psysiological processes. . . . Within a year the bulk of [a human being's] body tissues are renewed through metabolic changes" (p. 52).

4. Carter (2001) used the *yin-yang* dichotomy as an organizing principle to explain the laws of physics and the evolution of the universe. He classified the seven basic parameters of experimental physics as follows: inertial **mass** (*yin*) and kinetic **mass** (*yang*); inertial **space** (*yin*) and gravitational **space** (*yang*); inertial **time** (*yin*) and gravitational **time** (*yang*); circlon (*yin* **shape**) and photon (*yang* **shape**); mass x velocity x radius (*yin* angular **momentum**) and mass x velocity (*yang* **momentum**); spin **energy** $I\omega^2/2$ (*yin*) and kinetic **energy** $mv^2/2$ (*yang*); and proton (*yin* positive matter **charge**) and electron (*yang* negative matter **charge**).

Seven

Democracy-Journalism Connection

MYTH OF THE FOURTH ESTATE

The theoretical framework developed in the preceding chapter makes it clear that journalism practiced in any given nation-state is very much a reflection of the type of government of that nation-state. Our model presumes that the political system and the system of communication outlets are *operationally* coupled. (This is similar to the concept of *interpenetration* in Luhmann's paradigm, which uses this concept to show the relationship between what he defined as social systems [communications] and psychic systems [consciousness of persons]. Interpenetrating systems remain environments for each other. The Cartesian separation of mind and matter implicit in Luhmann's theory violates the basic presumption of the theory of living systems: the inseparability of the two.)

The communication outlets system has a parasitic dependence on the political system because journalism thrives on the ability to report on government. Similarly, the political system needs a cooperative communication outlets system to influence the public.

> What appears in the media establishes political priorities.
> Governments, as a matter of course, will as always seek to influence
> what media report. More than that, they increasingly understand
> that they have a stake in the process by which information and cul-
> tural signals are developed and communicated and the machinery
> through which that occurs. (Price, 2002, p. 198)

In his theory of communicative action, Habermas (1987) alluded to
this phenomenon as the state system's attempt to colonize the lifeworld
through instrumental reason. Because of this interpenetration, journalism's ability to function as the Fourth Estate is limited. Herman and
Chomsky (1988) offerred a propaganda model that explains how the
media tend to engage in propaganda to reaffirm the prevailing power
structure such that they fail to perform their role as watchdogs for
democracy. Kellner (1992) has documented that in the 1991 Gulf War,
the mainstream media parroted officials, never questioning the information they released. Gans (1979) concluded that American foreign news
follows American foreign policy very closely. The reporting of the
Watergate scandal and the Pentagon papers illustrates the exceptions
resulting from flagrant violations of the ethics of government. The gargantuan media conglomerates operating within the global capitalist
structure, as emphasized by world-systems analysis, are involved in
competitive capital accumulation. Tabloidization, or sensationalism, has
taken precedence over public-service journalism (McChesney, 1999).

Two American scholars have described the relationship between
democracy and journalism in the U.S. context as follows:

> A democracy is a system of government in which the ultimate politi-
> cal authority is vested in the people. . . . [R]eliable and unbiased
> information is vital to the health of the democratic state; information
> is the catalyst that allows democracies to function. . . . [T]he mass-
> communication media are the principle (sic) mechanism through
> which information is disseminated and learned as well [as] the
> means by which politicians and citizens communicate with each
> other. (McGraw & Holbrook, 2003, p. 399)

This assertion is predicated on the idea of the press as the Fourth
Estate, an Enlightenment concept on which Asian philosophy is silent.
Empirical studies conducted over 50 years show that the average
American is uninformed or underinformed about sociopolitical issues,
thereby raising doubts about the presumed connection between a more
or less libertarian press and liberal democracy (Delli Carpini & Keeter,
1996). Marcuse (1964) contended that the concerns of the advertising
industry shaped the mass media to a significant extent resulting in

"false consciousness"—a state of awareness in which people no longer consider or know what is their real interests.

As pointed out earlier, the East has more trust in government than the West but Eastern philosophy—Hindu, Buddhist, and Confucian—justifies the criticism and removal of rulers who have turned too autocratic. Sarkar (1918b) pointed out that the Chinese classics and the Hindu treatises on statecraft and law, and the Indian epics "contain frequent discussions as to the restraints on royal absolutism, the responsibility of ministers, and the authority of the people" (p. 583). Legge (1895) quoted Mencius thus: "The people are the most important element in a nation; . . . the sovereign is the lightest" (p. 483). In the West, the ideal of the Fourth Estate seems to have been eclipsed by the convergence of the vested interests of the government and the highly profit-motivated conglomerate media. Thus, American journalism failed to provide reliable and unbiased information on Iraq for the American public to determine the need to invade Iraq.

In this book, I have conceptualized journalism as an autopoietic self-referential *process* engendered by the interaction of the libertarian-authoritarian antinomies within the sociocultural boundaries of a nation-state (or its emerging variant) over space time. The ability of the environment, particularly the political system with which it is operationally coupled, to influence the nature of journalism within a nation-state depends on its cyclical movement along the n-dimensional libertarian–authoritarian continuum, within which a coherent superposition may show quantum jumps. The more these jumps shift toward the libertarian end, the more cognitively open a system would be to its environment, and vice versa. For example, journalism practice in Indonesia was cognitively less open to environmental influence under Sukarno or Suharto than under Habibie or Wahid. In other words, the coherent superposition of the communication outlets system experienced a quantum jump from the authoritarian side to the libertarian side. Because the relevant systems are dynamical, phase-space or state-space graphs, rather than the two-dimensional time-series graphs, are needed to illustrate these jumps (see Williams, 1997). This operational procedure does not violate the unity and mutual interrelation of all things and events.

Ette (2000) vividly described the operational coupling of the press and the state in Nigeria: "Its external source of support is the state, primarily through various forms of subsidies channeled through advertising revenue and sponsorships and, indirectly, through newspaper proprietors' dependence on the state for acquisition and accumulation of wealth" (p. 70). This situation holds true for many developing countries. In the developed countries, where the press has strong links to big business, late capitalism has produced another kind of relationship between the press and the state: a shift away from adversarial journalism by the press to accumulate capital through production and distribution of news as a commodity. The mainstream press generally follows the foreign policy dictates of the state.

I have already argued that the *Four Theories* and its subsequent improvements based on West-centric philosophy and history lack universal applicability because they ignore the holistic thinking of the East and emphasize the primacy of individual rights. From the West-centric perspective, *press freedom* primarily means the immunity of the communication outlets—newspapers, books, magazines, radio, TV, and so on—from government control or censorship implemented directly through laws and regulations or indirectly through economic and political pressures. (Fig. 7.1 and 7.2, which are linear, two-dimensional graphs used in the absence of phase-space graphs, show the distribution of press freedom scores estimated by Freedom House applying its West-centric criteria. The presentation of empirically contrived scores does not mean an endorsement. One cannot empirically measure nonphysical phenomena using the tools of positivism.) Because this perspective equates freedom with private ownership of communication outlets, it tends to downplay the inimical effects of private interests and the insatiable craving (*tanha*) for capital accumulation. It sees press freedom as a fundamental

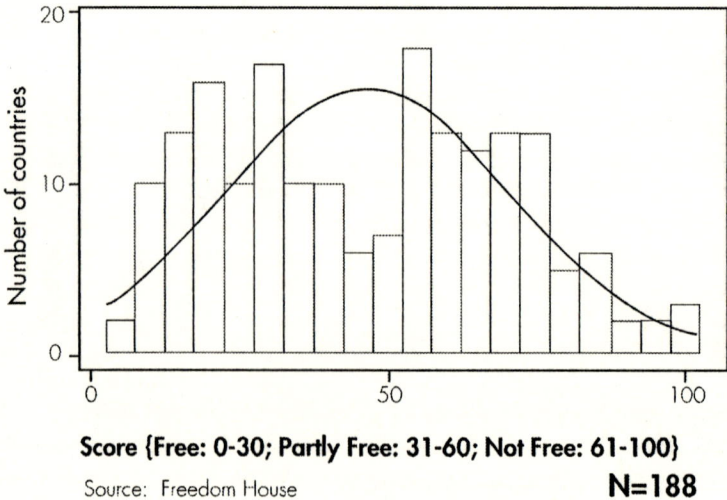

Score {Free: 0-30; Partly Free: 31-60; Not Free: 61-100}

Source: Freedom House   N=188

**Figure 7.1. Distribution of average PF scores, 1994-2002
Deviation from normal curve**

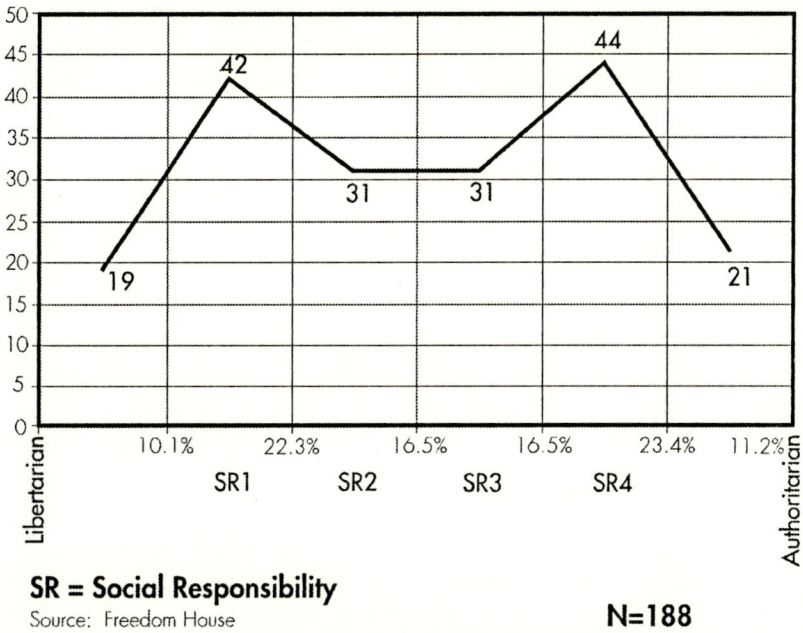

SR = Social Responsibility
Source: Freedom House

N=188

Figure 7.2. Distribution of countries on libertarian-authoritarian continuum based on average press scores, 1994-2002

individual right, although under contemporary capitalism it has metamorphosed into a conglomerate right. The West-centric approach is more concerned with negative freedom than with positive freedom (i.e., culture-specific social responsibility) of communication outlets.

Individualism and the profit motive lurk behind West-centric news values as well. In the 1930s, American journalist Stanley Walker defined these news values as the three Ws: women (sex), wampum (money), and wrong-doing (crime). Mencher (2000) identified seven news values—timeliness, impact, prominence, proximity, conflict, the unusual, and currency. The emphasis on conflict goes against Confucian harmony. Carrying these news values to the extreme signifies the treatment of news as a commodity rather than as a social good. Socially responsible journalism in the Asian context may mean following the Buddhist middle path. In practice, however, depending on the sociocultural context, news as a commodity exists in Asia as well (e.g., Hong Kong's *Apple Daily*, Japan's *Nikkan Gendai*, South Korea's *Ilyo Shinmun*, Thailand's *Thai Rath*, etc.).

Thus, although operationally closed, the pattern of journalism in Asia's freepress countries in particular is very much cognitively open to the powerful presence of West-centric journalism in their environment. However, broadly speaking, Asian journalism can never be the mirror image of Western journalism because of the socio-cultural distinction between the independent individual in the Western sense and the individual-within-networks in the Eastern sense. At the atomistic level of the individual, the former presumes the independence of the part (the individual) from the whole (or the environment) whereas the latter presumes a fundamental connection between the two. Hence, we see the arrogation of negative freedom for the former and the allocation of positive freedom for the latter. Western libertarianism, just as much as classical Daoism, stands for freedom devoid of any social shackles. However, the Daoist path of *wu-wei* (nonaction or not acting contrary to nature) recognizes the oneness of things. As Capra (1999) explained:

> The most important characteristic of the Eastern world view—one could almost say the essence of it—is the awareness of the unity and mutual interrelation of all things and events. . . . The Eastern traditions constantly refer to this ultimate, indivisible reality which manifests itself in all things, and of which all things are parts. It is called *Brahman* in Hinduism, *Dharmakaya* in Buddhism, [*D]ao* in [D]aoism. Because it transcends all concepts and categories, Buddhists also call it *Tathata*, or Suchness. . . . The basic oneness of the universe . . . is also one of the most important revelations of modern physics. (pp. 130–131)

The preceding analysis should make it clear that, from the Eastern perspective, both freedom *per se* and the process of journalism are associated with social responsibility—a concept that the East and West may understand differently. Thus, the Thai press will show the highest regard for the Thai king, and the Japanese press will not insult the Japanese emperor unlike the British press, which considers the British royal family fair game to make a fast buck. The values of Eastern philosophies—Hinduism, Buddhism, Confucianism, Daoism, and their offshoots—still have a pervasive effect on the communicative rationality of Asians in the so-called (Habermasian) *public sphere*. Asian philosophy encourages constructive criticism of the rulers and promotes pluralistic thinking. For example, pluralistic thinking is built into the Chinese personality—a product of a mixture of Confucianism, Daoism, Buddhism, and communism. This demonstrates the capacity of the Sinitic society to understand the extremes and follow the golden mean. The Chinese believe that flow and change are essential features of nature that follow a constant pattern. The communist experiment and the movement away from it are part of that flow and change.

Although from the West-centric perspective contemporary China is situated closer to the authoritarian end of the libertarian–authoritarian continuum (Fig. 7.3, a two-dimensional linear graph), both in relation to its structure of government and journalistic practice, it has incorporated a degree of democracy through the multiparty cooperation and political consultation system. Direct elections to people's congresses take place at the township and county levels of government in China, in contrast to indirect elections at the provincial and national levels. Thus, we see here the operation of the two faces of Confucianism—what scholar Tu Weiming called "political Confucianism," which legitimates a hierarchical political system culminating in the emperor or the oligarchy; and "Confucian personal ethic," which regulates day-to-day life (Fukuyama, 1995). The latter type of Confucianism is at work at the grassroots level, which P.C. Huang (1993) identified as the third realm—the space between state and society.

By recognizing the right to dissent, democratic governments encourage peaceful and orderly social and political change. Buddhism branched into several schools and sects quite early because of its tolerance of dissent. Thus, a journalism of pluralism would be consistent with Buddhist philosophy within the bounds of positive freedom. In practice, freedom of the press is never absolute. The principle has long been established that the press may not be used in circumstances that would create a "clear and present danger" of bringing about serious consequences to some significant interest that the government has a right or duty to protect. Another important limit on the free press is the law of libel, involving the defamation of a person, false accusations, or exposure of someone to hatred, ridicule, or pecuniary loss. Until about the mid-20th century, the law of obscenity was also a substantial limitation on freedom of the press. In the West, particularly in the United States, this exception, like the law of libel, has been narrowed so as to exclude from the constitutional guarantee only so-called *hard-core* pornography.

Social responsibility in journalism practice in Asia is consistent with the promotion of developmental journalism, which is vastly different from government-say-so journalism. The latter is a by-product of political Confucianism, which some Asian leaders are trying to falsely equate with Asian values. The major Asian philosophies do not condone the misuse of media by the rulers to suppress opposing views or muzzle constructive criticism. In the contemporary world, where Westernization has imposed itself in the garb of globalization, no country can avoid the influence of West-centric journalism. Autopoietic journalism processes within the sociocultural context of each nation-state are the natural defense against the inroads of globalization. Developmental journalism has engendered a counterpart in the West called *public journalism*, yet another outcome of the unity and mutual interrelation of all things and events.

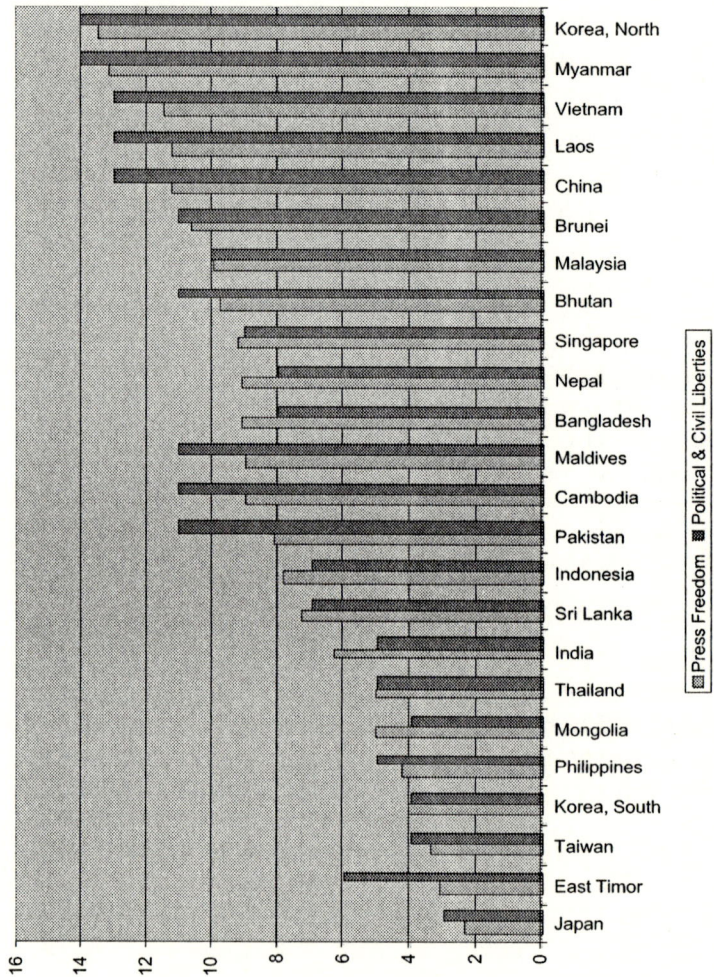

Fig. 7.3. An Occidental view of Asian democracy 2003 (Freedom House Ratings [adjusted for comparison]: 0 = free to 14 = not free)

Legend: Press Freedom ▨ Political & Civil Liberties ▩

Countries (top to bottom): Korea, North; Myanmar; Vietnam; Laos; China; Brunei; Malaysia; Bhutan; Singapore; Nepal; Bangladesh; Maldives; Cambodia; Pakistan; Indonesia; Sri Lanka; India; Thailand; Mongolia; Philippines; Korea, South; Taiwan; East Timor; Japan

In summary, the nature of journalism in a nation-state is a reflection of the shade of democracy it has chosen based on its sociocultural context. Various shades of democracy and socially responsible journalism occupy the four-dimensional continuum stretching from libertarianism (*yin*) to authoritarianism (*yang*). Each culture determines the meaning it gives to *social responsibility*. Because long-term research shows that the citizenry of the more or less libertarian free-press countries is ill informed about sociopolitical issues (as evident in the United States), doubts have arisen about a causal connection between press libertarianism and democracy. Therefore, our focus should shift from negative freedom of the press to positive (or socially responsible) freedom. In practical terms, purely libertarian or purely authoritarian press or political systems are rare and not viable in the long run. Autopoietic journalism processes within the sociocultural context in each nation-state have become the natural defense against the onslaught of globalization, a euphemism for Westernization. The holistic approach of the East should supplement the atomistic approach of the West to enhance our understanding of democracy and journalism. A more productive endeavor would be to focus on the broader concept of the right to communicate (Harms, 2003).

SYSTEMS THINKING

New insights emerge when we examine democracy and journalism from the perspective of new systems thinking incorporating the world-systems analysis[1] and the theory of living systems. Because the world is a complex adaptive system—a dissipative structure whose characteristics include nonlinearity, irreversibility, unpredictability, chaos, and far-from-equilibrium conditions—nomothetic science cannot provide any complete and definitive understanding of natural and social phenomena. *Democracy* and *press freedom* are abstract concepts that cannot be scientifically assessed with or without a sociocultural context. However, we can understand these nonphysical phenomena better through new systems thinking associated with nonlinear dynamics (Gunaratne, 2003c).

Capra (1996) identified six interdependent criteria of systems thinking: The first criterion is shifting our attention from the parts to the whole because parts do not have systemic properties. Dissecting a system into isolated elements destroys systemic properties. The world system as the superstructural unity is more than the sum of its parts or substructural unities (i.e., the nation-states). Applying Prigogine's theory of dissipative structures, we can surmise that the microchip (the attractor) engendered positive feedback (the butterfly effect), leading to the digital revolution that forced the far-from-equilibrium world system to self-organize into a more complex *structure* at a bifurcation point in the late 1980s. This self-organization engendered unpredictable nonlinear outcomes: It dismantled the communist bloc, created global networks of financial and information flows, produced giant global conglomerates, and curtailed the power of the nation-states to control their internal *processes*. The pattern of autopoiesis enabled the nation-states to put up a degree of defense. The nation-states have invoked closer structural coupling with relevant entities in their environment to prevent the erosion of sovereignty (Price, 2002).

The second criterion is the ability to shift attention back and forth between systems levels. (Capra explained that in the living world, systems nest within other systems. Different systems levels represent levels of differing complexity. Systemic properties of a particular level are called *emergent* properties because they emerge at that particular level. None of the levels is any more fundamental than the others.) Wallerstein's world-systems analysis identifies three systems levels—the center (roughly equivalent to the G-7 countries), the semiperiphery (roughly equivalent to countries constituting the Organization for Economic Cooperation and Development, excluding the G-7), and the periphery (the large group of developing countries). The *yin-yang* interaction, in its manifestation as the *centriphery* holon, recursively produces this triadic structure of the superstructural unity. Nation-states within each level may also nest in systems that cut across the three levels based on trade, economic, military, or other considerations (e.g., Asia-Pacific Economic Cooperation, British Commonwealth of Nations). The emergent property or the attractor that produced the digital revolution emerged at the center level. The patterns of relationships within and across these systems levels serve as the environment for each nation-state. (Note: Because the world system as the superstructural unity denotes the entire planet Earth, we can identify the three levels as system, rather than subsystem, levels. The Earth exchanges energy, matter and entropy with its immediate environment, the atmosphere, and the solar system.)

The third criterion is the shift from mechanistic thinking to contextual or environmental thinking. (Capra said living systems cannot be understood by analysis—in terms of the properties of a system's parts. Maturana asserted that autopoiesis is a generative mechanism, not an emergent property.) Applying Maturana and Varela's theory of autopoiesis, we can surmise that each nation-state, which can be compared to a cell in an organism, is operationally closed, but cognitively open to its environment—the systems level to which it belongs, the cross-level networks to which it belongs, and the world system as a whole. Thus, each nation-state recursively produces its own form of democracy and journalism (within the libertarian–authoritarian dichotomy) using the sociocultural context relevant to its boundary. However, it is very much influenced by its environment. The process of autopoiesis, which we can equate with the meeting of *yin* and *yang*, reacts both negatively and positively to its environment depending on the complex dimensions of space time. An example is the reaction of North Korea to the pressure from its environment.

The fourth criterion is the shift from objects to relationships. (Capra said that ultimately, as quantum physics has shown, there are no parts at all. A part is merely a pattern in an inseparable web of relationships.) A single cell alone cannot go through autopoiesis without all other cells operating simultaneously within the organism. This is true of all dissipative structures. Likewise, each nation-state is merely a pattern—constituting a vast conglomerate of atoms and their particles, which often metamorphose back and forth into waves or strings—in an inseparable web of relationships within the world system. (Throughout history, microsystems such as nations have disintegrated [e.g., Soviet Union, Yugoslavia, India] or merged [e.g., United Kingdom, Germany]. So have macrosystems such as empires [e.g., Neo-Assyrian, Achaemedes, Macedonian, Parthian, Sassanid, Mongol, Ottoman, Roman, Byzantine, Mauryan, Gupta, and Chinese]). The circular autopoietic patterns of nations within the world system generate different shades of democracy and journalism. These are natural patterns that reflect the diversity within the oneness of the world system, which would cease to operate if it were to reach thermodynamic equilibrium with just one shade of democracy and journalism. Thus, we cannot treat nation-states as objects outside the context of their complex relationships to the whole.

The fifth criterion is thinking in terms of networks (*vernetztes Denken*), another key characteristic of systems thinking. (Capra said the metaphor of knowledge as a building is being replaced by that of the network—the notion of scientific knowledge as a network of concepts, in which no part is any more fundamental than the others. The material universe is a dynamic web of interrelated events. It has no fundamental constants, laws, or equations.) The global networks are a systemic property of the world system. All microsystems are cognitively open to and influenced by the properties of the totality. Thus, no nation-state, however authoritarian it may be, can shut its citizenry off from the world system, which can use airwaves, satellites, fiber optics, and other technologies to transmit information.

The sixth criterion is the shift from objective to epistemic science. Capra said epistemology—understanding of the process of knowing—has to be included explicitly in the description of natural phenomena. Contrary to the Cartesian paradigm, scientific descriptions are not independent of the human observer and the process of knowing. Empirical science cannot ascertain the complex web of networks operating within the world system. Nomothetic science can never test the string theory of the universe, which combines the theories of gravity and relativity, electromagnetic field theory, and the theories of strong and weak forces. Neither can it test the complex web of networks that produces varying shades of democracy and journalism along the libertarian–authoritarian continuum elucidated in the present discussion. We need to shift to epistemic science to understand the complexities that defy empirical science.

Furthermore, Capra (1999) suggested that new-paradigm thinking in science should show a shift from thinking in terms of structure to thinking in terms of process (cognition) from which we derive meaning. He also suggested a shift from truth to approximate descriptions. In this discussion, we examined democracy and journalism as patterns connected with cognition encompassing a dissipative structure. Our conclusions are approximations, not truth, which defies all science.

PRICE'S PERSPECTIVE

We can now see how Price's (2002) analysis of media and sovereignty fits the theoretical framework developed in this book. We referred to the gist of Price's argument in chapter 4. Price contended that the information revolution has not necessarily diminished the sovereignty of the nation state, which has regained its power to control the flow of adverse information through extending its area of action beyond its national borders. States are deploying a mix of technology, law, force, and negotiation both unilaterally and consensually to protect their internal markets and alter their external markets. Price asserted that media structures, media spaces, and information policies are increasingly negotiated—the product of subtle arrangements between states and multinational corporations, between international entities and states, and encompassing other vectors.

Information intervention has become an important aspect of the center nation-states' foreign policy concerning global media-space. For example, NATO, led by the United States, resorted to information intervention in Bosnia-Herzegovina and Yugoslavia by using electronic warfare planes to block media outlets and seize TV towers using the Dayton Accords as the legal basis. Similar information intervention occurred against the hostile regimes in Afghanistan and Iraq. Price (2002) also pointed out the information foreign policies of several other nation-states (e.g., India's against Pakistan, Armenia's against Azerbaijan, and

Turkey's against use of media by Kurds abroad). Price also listed several techniques that nation-states use as part of their information and media foreign policy: providing subsidies, exerting pressure through the World Trade Organization, sponsoring and exporting media models, and so on.

Price (2002) highlighted seven main factors as determinants of a nation-state's approach to media: (a) sensitivity to international speech norms, (b) national security concerns, (c) tradition of private versus state media, (d) availability of new technology, (e) protectionism versus free trade, (f) nature and history of regime structure, and (g) isolation versus vulnerability to power realignments. These seven factors fit into the internal and external environments of the political system, which is operationally coupled with the system of communication outlets and free expression at the nation-state level. International speech norms, new technology, free trade, and power alignments, *inter alia*, form the external environments that the autopoietic political system of a nation-state cognitively draws on in determining its media-space policy along the libertarian–authoritarian continuum. National security concerns, tradition of media ownership, and the regime structure constitute aspects of the internal environment that are structurally coupled with the political system.

Autopoiesis of the system occurs through a continuous series of negative and positive feedback engendered by a multitude of factors giving rise to both chaos and order. The circular pattern of autopoiesis is what Chinese philosophy identifies as the interaction of *yin* and *yang*, which takes into account all relevant factors in the environment. The operationally coupled political and communication outlets systems in Bosnia-Herzegovina had reached the edge of chaos when the attractor, the external information intervention by NATO, a network of center states dominating the world system, set in motion the positive feedback that triggered the chaotic systems to cross the bifurcation point into a more complex state of emergence. Maturana (2002) pointed out that living systems are constitutively open to the flow of molecules (matter/energy) in the continuous realization of the recursive, closed, self-producing dynamics that constitutes them as singular entities. Our analogy of Bosnia-Herzegovina as a living system presumes that what applies to a human being as a singular living system is also applicable to a collectivity of human beings constituting a nation-state because they share meaning as close structurally coupled systems.

Thus, Price's analysis of contemporary state–media relations easily fits into our theory of living systems. Price implicitly recognized the oneness of the world system and the diversity within it, and the structural coupling of all living systems—whether in the form of individuals or collectivities such as communities or nation-states. What Price said is that collectivities of human beings, in their manifestation as nation-states, are establishing closer structural coupling with one another to establish their own controlled information space. Thus, Price implicitly conceded the operational coupling of the political and communication outlets systems, both at the world-system and nation-state levels. The freedom of communication outlets depends on the shade of democracy that the pattern of autopoiesis (*yin-yang* interaction) determines for each nation-state within the context of the world system. No system of communication outlets is free from the political system under which it has to operate. Hence, the myth of the Fourth Estate.

EXCURSUS: QUANTUM TELEDEMOCRACY

Some political scientists believe that quantum theory will become the physical basis "for an inevitable new transformational politics, government, and political science" (Becker & Slaton, 2000, p. 31). They see complexity science (or chaos theory) as a more modern offshoot of quantum theory because both are "post-Newtonian worldviews that share a great deal in their perception of all physical reality from supernovas to molecules" (p. 42). Both share several key elements: uncertainty, unpredictability, nonlinearity, and interactivity. The difference between the two is mostly philosophical. Complexity science presumes an ultimate or underlying order in the universe, whereas quantum theory makes no such presumption. Another difference is that complexity science applies irreversibility to all phenomena, whereas quantum theory excludes subatomic "particles" because no single particle can last long enough to gather a history. Thus, quantum theory does not emphasize entropy at the subatomic level.[2]

Synthesizing such post-Newtonian thinking, Becker and Slaton (2000) proposed a more participatory form of democracy (called teledemocracy) that, *inter alia*, emphasizes:

- processes and waves, not structure and matter;
- permeable and overlapping interaction, not separation and isolation;
- the inevitability and positive aspects of change, not stasis and order;
- randomness and change, not logic and law;
- the interdependence of everything, not the independence of individuals and component parts.

Becker and Slaton traced the origin of their notion of quantum democracy to Harvard professor W. B. Munro (1928), whom they call quantum political science's first voyager (see chap. 3). Furthermore, they cited the authority of political scientist and physicist R. J. Rummel (1977), who developed a field theory of international relations based on quantum theory. Political scientists Schubert (1983) and Dator (1987) also saw the relevance of quantum principles to achieve a form of "Athenian democracy." Architect and scientist R. Buckminster Fuller (1971) and political psychoanalyst Erich Fromm (1955) were early advocates of electronic democracy. Futurists Toffler and Toffler (1994) and Keskinen (1995) also enthusiastically embraced teledemocracy because they saw the "merits of a quantum correction to the Newtonian political thought" (Becker & Slaton, 2000, p. 153). A reviewer has summarized the main argument in Becker and Slaton's book on teledemocracy as follows:

> The dawn of the third millennium has brought with it an array of "uniquely menacing dilemmas" (p. 7)—civil war, poverty, environmental degradation, Third World debt, disaffected youth, etc.—with which representative democracy, dominated by "tiny cliques of economically powerful and well-organized interests who are, by and large, sexist, racist, and Social Darwinists at heart" (p. 6), is ill equipped to deal. The solution to these "threats to human viability" is teledemocracy: a "purer, future democracy" (p. 7) that makes liberal use of direct democratic instruments and new information and communication technologies. . . . [The] "New Democratic Paradigm" is imminent, especially in America, the progressive center of the "one continent on this globe generating a series of impulses that contain the best way for humankind to work together, live together, grow together, and govern together" (p. 8). This "wave of the future" (p. 9) is the political analog of the quantum revolution in physics . . ., its progress hindered by political, economic, and media elites whose interests are wedded to the current representative system and the outmoded "Newtonian paradigm" . . . upon which it is based and legitimated. (Barney, 2002, p. 171)

The quantum politics envisaged by Becker and Slaton (2000) include deliberative polling and televoting; electronic town meetings mediated by TV, telephone, and computer technology; and the integration of the Internet. The highly interactive core elements of the new democratic paradigm are (a) the global direct democracy movement, (b) the 21st-century democratic communication systems, (c) the modern mediation movement, and (d) transformational political organization via the Internet.

In direct democracy, Becker and Slaton (2000) said, "every citizen is equal as a law maker . . . [and] the flow of information and the deliberative process is lateral among citizens" (p. 158). Random selection of citizens would "make national legislatures more representative" (p. 157). The universally burgeoning traditional forms of citizens initiatives and referenda bode well for direct democracy. An essential tool of the new democratic paradigm's system of political communication is TV.

At the beginning of this chapter, I pointed out that the political system and the system of communication outlets are operationally coupled because of their close interdependence. Under quantum teledemocracy, this interdependence becomes even sharper because the mass media have to be more involved in the genre of journalism called *public journalism*. Becker and Slaton (2000) referred to the current system of communication-outlets as a Newtonian-style, "top-down flow of information and values from those who own and/or control" the media (p. 77). They said:

> whether capitalist, dynastic, communist, socialist, or social democratic, TV works to preserve the pyramidical nature of the society and its power elites by transmitting its electronic river of data and prejudices. (Becker & Slaton, 2000, p. 77)

They argued that under teledemocracy, "TV can be used as an interactive, upstream, and a lateral communications tool for positive economic, political, and social purposes—particularly when coupled with electronic communications devices like the telephone and, now, the Internet" (p. 79).

This idealistic teledemocracy, however, does not fit the model of the libertarian–authoritarian continuum developed in this book. Becker and Slaton (2000) presumed the world is ready for a quantum jump to teledemocracy, a pure form of democracy to replace Newtonian-style democracy. Their model is based on a continuum ranging from conventional democracy to teledemocracy. Theirs is thus another West-centric model that ignores all other philosophies. In the parlance of quantum theory, they have subjectively collapsed a coherent superposition (of the possibility waves of political and media systems) using a measuring device that changed the manifest form of the superposition's underlying reality. The principle of uncertainty applies here.

The interaction of quantum particles or the forces of the *yin* and *yang* will not cease on reaching a universal teledemocracy. The principle of irreversibility does not permit reverting to a two-millennia-old "Athenian democracy" or even a two-century-old liberal democracy that Habermas extolled. Moreover, the magnitude of global disparities in communication technologies is so vast (Gunaratne, 2002b) that a teledemocracy based on equality of every citizen is more like a pipe dream. Moreover, if every citizen were to be equal in all respects, humanity would reach thermodynamic equilibrium and cease to exist (with negentropy = entropy).

A permanent teledemocracy is incompatible with the theory of living systems, which is based on quantum theory and its offshoot called *complexity science*. Neither a West-centric nor an East-centric ideology can direct the transcendent reality of the Dao, the Brahman, the Dharmakaya, or God. Using quantum principles to promote a particular ideology or system is a self-defeating exercise. Because uncertainty, unpredictability, complementarity, nonlocality, and nonlinearity do not take sides.

NOTES

1. In a related endeavor, Gunaratne (2003b) analyzed the rise and fall of languages within the framework of world-systems analysis and Eastern philosophy.
2. However, this does not mean that quantum theorists ignored entropy. Schrödinger (1945) explained entropy as a measurable physical quantity: "When you melt a solid, its entropy increases by the amount of the heat of fusion divided by the temperature at the melting point" (p. 73).

Eight

Conclusions and Future Directions

To know the Way,
We go the Way;
We do the Way
The way we do
The things we do.
It's all there in front of you,
But if you try too hard to see it,
You'll only become Confused.
—*The Dao of Pooh* (Hoff, 1982, p. 158)

In this book, I have stepped into the minefield of Eastern mysticism that Enlightenment thinkers discarded as entropy because it did not fit reason-based science. Complexity science has reversed the arrogance of Enlightenment's rationalism and paved the way to see Eastern mysticism as transcendent reality, which could provide deep insights into the mystery of the subatomic universe unfolded by quantum physics. After all, despite the hostility of staunch Newtonians, one can talk about linking Eastern philosophy with Western science inasmuch as science cannot explain the mystery of the architect of universal laws.

The focus of this book was the development of a dynamic, humanocentric theory of communication outlets and free expression to replace the static, deontic normative theories of the press. In the process, *inter alia*, we elucidated the connection between democracy and journalism. Our conclusion was that individualism and self-interest dominated the Western concept of liberal democracy. Eastern thinking, in contrast, placed emphasis on interdependence and mutual causality. In particular reference to Buddhist philosophy, Joanna Macy (1991) explained this extremely well:

> In dependent co-arising, self, society, and world are reciprocally modified by their interaction, as they form relationships and are in turn conditioned by them. The Western idea contrasts with such a view to the extent that it assumes a free association between individuals who remain basically distinct and unaltered by such association. (Macy, 1991, p. 191)

In short, as Buddhadasa Bhikku put it, "The entire cosmos is a cooperative" (cited in Sivaraksa, 2002, p. 8).

Plainly, the disagreements on the nature of democracy boil down to the atomistic thinking of the West versus the systems thinking of the East. Thus, the notion that liberal democracy has universal validity reeks of what Tu Weiming called the Enlightenment's "arrogance of rationality" (in Yu & Lu, 2000, p. 379). Freedom House's exclusion of some countries from the fold of electoral democracies has a clear West-centric bias.

It follows that disagreement on the nature of press freedom, more precisely the freedom of communication outlets (Gunaratne, 2002a), also more or less boils down to atomistic thinking versus systems thinking. The West appears to think of press freedom as the negative freedom of expression by independent individuals. The West grudgingly concedes a degree of positive freedom associated with social responsibility, whereas the East's systems thinking promotes positive freedom as the more desirable approach. However, the Western and Eastern views of social responsibility may differ considerably in the context of culture.

Moreover, the digital revolution has created "global metanetworks of complex technological and human interactions, involving multiple feedback loops operating far from equilibrium, which produce a never-ending variety of emergent phenomena" (Capra, 2002, p. 140). Castells (1996) asserted that the global financial and information networks have rendered the governments of developing countries relatively powerless to control their economic and information policies, whereas Price (2002) documented that nation-states are reasserting their sovereignty by resorting to extraterritorial action to alter their external markets while protecting their internal markets. Held (1996, 2000), in contrast, saw the emergence of a cosmopolitan democracy at global and regional levels with the nation-states willingly relinquishing some degree of their sovereignty in the interest of global order while conceding greater autonomy at local levels. This is a phenomenon similar to the merging and splitting of cells within an organism. Therefore, the measurement of press freedom at the nation–state level, as Freedom House does, has become questionable without factoring in both the global and local contexts.

We can now summarize the principal conclusions derived from the review of the literature on West-centrism, theories of communication outlets, and Eastern philosophy within the contextual framework of the theory of living systems.

We have concluded that the normative West-centric theories of communication-outlets and free expression—the putative press theories—are inadequate to explain the dynamics of ongoing change at the main levels of the world system. They are founded on atomistic linear thinking, which pays no attention to system–environment interactions.

The *Four Theories of the Press*, as well as its subsequent improvements, has had a vast impact on communication scholars. "*Four Theories* was for several decades a basic framework for the macrosocial study of mass media systems" (Rogers & Chaffee, 1994, p. 20). However, our analysis has shown its limited applicability (even as *ideal type* models) across the three different levels of the world system, particularly with regard to the classification of social responsibility. Western scholars (e.g., Siebert, Peterson, & Schramm, 1956; Hachten, 2001) attached linear meanings consonant with Enlightenment thinking to the constructs of libertarianism and social responsibility without realizing how the meanings they attached to these constructs may run counter to the analogue style of thinking of the East associated with infinite interpretation, illusion, and intuition. Libertarian press philosophy is associated with liberal democracy. As subaltern scholars like Chakrabarty (2000) argued, the concept of *liberal democracy* provided the justification for India's struggle against British imperialism, thereby giving it the status of a universal concept. However, as Habermas (1987) lamented, the concept has changed under advanced capitalism, such that the media of money and power have colonized the lifeworld. The best a nation-state could do is glocalize the concept to suit its sociocultural context at a given time.

The theory developed in this book points out how the pattern of autopoiesis at the microlevel determines the nature of social responsibility appropriate for a particular system (community or nation-state) across space time. The scientific concept of autopoiesis is remarkably similar to the principle of the dialectical completion of relative polarities in Chinese metaphysics. I have adumbrated the essential philosophical elements pertaining to the notion of social responsibility from the Eastern perspective. Subaltern scholars (e.g., Chakrabarty, 2000) have emphasized the need to espouse the universalistic features of Enlightenment thought in the interest of modernity. The theory presented in this book merely examines the patterns and process of life that produce particular phenomena without attaching value judgments. We need to shift from objective to epistemic science when we analyze abstract concepts such as *democracy* and *social responsibility*. The revelations of quantum mechanics (e.g., uncertainty principle, complementarity, and nonlocality) have established that the claimed objectivity of nomothetic empiricism is mere wishful thinking.

Hachten (2001) discussed the theory and values of freedom of the press solely in terms of the Euro-American experience. The centerpiece of his discussion is the First Amendment to the U.S. Constitution and the constitutional law derived therefrom. His definition of *freedom of the press* is "the right of the press to report, to comment on, and to criticize its own government without retaliation or threat from that authority" (p. 31). This definition, however, emphasizes the nation-state level while ignoring the center-dominated world-system level, where governments, together with transnational media conglomerates, operate the system of communication outlets (Price, 2002). Under such circumstances, one may well ask: Is the Voice of America, for instance, free to criticize the U.S. government?

Furthermore, Hachten (2001) said that in U.S. law, "free speech and free press are identical rights" (p. 31) and "freedom of the press is an individual right, we are all protected by it" (p. 33). However, as Splichal (2002) pointed out, the 19th-century notion of the press as the Fourth Estate (i.e., the *corporate* entity serving collective interests) stood in contrast to the rationalistic and enlightenment conceptualization of freedom of the press as a *personal* freedom and right to publish opinions. Kant's idea of the "public use of reason" emphasized the personal right of publishing opinions. (The U.S. concept of freedom of the press was conceived as an individual right in the late 18th century when anyone could start a printing press to extend his or her freedom of speech. In the contemporary world, not everyone has equal access to the mainstream press.) The inclusion of the individual level in the three-tier model developed in this book provides for the restoration of the neo-Kantian notion of the right to communicate.

Another conclusion we have derived in the formulation of our theory is that the "improvements" to the *Four Theories* (e.g., developmental, public/civic, revolutionary, democratic socialist, etc.) merely describe varying shades of social responsibility determined by sociocultural factors at a particular juncture of space time.

These improvements describe shades of social responsibility, which are temporary phenomena (as evident in the evanescent communist formulation), and they lack mutually exclusive characteristics. Splichal (2002) implicitly recognized the truth of impermanence (*anicca*) when he asserted that "concepts and meanings vary with time and space, rather than progress in a linear manner" (p. 5). Therefore, these improvements belong to the passing parade of socially responsible public communication practices or genres of journalism distributed across the four-dimensional libertarian–authoritarian continuum. Elsewhere, I have shown the close connections of developmental and public journalism with the social responsibility theory (Gunaratne, 1998).

Hachten (2001), as well as Merrill, Gade, and Blevens (2001), has to varying degrees confused the systems of communication outlets with various genres of journalism. The humanocentric theory advanced in this book helps us see broad variations of middle-path systems of socially responsible communication outlets and free expression (broadly identifiable as SR1, SR2, SR3 in Newtonian linear terms) situated between the extremes of libertarianism and authoritarianism. From the perspective of new physics, these are clusters of possibility waves or wavicles, which behave in random fashion within the A–L continuum. Quantum jumps of these wavicles, which enable them to locate themselves simultaneously "here, there, and nowhere," render their accurate measurement impossible. Therefore, in this book, I have merely presented the *ideal-type* models for the epistemic understanding of the abstract concepts that constitute the main variables of my humanocentric theory. From the perspective of monistic idealism, we use our awareness, a function of consciousness shared by all sentient beings, to collapse the possibility waves of concepts. In this sense, an observer's subject–object dualism serves as the *yin-yang* antinomy that creates the concepts in consonance with the sociocultural values embedded in the quantum self of the observer. Winfield, Mizuno, and Beaudoin (2000) agreed that "the characteristics of a country's media depend on the culture in which they operate" (p. 323).

In the short-time scale, scholars can use the *ideal-type* models outlined in chapter 6 to develop broad categories of socially responsible systems of communication outlets for historically, culturally, and politically sensitive analyses of change. Using these categories, scholars could do three-pronged analyses of (a) changes within a nation-state in terms of social responsibility as defined by its own cultural values; (b) changes at the superstructural (world-system) level in terms of a more humanocentric (culturally inclusive) definition of social responsibility; and (c) changes at the individual level in terms of the right to communicate within the nation-state and across the world system. The more productive endeavor would be to focus on social responsibility, rather than on the negatives and positives of moving toward authoritarianism or libertarianism. Wahl-Jorgensen and Galperin (2000), who have analyzed the U.S. mass media within the framework of Habermas' communicative-action theory, concluded that the media of money and power associated with the economy and state systems have adversely impinged on the lifeworld's ability to use the public sphere for rational political discussion, thereby casting doubt on the desirability of the putative libertarian system of communication outlets as currently constituted.

I contend that the humanocentric theory of communication outlets and free expression developed in this book is consistent with the systems thinking associated with nonlinear dynamics reflecting the arrow of time (irreversibility) and the thermodynamically far-from-equilibrium state of dissipative structures.

The theory presented in this book is an attempt to go beyond the linear thinking associated with the *Four Theories* and their improvements. The theory incorporates the concepts of autopoiesis, cognition, structure, and meaning borrowed from the theory of living systems (Capra, 2002), as well as the *centriphery* concept borrowed from world-systems analysis (Baker, 1993a). These concepts are broadly consistent with Eastern philosophical thinking on the unity of the opposites, the intrinsically dynamic nature of the universe, and the interrelation of all phenomena. Autopoiesis is also a major feature of Luhmann's abstract social-system model. The classical Newtonian model, which presumes the reversibility of time, claims that it can apply the laws of nature to explain the past and the present, as well as predict the future. The Prigogine model, which has challenged this reductionism, asserts that nature spontaneously derives order out of chaos—a sort of harmony—that agrees with Eastern philosophy. Communication research encompassing this theoretical framework will enrich our understanding of communication phenomena in a universe where uncertainty and chance play a major role.

The humanocentric theory advanced in this book presumes a skewed distribution of systems of communication outlets and free expression consistent with the new science of complexity. Hachten's (2001) view of the triumph of Western journalism after the fall of communism gives the impression that the world's systems of communication outlets have moved toward the libertarian end of the continuum. Hachten claimed, "Non-Western nations have adopted not only the gadgets and equipment of the U.S. press and broadcasting but also its practices, norms, ethical standards, and ideology" (p. 18). In contrast, Sussman's (2000) grim picture of global press freedom gives us the impression that the distribution has moved toward the authoritarian end. Sussman referred to Freedom House's January 2000 press freedom survey, according to which "nearly two-thirds of countries (63 percent) restrict print and electronic journalism. Some 80 percent of the world's people live in nations with less than a free press" (p. 1). The January 2001 survey shows only a 1% reduction of each of these two figures.

The attempt to capture press freedom with precise scores based on the judgment of a few observers reflects Neo-Copenhagenism—the instrumentalist view that quantum mechanics is nothing but a set of rules to calculate what we can measure. Our observation collapses the quantum wave packet (e.g., concept of press freedom) to a localized particle, which is nothing but *maya* or illusion. So what happens to objectivity? Moreover, the principle of uncertainty has established that we can never determine both the particle's (concept's) position and momentum (initial condition) simultaneously with absolute accuracy. If we cannot do that, how can we apply causal determinism for predicting events? Furthermore, we know that quantum wave packets (e.g., concepts) spread over vast distances and instantly collapse when we take measurements. If this is the case, should we not acknowledge that what appears to be local is really an aspect of the whole?

Goswami (1993) said that data indicative of parallels between the mind (associated with concepts) and the quantum do exist. He said that the brain-mind can be looked at "as both a measuring apparatus and a quantum system" (p. 173).

> What we call the mind consists of objects that are akin to the objects of submicroscopic matter and that obey rules similar to those of quantum mechanics. (Goswami, 1993, p. 167)

We must bear in mind the reservations (already discussed earlier) when we assess the Freedom House annual surveys of press/media freedom. The discrete numerical scores these surveys have assigned to each nation-state give the appearance of strong objectivity, determinism, and locality although none applies. Moreover, the critique of the *Four Theories* in chapter 4 clearly applies to the Freedom House method of classifying press/media freedom because it is predicated on the belief that the Enlightenment libertarian philosophy—emphasizing liberal democracy, *laissez-faire* capitalism, and individualism—applies to the entire world-system (Gunaratne, 2002a).[1] Although it purports to uphold press freedom, it implicitly condemns pluralism. Furthermore, Freedom House merely presents just one actualized facet of the multi-faceted state that exists *in potentia* without revealing the statistical weight given by its probability wave amplitude. It makes no attempt to present four-dimensional phase-space or state-space profiles of the world's press.

Faulty as the Freedom House freedom scores are, we can use them to play a Newtonian statistical game. If you assemble them into a two-dimensional graph, you can derive the approximation of a normal curve (Fig. 8.1). Countries reflecting libertarian tendencies (with the minimum scores of 1–15) make up 11% of the total (21 out of 187) on the left tail of the distribution.[2] Countries reflecting authoritarian tendencies (with the maximum scores of 76–100) make up 13% of the total (24 out of 187) on the right tail.[3] The distribution of the other countries seems more or less to follow the pattern of a normal distribution. The three middle segments neatly make up three main shades of social responsibility. The "partly free" countries, which make up 28% (53 out of 187) of the total, are in the exact center (SR2) and represent the world's most prevalent shade of social responsibility.

However, Fig. 8.2 (based on the average of scores for a 9-year period) brings out the picture of a skewed distribution behind the façade of the normal curve when individual scores of countries are substituted for country classifications. Figure 8.2 shows the fit of the normal curve to a histogram of the average press-freedom scores assigned to each country by Freedom House during the 9-year period from 1994 to 2002. It presents the results of the Anderson-Darling Normality Test relating to the

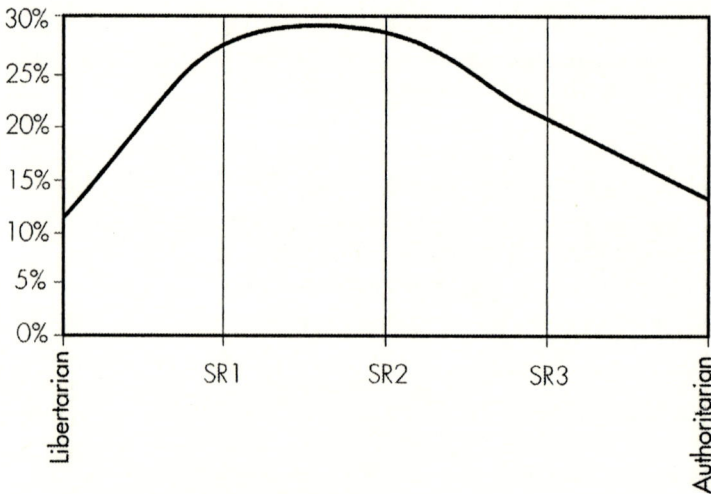

SR = Social Responsibility

Source: Freedom House

N=187

Figure 8.1. Distribution of countries based on freedom of press classifications, PF survey, 2001

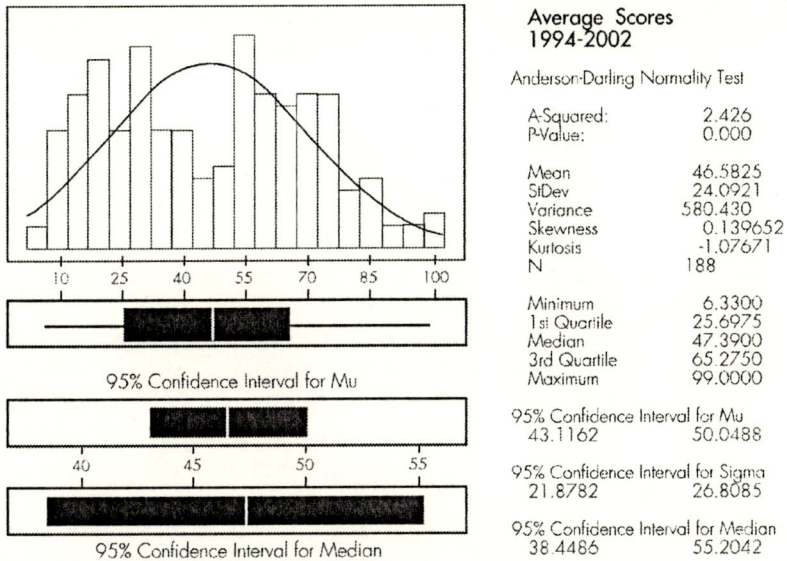

Average Scores
1994-2002

Anderson-Darling Normality Test

A-Squared:	2.426
P-Value:	0.000
Mean	46.5825
StDev	24.0921
Variance	580.430
Skewness	0.139652
Kurtosis	-1.07671
N	188
Minimum	6.3300
1st Quartile	25.6975
Median	47.3900
3rd Quartile	65.2750
Maximum	99.0000

95% Confidence Interval for Mu
43.1162   50.0488

95% Confidence Interval for Sigma
21.8782   26.8085

95% Confidence Interval for Median
38.4486   55.2042

95% Confidence Interval for Mu

95% Confidence Interval for Median

Source: Freedom House

Figure 8.2. Distribution of average PF scores, 1994-2002 (Statistical data)

same data. The test is statistically significant with $p < .01$. Although the mean score (46.7) and the median score (47.8) lie close to each other, the distribution is both positively and negatively skewed.

We just indulged in a statistical game, which befits Newtonian presumptions, but is inappropriate for quantum mechanics or complexity science. Nonlinear statistics—attractors, fractals, multifractals, normal forms, Lyapunov exponents, entropies, invariant measures, and correlation functions—remains an unfamiliar territory in the field of communication studies. As far as I am aware, phase-space press freedom scores do not exist. However, our brief game with linear statistics illustrated the *maya* of a far-from-equilibrium system of communication outlets at the world-system level. A related question arises on the reification of concepts related to higher ontological levels of dissipative systems by reducing them to quantitative measures (Gunaratne, 2004).

In terms of *future directions*, scholars from the "non-West" must lead the initiative to complement Occidental communication theory and research with humanocentric perspectives and approaches. This book has analyzed but one aspect of communication theory that is full of holes—a weakness that runs across the spectrum of the communication field. Because the so-called *human sciences* were born out of European thought in the 19th century, their West-centric bias was only natural. However, their resistance to incorporate non-Western ontology, epistemology, and methodology has merely weakened their ability to explain and analyze the non-Western world. Change is inevitable. The new systems thinking, exemplified by the theory of living systems, and the dialectical approach offer one avenue of linking the East West divide.

Merrill, Gade, and Blevens (2001) advanced the thesis that the press in the world, as well as in the United States, is losing its freedom and institutional importance. They added, "However, a corollary thesis is that with the loss of this freedom, the 21st century will see more social order and harmony and a more cooperative and a citizen-based press" (p. xvii). They saw the 18th-century Enlightenment liberalism giving way to the Eastern philosophy of harmony and cooperation. They are referring to the rise of communitarianism and its subgenre called *public* or *civic* journalism. Thus, they take the opposite view to that of Hachten and other "optimistic libertarian individualists" (p. xvii) when they foreshadow the reassertion of the spirit of communitarianism "that had hung around the periphery at least since the days of Plato and Confucius" (p. xxi). Rather than passing judgment on whether these developments are good or bad in terms of one's own cultural background, the social scientist should analyze the world at its various levels with a better understanding of the cultural contributions and differences of each civilization.

Although the application of post-Parsonsian systems thinking to theorize and research the relationship of communication and community may not be easy as the linear thinking associated with Newtonian mechanics, the future direction of the communication field lies in the first path. The theory presented in this book is three-dimensional. It enables us to analyze the system of communication outlets and free expression at all three levels of the world system using culture-inclusive criteria (Gunaratne, 2002a). If freedom from government interference is an essential element of freedom of communication outlets at the nation-state level, then that element is essential for determining freedom at the superstructural (world-system) level as well. However, considering the extent to which government-funded organizations are engaged in international broadcasting alone, coupled with the extent to which transnational corporations dominate the global communication outlets, one can attempt to fathom (and wonder about) the extent of freedom of communication outlets at the world-system level. However, the fact that such global communication outlets can reach people in nation-states where restrictions exist on domestic communication outlets makes those people freer at the individual level. Because nomothetic empiricism is a weak approach to apply at the higher ontological levels of dissipative systems (if for no other reason than the difficulties in finding valid and reliable data encompassing all systems), historians and philosophers can lead the social scientists at these levels.

As mentioned earlier, assessing the social responsibility of communication outlets should take precedence over assessing their freedom at the world-system and nation-state levels. Ownership by conglomerates in a profit-oriented commercial environment vis-àvis public ownership may not necessarily mean greater freedom of expression or a better informed public. From another angle, linking the Prigogine model with the world-system approach would enable researchers to explain the dynamics of the world's power structure and examine how the global system of communication outlets can produce both "chaos" and order in the international order through the recursive effects of message reproduction—an idea we owe to Luhmann (2000).

The theory of communication outlets and free expression adumbrated in this book differs from the four theories of the press and their subsequent improvements in significant ways. Our theory is dynamic, explanatory, humanocentric, and nonlinear; the latter is static, normative, West-centric, and linear. Our theory shows the continuous interaction of the two complements or antinomies—authoritarianism and libertarianism—to produce varying shades of social responsibility determined predominantly by socio-cultural values across space time. It views social responsibility in nonideological terms—not as an extension of libertarianism, but as an outcome of sociocultural factors shared by communities comprising the world system. Applying the principle of infinite interpretation, it looks at Peterson's "social responsibility theory" and Schramm's "Soviet communist theory" merely as descriptions of two of the several possible shades of social responsibility. Our formulation allows for a singular attractor to engender asymptotic behavior that pushes a system of communication outlets through a bifurcation point into a more complex reorganization.

Scholars can provide additional refinement to our model by incorporating parallel material from other pervasive cultures. Hamada (2001) already drew attention to the relevance of Islam, which he said, is not only a religion, but also a social order, a philosophy of life, a system of economic principles, and a rule of government. However, earlier attempts to define *Islamic communication* have run into severe dispute (Khiabany, 2003).

Communication scholars could apply our approach to refine other West-centric theories, such as Habermas' (1989) concept of the public sphere and his (Habermas, 1987) grand theory of communicative action, both of which have become popular among communication scholars.

Some have argued that Habermas' concepts presented as part of a theory of democracy are more universally applicable than the press theories we have analyzed. However, elsewhere I have pointed out that Habermas' concept of the public sphere, associated with the rise of the European bourgeoisie and the resulting emergence of civil society, ignores the developments in non-Western history (Gunaratne, 2005a). Habermas' concept of communicative rationality also conflicts with the principles of infinite interpretation and intuition associated with Eastern philosophy.

NOTES

1. Freedom House uses four criteria for measuring press freedom in each country: laws and regulations that influence media content; political pressures and controls on media content; economic influences over media content; and repressive actions (killing journalists, physical violence, censorship, self-censorship, arrests, etc.).
2. These countries are Australia, Austria, Bahamas, Belgium, Canada, Denmark, Finland, Germany, Jamaica, Luxembourg, Marshall Islands, Nauru, Netherlands, New Zealand, Norway, St. Lucia, Sweden, Switzerland, and United States.
3. These countries are Afghanistan, Angola, Azerbaijan, Belarus, Bhutan, Burundi, China, Congo (Kinshasa), Cote d'Ivorie, Cuba, Equatorial Guinea, Iraq, Koren (North), Libya, Myanmar, Saudi Arabia, Somalia, Sudan, Swaziland, Tajikistan, Turkmenistan, United Arab Emirates, Uzbekistan, and Vietnam.

References

Adams, J. (2001). Culture and economic development in South Asia. *The Annals of the American Academy of Political and Social Science, 573*, 152-175.

Altschull, J.H. (1984). *Agents of power*. White Plains, NY: Longman.

Amin, S. (1989). *Eurocentrism*. New York: Monthly Review Press.

Asante, C. E. (Comp.). (1997). *Press freedom and development: A research guide and selected bibliography*. Westport, CT: Greenwood.

Babbili, A. S. (1997). Ethics and the discourse on ethics in post-colonial India. In C. Christians & M. Traber (Eds.), *Communication ethics and universal values* (pp. 128-158). Thousand Oaks, CA: Sage.

Babbili, A. S. (2001). Culture, ethics, and burdens of history: Understanding the communications ethos of India. In S. R. Melkote & S. Rao (Eds.), *Critical issues in communication: Essays in honor of K.E. Eapen* (pp. 144-176). New Delhi: Sage.

Baert, P. (1998). *Social theory in the twentieth century*. New York: New York University Press.

Bahm, A. J. (1995). *Comparative philosophy: Western, Indian and Chinese philosophies compared* (rev. ed.). Albuquerque, NM: World Books.

Baker, P. L. (1993a). Chaos, order, and sociological theory. *Sociological Inquiry, 63*, 123–149.

Baker, P. L. (1993b). Space, time, space-time and society. *Sociological Inquiry, 63*, 408–424.

Baker, P. L. (1994). *Centering the periphery: Chaos, order, and the ethnohistory of Dominica*. Montreal: McGill University Press.

Bakker, J. I. (2003, July 27–30). *Community and the Luhmann-Habermas debate: A neo-Weberian Ideal Type solution*. Paper presented at the annual meeting of the Rural Sociological Society, Montreal.

Balagangadhara, S. N. (1994). *"The heathen in his blindness ..." Asia, the West and the dynamic of religion*. Leiden: E.J. Brill.

Barney, D. (2002). Political theory [Review of the book *The future of teledemocracy*]. *American Political Science Review, 96,* 171-172.

Bausch, K. (1997). The Habermas/Luhmann debate and subsequent Habermasian perspectives on systems theory. *Systems Research and Behavioral Science, 14*(5), 315-330.

Bausch, K. (2002). In response to Robert Kay: Luhmann's ontology, ontogeny, and epistemology. *Systems Research and Behavioral Science, 19*(6), 599-603.

Becker, T., & Slaton, C.D. (2000). *The future of teledemocracy*. Westport, CT: Praeger.

Becker, T. L. (Ed.). (1991). *Quantum politics: Applying quantum theory to political phenomena*. New York: Praeger.

Bernstein, J. (1979). Out of my mind . . . A cosmic flow. *The American Scholar, 48*(6), 6–9.

Billington, R. (1997). *Understanding Eastern philosophy*. London: Routledge.

Boron, A. A. (1999). A social theory for the 21st century? *Current Sociology, 47,* 47-60.

Braman, S. (2002). A pandemonic age: The future of international communication theory and research. In W. B. Gudykunst & B. Mody (Eds.), *Handbook of international and intercultural communication* (2nd ed., pp. 399-413). Thousand Oaks, CA: Sage.

Briggs, J., & Peat, F. D. (1989). *Turbulent mirror: An illustrated guide to chaos theory and the science of wholeness*. New York: Harper & Row.

Byeon, J. H. (1999). Non-equilibrium thermodynamic approach to the change in political systems. *Systems Research and Behavioral Science, 16*(3), 283–291.

Byun, D. H., & Lee, K. (2001, August 5). *Confucian values, ethics and legacies in history: Neo-Confucian debates and communication philosophy in Korea*. Paper presented to the Media Ethics and Cultural and Critical Studies divisions at the annual convention of the Association for Education in Journalism and Mass Communication, Washington, DC.

Cabezon, J. I. (2003). Buddhism and science: On the nature of the dialogue. In B.A. Wallace (Ed.), *Buddhism and science: Breaking new ground* (pp. 36-60). New York: Columbia University Press.

Capra, F. (1996). *The web of life: A new scientific understanding of living systems*. New York: Doubleday.

Capra, F. (1999). *The Tao of physics: An exploration of the parallels between modern physics and Eastern mysticism* (4th updated ed.). Boston: Shambhala. (Originally published in 1975)

Capra, F. (2002). *Hidden connections: Integrating the biological, cognitive, and social dimensions of life into a science of sustainability*. New York: Doubleday.

Carter, J. (2001). *The other theory of physics: A non-field unified theory of matter and motion* (2nd ed.). Franklin, WA: Absolute Motion Institute.

Carter, R. F. (1991). Comparative analysis, theory, and cross-cultural communication. *Communication Theory, 1*, 151-159.

Castells, M. (1996). *The Information Age: Vol. 1. The rise of network society*. London: Blackwell.

Chakrabarty, D. (2000). *Provincializing Europe: Postcolonial thought and historical difference*. Princeton, NJ: Princeton University Press.

Chang, J. H.-Y. (2003). Culture, state and economic development in Singapore. *Journal of Contemporary Asia, 33*(1), 85-106.

Charney, E. (1998). Political liberalism, deliberative democracy, and the public sphere. *American Political Science Review, 92*, 97-110.

Chen, E. M. (1989). *The Tao Te Ching [Dao De Jing]: A new translation with commentary*. New York: Paragon.

Chen, G.-M. & Starosta, W. J. (1996). Intercultural communication competence: A synthesis. In B. R. Burleson (Ed.), *Communication Yearbook 19* (pp. 353-383). Thousand Oaks, CA: Sage.

Chen, G.-M., & Starosta, W. J. (2003). Asian approaches to human communication: A dialogue. *Intercultural Communication Studies, 12*(4), 1-15.

Cheng, C.-Y. (1987). Chinese philosophy and contemporary human communication theory. In D. L. Kincaid (Ed.), *Communication theory: Eastern and Western perspectives* (pp. 23-43). San Diego, CA: Academic Press.

Cheng, C.-Y. (1988). The *I Ching [Yijing]* as a symbolic system of integrated communication. In W. Dissanayake (Ed.), *Communication theory: The Asian perspective* (pp. 79-104). Singapore: Amic.

Cheng, C.-Y. (1998). Reality and divinity in Chinese philosophy. In E. Deutsch & R. Bontekoe (Eds.), *A companion to world philosophies* (pp. 185-200). Malden, MA: Blackwell.

Chuang, R., & Chen, G. -M. (2003). Buddhist perspectives and human communication. *Intercultural Communication Studies, 12*(4), 65-80.

Cilliers, P. (1998). *Complexity and postmodernism: Understanding complex systems*. London: Routledge.

Collier, M. J., Hegde, R. S., Lee, W., Nakayama, T. K., & Yep, G. A. (2002). Dialogue on the edges: Ferment in communication and culture. In M. J. Collier (Ed.), *Transforming communication about culture: Critical new directions* (pp. 219–280). Thousand Oaks, CA: Sage.

Copleston, F. C. (1982). *Religion and the one: Philosophies east and west*. New York: Crossroad.

Curran, J., & Seaton, J. (2003). *Power without responsibility: The press, broadcasting, and new media in Britain* (6th ed.). London: Routledge.

Dahl, R. A. (1963). *Preface to democratic theory*. Chicago: University of Chicago Press.

Dahlke, P. (1913). *Buddhism and science* (Bhikku Silacara, Trans.). London: Macmillan.

Dasgupta, S. (1922). *A history of Indian philosophy* (Vol. 1). Cambridge, England: Cambridge University Press.

Dator, J. A. (1987, September). *Transforming the constitution: A quantum leap*. Paper presented to the annual meeting of the American Political Science Association, Chicago.

De Bary, T. (Ed.). (1958). *Sources of Indian tradition*. New York: Columbia University Press.

De Bary, T., & Bloom, I. (Eds.). (1999). *Sources of Chinese tradition* (Vol. 1, 2nd ed.). New York: Columbia University Press.

Delli Carpini, M., & Keeter, S. (1996). *What Americans know about politics and why it matters*. New Haven, CT: Yale University Press.

Dervin, B. (1991). Comparative theory reconceptualized: From entities and states to processes and dynamics. *Communication Theory, 1,* 59-69.

De Smaele, H. (1999). The applicability of Western media models on the Russian media system. *European Journal of Communication, 14,* 173–189.

Dewey, J. (1948). *Reconstruction in philosophy*. Boston: Beacon.

Dilworth, D. A. (1989). *Philosophy in world perspective: A comparative hermeneutic of the major theories*. New Haven, CT: Yale University Press.

Dirlik, A. (2000). Reversals, ironies, hegemonies: Notes on the contemporary historiography of modern China. In A. Dirlik, V. Bahl, & P. Gran (Eds.), *History after the three worlds: Post-Eurocentric historiographies* (pp. 125-156). Lanham, MD: Rowman & Littlefield.

Dissanayake, W. (1987). The guiding image of Indian culture and its implications for communication. In D. L. Kincaid (Ed.), *Communication theory: Eastern and western Perspectives* (pp. 151-160). San Diego, CA: Academic Press.

Dissanayake, W. (2003). Asian approaches to human communication: Retrospect and prospect. *Intercultural Communication Studies, 12*(4), 17-37.

Docherty, T. (1994). Postmodernist theory: Lyotard, Baudrillard and others. In R. Kearney (Ed.), *Continental philosophy in the 20th century* (pp. 474-505). London: Routledge.

Donohew, L., & Palmgreen, P. (1989). Theory construction. In G. H. Stempel III & B. H. Westley (Eds.), *Research methods in mass communication* (2nd ed., pp. 30-48). Englewood Cliffs, NJ: Prentice-Hall.

Downing, J. D. H. ((2002). Drawing a bead on global communication theories. In Y. R. Kamalipour (Ed.), *Global communication* (pp. 21-34). Belmont, CA: Wadsworth/Thomson Learning.

Dussel, E. (2002). World-system and "trans"-modernity. *Nepantla: Views from South, 3,* 221-244.

Embree, A. T. (Ed.). (1988). *Sources of Indian tradition* (Vol. 1, 2nd ed.). New York: Columbia University Press.

Ette, M. (2000). Agent of change or stability? The Nigerian press undermines democracy. *Harvard International Journal of Press/Politics, 5*(3), 67-86.

Fals-Borda, O., & Mora-Osejo, L. E. (2003). Context and differences in knowledge: A critique of Eurocentrism. *Action Research, 1,* 29-37.

Farazmand, A. (2003). Chaos and transformation theories: A theoretical analysis with implications for organization theory and public management. *Public Organization Review: A Global Journal, 3*, 339-372.

Fletcher, J. (1985). Integrative history: Parallels and interconnections in the early modern period, 1500-1800. *Journal of Turkish Studies, 9*, 37-58.

Francis, R. G. (1983). *Sociology in a different key: Essays in non-linear sociology.* Houston: Cap and Gown Press.

Frank, A. G. (1998). *Re-ORIENT: Global economy in the Asian age.* Berkeley: University of California Press.

Frank, A. G., & Gills, B. K. (Eds.). (1993). *The world system: Five hundred years or five thousand?* London: Routledge.

Freedom House. (2003). Freedom in the world 2003: Tables and charts. Available from http://www.freedomhouse.org/research/freeworld/2003/tables.htm

Freeman, C. (1996). *Egypt Greece and Rome: Civilizations of the ancient Mediterranean.* Oxford, England: Oxford University Press.

Fromm, E. (1955). *The sane society.* New York: Rinehart.

Fukuyama, F. (1995). Confucianism and democracy. *Journal of Democracy, 6*(2), 20-33.

Fuller, R. B. (1971). *No more secondhand God.* Garden City, NY: Doubleday.

Gans, H. (1979). *Deciding what's news: A study of CBS evening news, NBC nightly news, Newsweek, and Time.* New York: Pantheon.

Giddens, A. (1984). *The constitution of society: Outline of the theory of structuration.* Berkeley: University of California Press.

Gleick, J. (1987). *Chaos: Making a new science.* New York: Viking.

Godin, C. (2000). The notion of totality in Indian thought. *Diogenes, 48*(189), 58-69.

Gokhale, B. G. (1966). *Asoka Maurya.* New York: Twayne.

Goldfrank, W. L. (2000). Paradigm regained? The rules of Wallerstein's world-system method. *Journal of World-Systems Research, 6*, 150-195.

Goonatilake, S. (1998). *Toward a global science: Mining civilizational knowledge.* Bloomington: Indiana University Press.

Goonatilake, S. (1999). *Merged evolution: Long-term implications of biotechnology and information technology.* Amsterdam: Gordon & Breach.

Goonatilake, S. (2001). *Anthropologizing Sri Lanka: A Eurocentric misadventure.* Bloomington: Indiana University Press.

Gordon, K. (2002). Worlds within worlds: Kabbalah and the new scientific paradigm. *Zygon, 37*, 963-983.

Goswami, A. (1993). *The self-aware universe: How consciousness creates the material world.* New York: Jeremy P. Tarcher/Putnam.

Goswami, A. (2000). *The visionary window: A quantum physicist's guide to enlightenment.* Wheaton, IL: Quest Books.

Gowen, H. H. (1929). "The Indian Machiavelli" or political theory in India two thousand years ago. *Political Science Quarterly, 44*, 173-192.

Gunaratne, S. A. (1998). Old wine in a new bottle: Public journalism, developmental journalism, and social responsibility. In M. E. Roloff (Ed.), *Communication Yearbook 21* (pp. 277-321). Thousand Oaks, CA: Sage.

Gunaratne, S. A. (2001). Paper, printing, and the printing press: A horizontally integrative macrohistory analysis. *Gazette, 63*, 459-479.

Gunaratne, S. A. (2002a). Freedom of the press: A world system perspective. *Gazette, 64*, 343–369.

Gunaratne, S. A. (2002b). An evolving triadic world: A theoretical framework for global communication research. *Journal of World-Systems Research, 8*, 329-365.

Gunaratne, S. A. (2003a). Freedom of the press in Asia. In D. H. Johnston (Ed.), *Encyclopedia of International Media and Communications* (Vol. 2, pp. 117-125). San Diego, CA: Academic Press.

Gunaratne, S. A. (2003b). Proto-Indo-European expansion, rise of English, and the international language order: A humanocentric analysis. *International Journal of the Sociology of Language, 164*, 1-32.

Gunaratne, S. A. (2003c). Thank you Newton, welcome Prigogine: "Unthinking"' old paradigms and embracing new directions—Part 1: Theoretical distinctions. *Communications, 28*, 435-455.

Gunaratne, S. A. (2004). Thank you Newton, welcome Prigogine: "Unthinking" old paradigms and embracing new directions—Part 2: The pragmatics. *Communications, 29*, 113-132.

Gunaratne, S. A. (2005a). Public sphere and communicative-action theory: Interrogating Habermas' Eurocentrism. *Journalism & Communication Monographs, 7*.

Gunaratne, S. A. (2005b). *World system as a dissipative structure: Ties with Eastern philosophy.* Manuscript submitted for publication.

Gunaratne, S. A. (in press). Democracy, journalism, and systems: Perspectives from East and West. In Hao Xiaoming & S. K. Datta-Ray (Eds.), *Issues and challenges in Asian journalism.* Singapore: Marshall Cavendish Academic.

Habermas, J. (1987). *The theory of communicative action: Lifeworld and system—a critique of functionalist reason* (Vol. 2, T. McCarthy, Trans.). Boston: Beacon. (Original publication 1981)

Habermas, J. (1989). *The structural transformation of the public sphere* (T. Burger, Trans.). Cambridge, MA: MIT Press. (Original publication 1962)

Hachten, W. A. (1999). *The world news prism: Changing media of international communication* (5th ed.). Ames: Iowa State University Press. (First edition published 1981)

Hachten, W. A. (2001). *The troubles of journalism: A critical look at what's right and wrong with the press* (2nd ed.). Mahwah, NJ: Erlbaum.

Hamada, B. I. (2001). Islamic cultural theory: Arab media performance and public opinion. In S. Splichal (Ed.), *Public opinion and democracy: Vox populi—vox dei?* (pp. 215-239). Cresskill, NJ: Hampton Press.

Hardt, M. (2001). The eurocentrism of history. *Postcolonial Studies, 4*, 243-249.

Harms, L. S. (2003). *Some essentials of the right to communicate.* Retrieved January 22, 2004, from the Right to Communicate Group Web site: http://www. righttocommunicate.org/viewReference.atm?id=35

Harvey, D. L., & Reed, M. H. (1994). The evolution of dissipative social systems. *Journal of Social and Evolutionary Systems, 17,* 371-411.

Held, D. (1995). *Democracy and the global order: From the modern state to cosmopolitan governance.* Stanford, CA: Stanford University Press.

Held, D. (1996). *Models of democracy* (2nd ed.). Stanford, CA: Stanford University Press.

Held, D. (2000). Regulating globalization? The reinvention of politics. *International Sociology, 15,* 394-408.

Herman, E., & Chomsky, N. (1988). *Manufacturing consent: The political economy of the mass media.* New York: Pantheon.

Hoff, B. (1982). *The Tao[Dao] of Pooh.* New York: E. P. Dutton.

Hoffmann, Y. (1978). The possibility of knowledge: Kant and Nagarjuna. In B. Scharfstein (Ed.), *Philosophy East/philosophy West: A critical comparison of Indian, Chinese, Islamic, and European philosophy* (pp. 269-290). New York: Oxford University Press.

Holcombe, C. (2001). *The genesis of East Asia, 221 B.C.–A.D. 907.* Honolulu: University of Hawaii Press.

Hornung, B. R. (2001). Structural coupling and concepts of data and information exchange: Integrating Luhmann into information science. *Journal of Sociocybernetics, 2*(2), 1-12.

Huang, C. J. (2003). Transitional media vs. normative theories: Schramm, Altschull, and China. *Journal of Communication, 53,* 444-459.

Huang, P. C. (1993). "Public sphere"/"civil society" in China? The third realm between state and society. *Modern China, 19*(2), 216-240.

Huysmans, F. (2003). The foundation of communication and action in consciousness: Confronting action theory with systems theoretical arguments. *Communications, 28,* 17-31.

Inden, R. B. (1990). *Imagining India.* Cambridge, MA: Basil Blackwell.

Ishii, S. (1984). *Enryo-sasshi* communication: A key to understanding Japanese interpersonal relations. *Cross Currents, 11*(1), 49-58.

Ishii, S. (1988). *Nonverbal communication in Japan* (Orientation seminars on Japan: 28). Tokyo: Office of the Japanese Studies Center of the Japan Foundation.

Ishii, S. (1992). Buddhist preaching: The persistent main undercurrent of Japanese traditional rhetorical communication. *Communication Quarterly, 40*(4), 391-397.

Ishii, S. (1998). Developing a Buddhist *en*-based systems paradigm for the study of Japanese human relationships. *Japan Review, 10,* 109-122.

Jacobson, T. L. (1991). Theories as communications. *Communication Theory, 1,* 145-150.

Jaspers, K. (1981/1993). *The great philosophers* (E. & L. H. Ehrlich, Trans.). New York: Harcourt Brace.

Jayatilleke, K. N. (1963). *Early Buddhist theory of knowledge.* London: George Allen & Unwin.

Jayatilleke, K. N. (1974). *The message of the Buddha.* New York: The Free Press.

Jayatilleke, K. N. (1984). Buddhism and the scientific revolution. In B. P. Kirthisinghe (Ed.), *Buddhism and science* (pp. 8-16). Delhi: Motilal Banarsidass.

Jia, W., Lu, X., & Heisey, D. R. (2002). *Chinese communication theory and research: Reflections, new frontiers, and new directions.* Westport, CT: Ablex.

Jones, D., & Culliney, J. (1999). The fractal self and the organization of nature: The Daoist sage and chaos theory. *Zygon, 34*, 643-655.

Jung, H. Y. (1999). Postmodernity, Eurocentrism, and the future of political philosophy. In F. Dallmayr (Ed.), *Border crossings: Toward a comparative political theory* (pp. 277-296). Lanham, MD: Lexington.

Kalupahana, D. J. (1976). *Buddhist philosophy: A historical analysis.* Honolulu: The University Press of Hawaii.

Kamhawi, R., & Weaver, D. (2003). Mass communication research trends from 1980 to 1999. *Journalism & Mass Communication Quarterly, 80*, 7-27.

Kaplan, A. (1964). *The conduct of inquiry: Methodology for behavioral science.* San Francisco: Chandler.

Kaza, S. (2002). Green Buddhism. In C. N. Matthews, M. E. Tucker, & P. Hefner (Eds.), *When worlds converge: What science and religion tell us about the story of the universe and our place in it* (pp. 293-309). Chicago: Open Court.

Kellner, D. (1992). *The Persian Gulf TV war.* Boulder, CO: Westview.

Kerlinger, F.N. (1986). *Foundations of behavioral research.* New York: Holt, Rinehart.

Keskinen, A. (1995). *Teledemokratia.* Helsinki: Painatuskeskus.

Khiabany, G. (2003). De-Westernizing media theory, or reverse Orientalism: "Islamic communication" as theorized by Hamid Mowlana. *Media, Culture & Society, 25*, 415-422.

Kim, M.-S. (2002). *Non-Western perspectives on human communication: Implications for theory and practice.* Thousand Oaks, CA: Sage.

Kim, Y. Y. (2000). Intercultural personhood: An integration of Eastern and Western perspectives. In L. A. Samovar & R. E. Porter (Eds.), *Intercultural communication: A reader* (9th ed., pp. 431-443). Belmont, CA: Wadsworth.

King, R. (1999). *Indian philosophy: An introduction to Hindu and Buddhist thought.* Washington, DC: Georgetown University Press.

Klostermaier, K. (1991). The nature of Buddhism. *Asian Philosophy, 1*(1), 29-37.

Konsky, C., Kapoor, U., Blue, J., & Kapoor, S. (2000). Religion and communication: A study of Hinduism, Buddhism and Christianity. *Intercultural Communication Studies, 10*(2), 235-251.

Krippendorff, K. (1993). Conversation or intellectual imperialism in comparing communication (theories). *Communication Theory, 3*, 252-266.

Lai, P.-C. (2002). Buddhist-Christian complementarity in the perspective of quantum physics. *Buddhist-Christian Studies, 22*, 149-162.

Lambeth, E. B. (1995). Global media philosophies. In J. C. Merrill (Ed.), *Global journalism: Survey of international communication* (pp. 3-18). White Plains, NY: Longman.

Larson, G. J. (1998). Indian conceptions of reality and divinity. In E. Deutsch & R. Bontekoe (Eds.), *A companion to world philosophies* (pp. 248-258). Malden, MA: Blackwell.

Lasswell, H. D. (1948). The structure and function of communication in society. In L. Bryson (Ed.), *Communication of ideas* (pp. 37-51) New York: Harper & Brothers.

Laszlo, E. (1998). Systems and societies: The logic of sociocultural evolution. In G. Altmann & W. A. Koch (Eds.), *Systems: New paradigms for the human sciences* (pp. 104-125). Berlin: Walter de Gruyter.

Lazarsfeld, P. F., & Merton, R. K. (1948). Mass communication, popular taste, and organized social action. In L. Bryson (Ed.), *Communication of ideas* (pp. 95-118). New York: Harper & Brothers.

Legge, J. (1893). *The Chinese classics: Confucian analects, the great learning, and the doctrine of the mean* (Vol. 1). Oxford: Clarendon.

Legge, J. (1895). *The Chinese classics: The works of Mencius* (Vol. 2). Oxford: Clarendon.

Leydesdorff, L. (2003). *A sociological theory of communication: The self-organization of the knowledge-based society* (2nd ed.). Parkland, FL: Universal Publishers.

Li, C. (1999). *The Tao encounters the West: Explorations in comparative philosophy.* Albany: State University of New York Press.

Lin, T., Rosemont, H., & Ames, R. T. (1995). Chinese philosophy: A philosophical essay on the "state-of-the-art." *Journal of Asian Studies, 54,* 727-758.

Lin, T. C. (1947). The Chinese mind: Its Daoist substratum. *Journal of the History of Ideas, 8*(3), 259-272.

Lowenstein, R. L. (1970). Press freedom as a political indicator. In H-D. Fischer & J. C. Merrill (Eds.), *International communication: Media, channels, functions* (pp. 129-140). New York: Hastings House.

Lu, X., Jia, W., & Heisey, D. R. (2002). *Chinese communication studies: Contexts and comparisons.* Westport, CT: Ablex.

Luhmann, N. (1989). *Ecological communication* (J. Bednarz, Trans.). Cambridge: Polity. (Originally published 1986)

Luhmann, N. (1992). Autopoiesis: What is communication? *Communication Theory, 2,* 251-258.

Luhmann, N. (1995). *Social systems* (J. Bednarz, Jr., with D. Baecker, Trans.). Stanford, CA: Stanford University Press. (Originally published 1984)

Luhmann, N. (2000). *The reality of the mass media* (K. Cross, Trans.). Stanford, CA: Stanford University Press. (Originally published 1996)

Luksha, P.O. (2001). Society as a self-reproducing system. *Journal of Sociocybernetics, 2*(2), 13-36.

Macy, J. (1991). *Mutual causality in Buddhism and general systems theory: The dharma of natural systems.* Albany: State University of New York Press.

Mansfield, V. N. (1976). [Review of the book *The Dao of physics*]. *Physics Today, 29*(8), 56.

Marcuse, H. (1964). *One-dimensional man*, Boston: Beacon.

Matilal, B. K. (1989). Caste, karma and the Gita. In R. W. Perrett (Ed.), *Indian philosophy of religion* (pp. 195-201). Dordrecht: Kluwer Academic Publishers.

Maturana, H. (1980). Man and society. In F. Benseler, P. Hejl, & W. Knock (Eds), *Autopoietic systems in the social sciences* (pp. 11-31). Frankfurt: Campus Verlag.

Maturana, H. ([1974]1999). The organization of the living: A theory of the living organization. *International Journal of Human-Computer Studies, 51*(2), 149-168.

Maturana, H. (2002). Autopoiesis, structural coupling and cognition: A history of these and other notions in the biology of cognition. *Cybernetics & Human Knowing, 9*(3), 5-34.

Maturana, H., & Varela, F. (1980). *Autopoiesis and cognition: The realization of the living*. Dordrecht: Reidel.

McChesney, R. W. (1999). *Rich media, poor democracy: Communication politics in dubious times*. Urbana: University of Illinois Press.

McGraw, K. M., & Holbrook, R. A. (2003). Democracy and the media. In D. H. Johnston (Ed.), *Encyclopedia of International Media and Communications* (Vol. 1, pp. 399-408). San Diego, CA: Academic Press.

McQuail, D. (1984/1987). *Mass communication theory: An introduction*. London: Sage.

Medd, W. (2001). Making (dis)connections. Complexity and the policy process. *Social Issues, 1*(2). Retrieved from http://www.whb.co.uk/socialissues/wm.htm

Mencher, M. (2000). *News reporting and writing* (8th ed.). Boston: McGraw-Hill.

Merrill, J. C. (1970). The press and social responsibility. In H.-D. Fischer & J. C. Merrill (Eds.), *International communication: Media, channels, functions* (pp. 15-20). New York: Hastings House.

Merrill, J. C., Gade, P. J., & Blevens, F. R. (2001). *Twilight of press freedom: The role of people's journalism*. Mahwah, NJ: Erlbaum.

Merrill, J. C., & Lowenstein, R. L. (1979). *Media, messages, and men: New perspectives in communication* (2nd ed.). New York: Longman.

Miike, Y. (2003a). Beyond Eurocentrism in the intercultural field: Searching for an Asiacentric paradigm. In W. J. Starosta & G.-M. Chen (Eds.), *Ferment in the intercultural field: Axiology/value/praxis* (pp. 243-276). Thousand Oaks, CA: Sage.

Miike, Y. (2003b). Toward an alternative metatheory of human communication: An Asiacentric vision. *Intercultural Communication Studies, 12*(4), 39-63.

Miike, Y., & Chen, G.-M. (2003). Asian approaches to human communication: A selected bibliography. *Intercultural Communication Studies, 12*(4), 209-218.

Miller, J. G. (1978). *Living systems*. New York: McGraw-Hill.

Milner, M. (1993). Hindu eschatology and the Indian caste system: An example of structural reversal. *The Journal of Asian Studies, 52,* 298-319.

Mingers, J. (2002). Can social systems be autopoietic? Assessing Luhmann's social theory. *The Sociological Review, 50,* 278-279.

Mirsepassi, A. (2000). *Intellectual discourse and the politics of modernization: Negotiating modernity in Iran.* Cambridge, UK: Cambridge University Press.

Modelski, G. (1964). Kautilya: Foreign policy and international system in the ancient Hindu world. *The American Political Science Review, 58,* 549-560.

Mohanty, J. N. (1998). Indian philosophy. In *The new encyclopedia Britannica* (Vol. 21, pp. 191-212). Chicago: Encyclopedia Britannica.

Mohanty, J. N. (2000). *Classical Indian philosophy.* Lanham, MD: Rowman & Littlefield.

Mosco, V. (2004). *The digital sublime: Myth, power, and cyberspace.* Cambridge, MA: MIT Press.

Mote, F. W. (1989). *Intellectual foundations of China* (2nd ed.). New York: Alfred A. Knopf.

Moussalli, A.S. (2001). *The Islamic quest for democracy, pluralism, and human rights.* Gainesville: University Press of Florida.

Mowlana, H. (1996). *Global communication in transition: The end of diversity?* Thousand Oaks, CA: Sage.

Mueller, G. E. (1958). The Hegel legend of "thesis-antithesis-synthesis." *Journal of the History of Ideas, 19,* 411-414.

Muhlberger, S. (1998). *Democracy in ancient India.* Retrieved July 18, 2004, from http://www.nipissingu.ca/department/history/muhlberger/histdem/indiadem.htm

Munro, W. B. (1928). Physics and politics—An old analogy revisited. *The American Political Science Review, 22,* 1-11.

Needham, J. (1956). *Science and civilization in China: History of scientific thought* (Vol. 2). Cambridge: University Press.

Nerone, J. C. (Ed.). (1995). *Last rights: Revisiting four theories of the press.* Urbana: University of Illinois Press.

Nikam, N. A., & McKeon, R. (Eds.). (1958). *The edicts of Asoka.* Chicago: The University of Chicago Press.

Nordenstreng, K. (1997). Beyond the four theories of the press. In J. Servaes & R. Lie (Eds.), *Media and politics in transition: Cultural identity in the age of globalization* (pp. 97-112). Leuven, Belgium: Acco.

Northrop, F. (1966). *The meeting of the East and the West.* New York: Collier Books. (Originally published 1946)

Nuyen, A. T. (2001). Confucianism and the idea of equality. *Asian Philosophy, 11*(2), 61-71.

Olcott, H.S. (1885). *A Buddhist catechism.* Boston: Estes & Lauriat.

Oliver, R. T. (1971). *Communication and culture in ancient India and China.* Syracuse, NY: Syracuse University Press.

Ostini, J., & Fung, A. Y. H. (2002). Beyond the four theories of the press: A new model of national media systems. *Mass Communication and Society, 5*(1), 41-56.

Overman, E.S. (1991). Policy physics. In T. L. Becker (Ed.), *Quantum politics: Applying quantum theory to political phenomena* (pp. 151-167). New York: Praeger.

Paranjpe, A. C., Ho, D. Y. F., & Rieber, R. W. (1988). *Asian contributions to psychology*. New York: Praeger.

Parsons, T. (1971). *The system of modern societies*. Englewood Cliffs, NJ: Prentice-Hall.

Pearce, W. B. (1991). On comparing theories: Treating theories as commensurate and incommensurate. *Communication Theory, 1*, 159-164.

Peek, J. M. (1995). Buddhism, human rights and the Japanese state. *Human Rights Quarterly, 17*, 527-540.

Penrose, R. (1989). *The emperor's new mind: Concerning computers, minds, and the laws of physics*. New York: Oxford University Press.

Perera, L. P. N. (1989). Democracy. In A. W. P. Guruge (Ed.), *Encyclopedia of Buddhism* (Vol. IV, pp. 363-369). Colombo: Ministry of Cultural Affairs, Government of Ceylon (Sri Lanka).

Picard, R. G. (1985). *The press and the decline of democracy*. Westport, CT: Greenwood.

Popper, K. P. (1962). *Conjectures and refutations: The growth of scientific knowledge*. New York: Basic Books.

Price, M. E. (2002). *Media and sovereignty: The global information revolution and its challenge to state power*. Cambridge, MA: MIT Press.

Prigogine, I. (1996). *The end of certainty: Time, chaos, and the new laws of nature*. New York: The Free Press.

Prigogine, I., & Stengers, I. (1984). *Order out of chaos: Man's new dialogue with nature*. Toronto: Bantam.

Putuwar, S. (1988). The Buddhist Sangha: Paradigm of the ideal human society (Doctoral dissertation, The American University, 1988). *Dissertation Abstracts International, 49*, 1177.

Radhakrishnan, S. (1940). *Eastern religions and Western thought* (2nd ed.). London: Oxford University Press.

Radhakrishnan, S. (Ed.). (1952). *History of philosophy Eastern and Western* (Vol. 1). London: George Allen & Unwin.

Raman, V. V. (2003). Hindu perspectives on the thirst for transcendence. *Zygon, 38*, 821–837.

Ratanakul, P. (2002). Buddhism and science: Allies or enemies. *Zygon, 37*, 115-120.

Rhee, Y. P. (1997). Synthetic systems theory: Linkage between Western theory of physics and Eastern thought. *System Research and Behavioral Science, 13*(3), 211-221.

Ritzer, G. (2003). The globalization of nothing. *SAIS Review, 23*(2), 189-200.

Robertson, R. (1994). Globalization or glocalization? *The Journal of International Communication, 1*, 33-52.

Robinson, R. H. (1969). Early Buddhist theory of knowledge [Review of the book *Early Buddhist theory of knowledge*]. *Journal of Asian Studies, 28*, 380-390.

Rogers, E. M., & Chaffee, S. H. (1994). Communication and journalism from "Daddy" Bleyer to Wilbur Schramm. *Journalism Monographs, 148*.

Rorty, R. (1983). *Consequences of pragmatism: Essays, 1972-1980.* Minneapolis: University of Minnesota Press.

Rosen, J. (1999). *What are journalists for?* New Haven, CT: Yale University Press.

Rubin, V. A. (1976). *Individual and state in ancient China: Essays on four Chinese philosophers* (S. I. Levine, Trans.). New York: Columbia University Press.

Rummel, R. J. (1977). *Field theory evolving.* Beverley Hills, CA: Sage.

Russell, R. J., Clayton, P., McNelly, K. W., & Polkinghorne, J. (Eds.). (2001). *Quantum mechanics: Scientific perspectives on divine action, Vol. 5.* Berkeley, CA: Center for Theology and the Natural Sciences & Vatican Observatory.

Saher, P. J. (1970). *Eastern wisdom and Western thought: A comparative study in the modern philosophy of religion.* New York: Barnes & Noble.

Said, E. (1978). *Orientalism.* New York: Random House.

Sarkar, B. K. (1918a). Hindu political philosophy. *Political Science Quarterly, 33,* 482–500.

Sarkar, B. K. (1918b). Democratic ideals and republican institutions in India. *The American Political Science Review, 12,* 581-606.

Sarkar, B. K. (1921). The Hindu theory of the state. *Political Science Quarterly, 36,* 79–90.

Schrödinger, E. (1945). *What is life? The physical aspect of the living cell.* New York: Macmillan.

Schubert, G. (1983). The evolution of political science: Paradigms of physics, biology, and politics. *Politics and the Life Sciences, 1,* 97-110.

Sen, A. (2001). Democracy as a universal value. In L. Diamond & M.F. Plattner (Eds.), *The global divergence of democracies* (pp. 3-17). Baltimore, MD: Johns Hopkins University Press.

Servaes, J. (1999). *Communication for development: One world, multiple cultures.* Cresskill, NJ: Hampton.

Sharma, J. P. (1968). *Republics in ancient India, c. 1500 B.C.-500 B.C.* Leiden: E. J. Brill.

Sheth, N. (2004, June 5–9). *Buddhism and science.* Paper presented at the Science and Religion in Context conference, Philadelphia.

Shuter, R. (2000a). Ethical issues in global communication. In G.-M. Chen & W. J. Starosta (Eds.), *Communication and global society* (pp. 181-190). New York: Peter Lang.

Shuter, R. (2000b). Ethics, culture, and communication: An intercultural perspective. In L. A. Samovar & R. E. Porter (Eds.), *Intercultural communication: A reader* (9th ed., pp. 443-450). Belmont, CA: Wadsworth.

Siebert, F. S., Peterson, T., & Schramm, W. (1956). *Four theories of the press.* Urbana: University of Illinois Press.

Siu, R.G. H. (1957). *The Tao of science: An essay on Western knowledge and Eastern wisdom.* Cambridge, MA: The MIT Press.

Sivaraksa, S. (2002). Economic aspects of social and environmental violence from a Buddhist perspective. *Buddhist-Christian Studies, 22,* 47-60.

Slaton, C.D. (1992). *Televote: Expanding citizen participation in the quantum age.* New York: Praeger.

Splichal, S. (2002). *Principles of publicity and press freedom.* Lanham, MD: Rowman & Littlefield.

Srinivasiengar, K. R. (1934). Emergent evolution: An Indian view. *The Philosophical Review, 43*(6), 598-606.

Stichweh, R. (1998). Systems theory and the evolution of science. In G. Altmann & W. Koch (Eds.), *Systems: New paradigms for the human sciences* (pp. 303-317). Berlin: Walter de Gruyter.

Stichweh, R. (2000). Systems theory as an alternative to action theory? The rise of "communication" as theoretical option. *Acta Sociologica, 43*, 5-13.

Straussfogel, D. (2000). World-systems theory in the context of systems theory: An overview. In T. D. Hall (Ed.), *A world-systems reader: New perspectives on gender, urbanism, cultures, indigenous peoples, and ecology* (pp. 169-180). Lanham, MD: Rowman & Littlefield.

Sussman, L. R. (2000). *Censor dot gov: The Internet and press freedom.* New York: Freedom House.

Tambiah, S. J. (2003). Transnational movements, diaspora, and multiple modernities. *Daedalus, 129*(1), 163-194.

Tan, S. H. (2003). *Confucian democracy: A Deweyan reconstruction.* Albany: State University of New York Press.

Tang, Y. J. (1991). *Confucianism, Buddhism, Daoism, Christianity and Chinese culture.* Washington, DC: The Council for Research in Values and Philosophy.

Tehranian, M. (1991). Is comparative communication theory possible/desirable? *Communication Theory, 1*, 44-59.

Terchek, R. J., & Conte, T. C. (2001). *Theories of democracy: A reader.* Lanham, MD: Rowman & Littlefield.

Tetenbaum, T. J. (1998). Shifting paradigms: From Newton to chaos. *Organizational Dynamics, 26*(4), 21-32.

Thapar, R. (1961). *Asoka and the decline of the Mauryas.* New York: Oxford University Press.

Thayer-Bacon, B. J. (2003). Buddhism as an example of a holistic, relational epistemology. *Encounter, 16*(2), 27-38.

Tillis, S. (2003). East, West, and world theatre. *Asian Theatre Journal, 20,* 71-87.

Toffler, A., & Toffler, H. (1994). *Creating a new civilization.* Atlanta, GA: Turner.

Tu Weiming (1997). Chinese philosophy: A synoptic view. In E. Deutsch & R. Bontekoe (Eds.), *A companion to world philosophies* (pp. 3-23). Malden, MA: Blackwell.

Tu Weiming. (2000). Implications of the rise of "Confucian" East Asia. *Daedalus, 129*(1), 195-218.

Tu Weiming. (2001). The ecological turn in new Confucian humanism: Implications for China and the world. *Daedalus, 130*(4), 243-264.

Tucker, R. B. (1983, May). Ilya Prigogine: Wizard of time. *OMNI.* Available [02.06.2002] at http://www.omnimag.com/archives/interviews/prigogin.html

Urry, J. (2003). *Global complexity*. Cambridge: Polity.

Verdu, A. (1981). *The philosophy of Buddhism: A "totalistic" synthesis*. The Hague: Martinus Nijhoff.

Villa, D. R. (1992). Postmodernism and the public sphere. *American Political Science Review, 86*, 712-721.

Wahl-Jorgensen, K., & Galperin, H. (2000). Discourse ethics and the regulation of media. *Journal of Communication Inquiry, 24*, 19-40.

Walby, S. (2003, April). *Complexity theory, globalization and diversity*. Paper presented to conference of the British Sociological Association, University of York.

Wallace, B. A. (Ed.). (2003). *Buddhism and science: Breaking new ground*. New York: Columbia University Press.

Wallerstein, I. (1974). *The modern world-system: Capitalist agriculture and the origins of the European world economy in the sixteenth century*. New York: Academic Press.

Wallerstein, I. (1999). *The end of the world as we know it: Social science for the twenty-first century*. Minneapolis: University of Minnesota Press.

Walter, K. (1994). *Tao of chaos: Merging East and West*. Austin, TX: Kairos Center.

Wang, G., & Shen, V. (2000). East, West, communication, and theory: Searching for the meaning of searching for Asian communication theories. *Asian Journal of Communication, 10*(2), 14-32.

Wang, R. R. (Ed.). (2004). *Chinese philosophy in an era of globalization*. Albany: State University of New York Press.

Weber, M. (1951). *The religion of China: Confucianism and Taoism* (H. H. Gerth, Trans.). New York: The Free Press.

Weber, M. ([1921]1958). *The religion of India: The sociology of Hinduism and Buddhism* (H.H. Gerth & D. Martinsdale, Trans.). Glencoe, IL: The Free Press.

White, D. H. (1979). [Review of the book *The Dao of physics*]. *Contemporary Sociology, 8*, 586-587.

Williams, G. P. (1997). *Chaos theory tamed*. Washington, DC: National Academies Press.

Winfield, B. H., Mizuno, T., & Beaudoin, C. E. (2000). Confucianism, collectivism and constitutions: Press systems in China and Japan. *Communication Law & Policy, 5*, 323-347.

Wittgenstein, L. (1953). *Philosophical investigations* (G. E. M. Anscombe, Trans.). New York: Macmillan.

Woelfel, J. (1987). Development of the Western model: Toward a reconciliation of Eastern and Western perspectives. In D. L. Kincaid (Ed.), *Communication theory: Eastern and Western perspectives* (pp. 299-318). San Diego, CA: Academic Press.

Wolf, E. R. (1982). *Europe and the people without history*. Berkeley: University of California Press.

Yin, J. F. (2003, August). *Press freedom in Asia: New paradigm needed in building theories*. Paper presented at the annual convention of the Association for Education in Journalism and Mass Communication, Kansas City, MO.

Yu, B., & Lu, Z. (2000). Confucianism and modernity—insights from an interview with Tu Wei-ming. *China Review International, 7*, 377-387.

Yum, J. O. (2000). The impact of Confucianism on interpersonal relationships and communication patterns in East Asia. In L. A. Samovar & R. E. Porter (Eds.), *Intercultural communication: A reader* (9th ed., pp. 63-73). Belmont, CA: Wadsworth.

Zukav, G. (1979). *The dancing Wu Li masters: An overview of the new physics*. New York: William Morrow & Co.

Author Index

Subject Index

Printed in the United States
29773LVS00001B/61-99

9 781572 736160